Fault-tolerant Agreement in Synchronous Message-passing Systems

Synthesis Lectures on Distributed Computing Theory

Editor
Nancy Lynch, *Massachusetts Institute of Technology*

Synthesis Lectures on Distributed Computing Theory is edited by Nancy Lynch of the Massachusetts Institute of Technology. The series will publish 50- to 150 page publications on topics pertaining to distributed computing theory. The scope will largely follow the purview of premier information and computer science conferences, such as ACM PODC, DISC, SPAA, OPODIS, CONCUR, DialM-POMC, ICDCS, SODA, Sirocco, SSS, and related conferences. Potential topics include, but not are limited to: distributed algorithms and lower bounds, algorithm design methods, formal modeling and verification of distributed algorithms, and concurrent data structures.

Fault-tolerant Agreement in Synchronous Message-passing Systems
Michel Raynal
2010

Communication and Agreement Abstractions for Fault-Tolerant Asynchronous Distributed Systems
Michel Raynal
2010

The Mobile Agent Rendezvous Problem in the Ring
Evangelos Kranakis, Danny Krizanc, Euripides Markou
2010

Fault-tolerant Agreement in Synchronous Message-passing Systems

Michel Raynal

ISBN: 978-3-031-00873-3 paperback
ISBN: 978-3-031-02001-8   ebook

DOI 10.1007/978-3-031-02001-8

A Publication in the Springer series
SYNTHESIS LECTURES ON DISTRIBUTED COMPUTING THEORY

Lecture #3
Series Editor: Nancy Lynch, *Massachusetts Institute of Technology*
Series ISSN
Synthesis Lectures on Distributed Computing Theory
Print 2155-1626   Electronic 2155-1634

Fault-tolerant Agreement in Synchronous Message-passing Systems

Michel Raynal
IRISA, Université de Rennes

SYNTHESIS LECTURES ON DISTRIBUTED COMPUTING THEORY #3

ABSTRACT

Understanding distributed computing is not an easy task. This is due to the many facets of uncertainty one has to cope with and master in order to produce correct distributed software. A previous book *Communication and Agreement Abstraction for Fault-tolerant Asynchronous Distributed Systems* (published by Morgan & Claypool, 2010) was devoted to the problems created by crash failures in asynchronous message-passing systems.

The present book focuses on the way to cope with the uncertainty created by process failures (crash, omission failures and Byzantine behavior) in synchronous message-passing systems (i.e., systems whose progress is governed by the passage of time). To that end, the book considers fundamental problems that distributed synchronous processes have to solve. These fundamental problems concern agreement among processes (if processes are unable to agree in one way or another in presence of failures, no non-trivial problem can be solved). They are consensus, interactive consistency, k-set agreement and non-blocking atomic commit.

Being able to solve these basic problems efficiently with provable guarantees allows applications designers to give a precise meaning to the words "cooperate " and "agree" despite failures, and write distributed synchronous programs with properties that can be stated and proved.

Hence, the aim of the book is to present a comprehensive view of agreement problems, algorithms that solve them and associated computability bounds in synchronous message-passing distributed systems.

KEYWORDS

agreement problem, Byzantine failure, consensus, interactive consistency, lower bound, non-blocking atomic commit, process crash, omission failure, synchronous message-passing system

Contents

Notations

n	number of processes
t	upper bound on the number of faulty processes
f	actual number of faulty processes
r	round number
$\#_v(S)$	occurrence number of value v in the array or multiset S

Multiset   Some algorithms described in the book use *multisets*. Differently from a set where each member has only one membership, a member of a multiset can have more than one membership. Hence its occurrence number is associated with each member of a multiset. As an example, $\{a, b, a, c\}$ is a multiset that contains four values, a that appears twice, b that appears once and c that appears once. This means that $\{a, b, a, c\}$ and $\{a, b, c\}$ are different multisets, while they are equal from a set point of view.

List of Figures

Preface

What distributed computing is   Distributed computing arises when one has to solve a problem in terms of entities (usually called processes, agents, sensors, peers, actors, processors, nodes, etc.) such that each entity has only a partial knowledge of the many parameters involved in the problem that has to be solved. While parallelism and real-time can be characterized by the words *efficiency* and on time computing, respectively, distributed computing can be characterized by the word *uncertainty*. This uncertainty is created by asynchrony, failures, unstable behaviors, non-monotonicity, system dynamism, mobility, low computing capability, scalability requirements, etc. Mastering one form or another of uncertainty is pervasive in all distributed computing problems.

Distributed computing is pervasive everywhere and computing applications are more and more distributed. It becomes, consequently, more important than ever not only to understand the fundamental principles on which the design of distributed applications are based, but also to have a precise knowledge of what can be done and what cannot be done in a distributed system, and (when it can be done) how efficiently it can be done. Hence, as the aim of a theory is to codify knowledge in order it can be transmitted (to students, engineers, practitioners, etc), basic knowledge in distributed computing theory is fundamental. When something works, we must know why it works, and when something does not work ... we must know why it does not work.

Asynchronous distributed systems   Asynchronous message-passing systems (also called time-free systems) are characterized by the fact that there are bounds neither on message transfer delays nor on the speed of processes. The combined effect of asynchrony and failures creates an "uncertainty" on the system state that makes problems very difficult or even impossible to solve. These topics are addressed in the companion book *"Communication and agreement abstractions for fault-tolerant asynchronous distributed systems"* (Morgan & Claypool, 2010).

Synchronous distributed systems   This book is on synchronous message-passing distributed systems where the processes are prone to different types of failures (crash failures, omission failures and Byzantine failures). *Synchronous* means that these systems are characterized by the fact that there are bounds on both message transit delay and process speed, and these bounds are known by the processes. This means that the timing uncertainty that makes things difficult (or even impossible) in failure-prone asynchronous systems is partially absent in the synchronous computation model. Hence, problems impossible to solve in pure asynchronous systems can be solved in synchronous systems.

The synchronous message-passing computation model can be seen as an idealized distributed computation model in which processes progress in a lock-step manner and where an execution can be represented as a sequence of rounds. During a round, each process first sends messages, then receives messages and finally executes local computation before it is allowed to proceed to the next round. The fundamental synchrony property is that a message is received in the very same round during which it is sent. This is the basic synchrony assumption.

Albeit it is an idealized computation model, the synchronous model is important because it is a very good approximation of a lot of systems encountered in practical settings (e.g., "closed" systems or embedded systems). Hence, once an algorithm has been designed for the synchronous model, it can be easily adapted and transported to work in a more realistic setting. Said in another way, the synchronous system model is an appropriate model abstraction for a lot of distributed applications.

This book is on fundamental principles of synchronous distributed systems. To present these principles, it focuses on a family of problems that are considered as the most important distributed computing problems, namely the family of distributed agreement problems (consensus, interactive consistency, non-blocking atomic commit and the Byzantine general problem). The book studies these problems in three different process failure models (crash, omission and Byzantine failures).

Readership   This book has been written first for people who are not familiar with the topic and the concepts that are exposed. This includes mainly:

- Graduate students and senior level undergraduate students in computer science, computer engineering, and graduate students in mathematics who are interested in the foundations of fault-tolerant distributed computing.

- Practitioners and engineers who want to be aware of state-of-the-art fault-tolerant distributed algorithms and basic principles that underlie their design.

Prerequisites for this book includes undergraduate courses on algorithms and synchronization. Knowledge of distributed systems can be helpful but is not necessary.

Acknowledgments   This book originated from lecture notes for graduate courses on distributed computing that I give at the University of Rennes (France) and, as an invited professor, in several other universities all over the world. I would like to thank all the graduate students for their questions that, in one way or another, have contributed to this book.

I would also thank all the researchers whose results are exposed in this book. Without their work, this book would not exist. I thank my colleagues of the distributed computing area with whom I worked on topics discussed in this book and more particularly Yoram Moses, Achour Mostéfaoui, Philippe Raïpin Parvédy, Sergio Rajsbaum and Corentin Travers with whom I have developed several results presented here. I want also to thank my colleagues of the distributed computing area with whom I had a lot of fascinating discussions on topics addressed in this book. I also thank Jiannong

Cao, Hong-Kong Polytechnic University, who hosted me while I was writing parts of this book. I want also thank Soma Chaudhuri for her constructive comments on a first draft of this book.

Finally, I would like to thank Nancy Lynch for her kind invitation to write a book for the *Synthesis Lectures on Distributed Computing Theory* series she is editing for Morgan & Claypool Publishers and Diane Cerra for her support as well as the support staff at Morgan and Claypool for their help in putting it all together.

Michel Raynal

February - March, 2010
Rennes, Hong-Kong, Saint-Grégoire

PART I

Definitions

CHAPTER 1

Synchronous Model, Failure Models, and Agreement Problems

This chapter introduces basic definitions: synchronous message-passing model, failure models, and the agreement problems we are interested in.

1.1 COMPUTATION MODEL: DEFINITIONS

1.1.1 SYNCHRONOUS MESSAGE-PASSING MODEL

Message-passing system   We consider systems made up of a fixed number n of processors (nodes) that communicate by sending and receiving messages through bidirectional communication channels. The network is assumed to be fully connected: there is a bidirectional channel that connects every pair nodes. Moreover, each channel is reliable (no loss, duplication or alteration of message).

Each processor locally executes a sequential algorithm. Its power is the one of a Turing machine enriched with two communication operations. By a slight abuse of language, we use the term "process" instead of "processor" in the book.

Communication operations   When invoked by a process p_i, the operation "send m to p_j" allows it to send a message m to a process p_j. Such an operation is atomic in the sense that, whatever the size of m, it is executed entirely or not at all (the case where "half a message" only is sent cannot occur). In a failure-free context, every invocation of this operation terminates.

The notation "broadcast m" is used as a shortcut for
"**for each** $j \in \{1, \ldots, n\}$ **for do** send m to p_j **end for**".

Different from the operation " send m to p" that is atomic (it is executed entirely or not all), the operation " broadcast m" is not atomic (see below the section on failures). Moreover, there is no predetermined sending order (this is emphasized by the statement $j \in \{1, \ldots, n\}$ and the fact that the elements of a set are not ordered). When an invocation " broadcast m" terminates, we know that m has been sent to each processes, but we do not know if it has been sent first to p_a, then to p_b, etc., or in another order.

To receive a message, a process invokes the operation " receive () ". As we will see below, due to the underlying synchrony assumption, this operation can never block a process forever. Moreover, it appears only in an implicit way in an algorithm description.

Synchronous system   *Synchrony* is an abstraction that encapsulates (and hides) specific timing assumptions. It states that there are known upper bounds on both message transfer delays and durations to perform actions by processes. Hence, a synchronous model eliminates all the timing uncertainties encountered in asynchronous systems. This allows us to assume that, at the programming abstraction level, one can consider that the processes progress in a lock-step manner.

1.1.2   THE SYNCHRONOUS ROUND-BASED MODEL

"Lock-step" means that the following *round-based* model can be used to write distributed synchronous algorithms. Each execution (run) consists of a sequence of rounds. Those are identified by the successive integers 1, 2, etc. For each process, the current round number appears as a global variable r that it can only read, and whose progress is implicitly guaranteed by the synchrony assumption. This means that the round number variable r can be seen as global clock that automatically ensures the algorithm liveness. A round is made up of three consecutive phases.

- A send phase during which each process p_i can broadcast a message (i.e., send the message to all processes including itself). The fact that a message is broadcast or not by p_i during a round r is specified by the local algorithm it executes.

- A receive phase during which each process receives messages.

  The fundamental property of the round-based synchronous model lies in the fact that a message sent by a process p_i to a process p_j during a round r is received by p_j at the very same round r.

- Finally, a local computation phase during which a process p_i modifies its local state according to its current local state and the messages it has received. During that phase, a process p_i computes the message (if any) that it will to broadcast during the next round.

The corresponding algorithmic skeleton is described in Figure 1.1. It is easy to see that the receive statements are implicit. σ_i^{r-1} is the local state of p_i at the end of round $r-1$, or equivalently at the beginning of round r; $\delta_i(r, \sigma_i^{r-1}, rec_i^r)$ is the transition function that defines the new local state of p_i at the end of round r (i.e., σ_i^r).

Given a run of an algorithm, the number of rounds is finite. A process stops executing when it invokes the statement return(). Albeit it is not explicitly indicated in the skeleton, in some algorithms, a process p_i can stop after executing the send phase. (This occurs in early-deciding algorithms where a process is required to inform the other processes before deciding and stopping.)

Synchronous space-time diagram   An easy way to represent a synchronous execution is given on Figure 1.2. In that example, (a) there are three processes, and (b) each process broadcasts a message at every round. The execution is failure-free. Each process first broadcasts a message, then waits for

```
algorithm skeleton ():
    Initialization of local variables; let σ⁰ᵢ be pᵢ's initial local state;
    when = 1, 2, ... do % r is the round number %
    begin synchronous round
        Send phase: if pᵢ has to broadcast a round r message m, it does it.
                        In that case, the content of the message is part of σᵢʳ⁻¹;
        Receive phase: let recᵢʳ be the set of messages received during this round;
        Local computation phase: σᵢʳ = δᵢ(r, σᵢʳ⁻¹, recᵢʳ)
    end synchronous round.
```

Figure 1.1: Algorithmic skeleton for the round-based synchronous model (code for p_i)

messages, and finally executes a local computation before the system model forces all the processes to proceed to the next round.

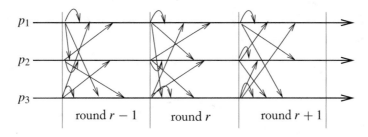

p_1

p_2

p_3

round $r - 1$ round r round $r + 1$

Figure 1.2: A space-time diagram of a synchronous execution

1.1.3 FAILURE MODELS

Process failure   Given a run of a distributed algorithm, a process is *faulty* in that run if its behavior deviates from the one defined by its algorithm. Otherwise, the process is *correct* in the considered run.

A *process failure model* specifies in what way a faulty process can deviate from the behavior specified by its algorithm. (Let us notice that, if a process p_i deviates "more" than allowed by the considered failure model, the failure is outside the failure model, and it might be impossible to design a correct algorithm that tolerates this failure.)

A hierarchy of failure models
- *Crash failure* model. In that case, a faulty process stops executing prematurely. After it has crashed, a process does nothing. Before crashing (if it ever does), a process behaves correctly.
- *Omission failure* models.
    - *Send omission failure* model. In that case, a faulty process intermittently omits to send messages it was supposed to send, or crashes, or both.

- *Receive omission failure* model. In that case, a process intermittently omits to receive messages sent to it, or crashes, or both.
- *General omission failure* model. In that case, a faulty process is subject to send or receive omission failures, or both.

• *Byzantine failure* model.

In that case, a faulty process can exhibit any behavior. As an example, a faulty process can change its state arbitrarily, send messages with erroneous content, or send different messages to distinct processes and no message to others when it should send the same message to all.

The previous failure models can be compared on terms of *severity*. Failure model $\mathcal{F}$ is more *severe* than failure model $\mathcal{G}$ if the sets of faulty behaviors allowed by $\mathcal{G}$ is a proper subset of the sets of faulty behaviors allowed by $\mathcal{F}$. We also say that $\mathcal{G}$ is less severe than $\mathcal{F}$. This means that an algorithm that tolerates failures of type $\mathcal{F}$ also tolerates those of type $\mathcal{G}$ while the opposite is not true.

It is easy to see that crash failures are the less severe while Byzantine failures are the most severe. The hierarchy of the previous failure models is described in Figure 1.3 where an arrow from $\mathcal{G}$ to $\mathcal{F}$ means that $\mathcal{G}$ is less severe than $\mathcal{F}$.

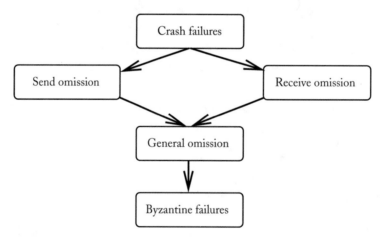

Figure 1.3: Failure model hierarchy

Where is the difficulty created by a given type of failures? Let us consider a process p that, during a round r, crashes while it is broadcasting a message m. As the broadcast operation is not atomic, and there is no predetermined sending order with respect to the destination processes, the message m can be received by any subset of processes. This subset is totally arbitrary (and can be the empty set).

This means that the crash of a process in a send phase of a round creates non-determinism. Contrarily to the failure-free case, it is impossible to know a priori which are the processes that will receive message m. Mastering this uncertainty is the main problem a synchronous distributed algorithm has to cope with when considering the crash failure model.

The additional difficulty in the omission model comes from the fact that a process can on the one hand commit a send (or receive) omission failure with respect to some processes and behave correctly with respect to other processes, and on the other hand commit a send (or receive) omission failure with respect to a given process during some rounds and not during other rounds. This type of failures destroys the communication determinism as described by the algorithm.

Moreover, there is a strong difference between the send omission model and the receive omission model. A process that commits only send omission failures receives all the messages sent to it by correct processes. Hence, it can adopt the point of view of a correct process. Differently, a process that commits receive omission failures can miss messages from correct processes. In the worst case, a faulty process might receive no messages at all.

Send (receive) omission failures model failure of output (input) buffers. Overwriting a message before it is sent by the communication network is a send omission failure. The overwriting of a message m in an input buffer before m has been read is a receive omission failure. In the same vein, the loss of a message can be considered as a send omission failure or a receive omission failure.

In the case of Byzantine faults, a faulty process can create additional "noise" with respect to both communication and the content of values it sends. This creates additional non-determinism that the correct processes have to cope with.

Notation   Given a failure model $\mathcal{F}$, t denotes the maximum number of processes that can fail according to $\mathcal{F}$, and f denotes the number of processes that actually fail in the run we consider. If there are n processes, we have $0 \leq f \leq t < n$.

As we will see, solving a problem P in presence of up to t processes that can fail according to a failure model $\mathcal{F}$ usually requires t to satisfy some constraint with respect to n. The constraint on t can be stronger when P has to be solved in a failure model more severe than $\mathcal{F}$.

1.2   THE CONSENSUS PROBLEM

This section defines the consensus problem. This a fundamental problem of distributed computing: it requires that the processes agree. In one way or another, any distributed application needs some form of agreement; otherwise, the application would not be an application but a set of unrelated applications.

1.2.1   CONSENSUS IN THE CRASH FAILURE MODEL

Base definition   In the consensus problem, each process proposes a value, and the processes have to collectively agree on the same value. Of course, a process can crash before deciding a value. Moreover, in order to be meaningful, the value that is decided has to be related to the values that are proposed. This is captured by the following specification.

- Validity. A decided value is a proposed value.

- Agreement. No two processes decide different values.

- Termination. Every correct process decides.

The validity and agreement properties define the safety property of the consensus problem. Validity relates the output to the inputs, while agreement captures the difficulty of the problem. Termination is a the liveness property of the consensus problem. It states that at least the processes that do not crash have to decide.

Non-uniform consensus   The previous definition is sometimes called uniform consensus, in the sense that it does prevent a process that decides and then crashes from deciding differently from the correct processes. A weaker version of the problem, called non-uniform consensus, allows a process that crashes to decide differently from the other processes. It is defined by the same validity and termination properties plus the following agreement property.

- Agreement. No two correct processes decide different values.

In the following, except when explicitly indicated, we always consider the base (uniform) consensus problem.

Lower bound   As we will see, consensus can always be solved in crash failure model, i.e., for any $t < n$.

Binary vs multivalued consensus   Let $\mathcal{V}$ be the set of values that can be proposed to a consensus instance. If $|\mathcal{V}| = 2$, the consensus is binary. In that case, it is usually considered that $\mathcal{V} = \{0, 1\}$. If $|\mathcal{V}| > 2$, the consensus is multivalued. In that case, the set V can be finite or infinite.

1.2.2   THE SIMULTANEOUS CONSENSUS PROBLEM

The simultaneous consensus problem is a strengthening of the base consensus problem. In base consensus, the agreement property is only on the decided value. Simultaneous consensus adds another agreement constraint on the time (round number) at which processes decide. It is defined by the following properties.

- Validity. A decided value is a proposed value.

- Data agreement. No two processes decide on different values.

- Simultaneous agreement. No two processes decide at different rounds.

- Termination. Every correct process decides a value.

1.2.3   THE k-SET AGREEMENT PROBLEM

This problem is a weakened variant of the consensus problem. It allowed up to k different values to be decided by the processes, each process deciding a single value. Hence, the 1-set agreement problem is consensus. This problem is mainly considered in the crash and omission failure models. In the crash failure model, it is defined by the following properties.

- Validity. A decided value is a proposed value.
- Agreement. At most k different values are decided.
- Termination. Every correct process decides a value.

1.2.4   CONSENSUS IN THE OMISSION FAILURE MODEL

In the omission failure model, the definition of the consensus problem is similar to the one in the crash failure model.

Faulty but not crashed   In the omission failure model, a process can be faulty without ever crashing. Moreover, a faulty process is not required to decide. Due to the synchrony of the computation model, a faulty process that does not crash terminates its algorithm. To prevent ambiguities, let us consider a default value (denoted $\bot$) whose meaning is "no decision". A faulty process that does not crash is required to return either the same value v as correct processes (in that case it "decides v") or the default value $\bot$ (by a slight abuse of language, we then say that it "decides $\bot$"). Let us notice that, according to this specification, a process that decides $\bot$ learns that it has committed omission failures.

Considering the meaning of "decide" that has been introduced in the previous paragraph, the definition of the consensus problem suited to the omission failure model is the following one.

- Validity. A decided value is a proposed value or $\bot$. No correct process decides $\bot$.
- Agreement. No two processes decide different non-$\bot$ values.
- Termination. Every process that does not crash decides.

Good and bad processes   As already indicated, in the worst case, it is possible that a process that commits receive omission failures never receive a message. As it receives no message, is impossible for it to decide a non-$\bot$ value. The situation is different for the processes that commit only send omission failures. They receive all messages sent by correct processes. Hence, these processes can be forced to decide as the correct processes.

Let a *good* process be a process that neither crashes nor commits receive omission failure. This means that a good process is either a correct process or a process that does not crash and commits only send omission failures. The other processes are *bad* processes. Hence, a bad process is a process that crashes or a process that commits receive omission failures.

It is possible to define a stronger version of the consensus problem for the omission failure model. This version is defined by the same agreement and termination properties as before and the following validity property.

- Validity. A decided value is a proposed value or $\bot$. No good process decides $\bot$.

Lower bound   As we will see, consensus can always be solved in the send omission failure model i.e., for any $t < n$. Differently, it can be solved in the receive omission and general omission failure models only for $t < n/2$, which means that there is no algorithm that always works when half or more processes can commit receive omission failures.

1.2.5   CONSENSUS IN THE BYZANTINE FAILURE MODEL

Due to the very nature of faults allowed in this failure model, it is not possible to force a faulty process to decide a default value. Due to its Byzantine behavior, a faulty process can "decide" any value. In the following, the word "decide" applies only to correct processes.

All the consensus specifications for the Byzantine fault model share the same agreement and termination processes that are only on correct processes. As far as the validity property is concerned, there are several possibilities. The choice of one of them depends on the problem one has to solve. We consider here the one that, while remaining meaningful, is the less constraining.

- Strong   validity. If all correct processes propose the same value v, they can decide only v.
- Agreement. No two correct processes decide different values.
- Termination. Every correct process decides.

It is important to notice that when not all correct processes propose the same value, the previous specification does not prevent them to decide any value. As we will, see this cannot cause problem when the consensus is binary.

Lower bound   As we will see, consensus can be solved in Byzantine failure model only when $t < n/3$. This means that if one third or more processes can commit Byzantine failures, it impossible to design a consensus algorithm that always satisfies the previous specification.

1.3   THE INTERACTIVE CONSISTENCY PROBLEM

1.3.1   DEFINITION IN THE CRASH FAILURE MODEL

The *Interactive Consistency* (IC) problem is an agreement problem stronger than consensus in the sense that any IC algorithm can be used to solve consensus, while the opposite is not true. We consider this problem in the context of crash failures.

Similarly to consensus, each process proposes a value. Differently from consensus, the processes have now to agree on the vector of proposed values. A process can crash before or while it is executing the algorithm. In that case, its entry in the decided vector can be $\perp$. More precisely, IC is defined by the following properties.

- Validity. Let $D[1..n]$ be the vector decided by a process. $\forall i \in [1..n]: D[i] \in \{v_i, \perp\}$ where v_i is the value proposed by p_i. Moreover, $D[i] = v_i$ if p_i is correct.
- Agreement. No two processes decide different vectors.
- Termination. Every correct process decides.

It is easy to see solve consensus from IC. As all the processes that decide obtain the same vector, they can use the same deterministic rule to select one of its non-$\perp$ value.

1.3.2   DEFINITION IN THE BYZANTINE MODEL

The Byzantine general (BG) problem has been defined in the Byzantine failure model. A given process (the general) is assumed to send the same message (order) to the other processes (the lieutenants). The BG problem is defined by the following properties.

- Validity. If the sender process is correct, all correct processes deliver the message it has sent.
- Agreement. No two correct processes deliver different messages.
- Termination. Every correct process delivers a message.

It is easy to see that the processes can deliver any value when the sender is Byzantine.

When considering the Byzantine failure model, the interactive consistency problem consists in n instances of the BG problem (each process is the sender in a separate BG instance, and all instances can be executed simultaneously).

1.4   THE NON-BLOCKING ATOMIC COMMIT PROBLEM

Motivation   The *Non-blocking Atomic Commit* problem, that originated in databases, is pervasive in a lot of distributed applications. This problem is addressed in the context of crash failures. It is a basic agreement problem. A task has been split into n subtasks, each executed by a process. When, they have executed their subtasks, the processes have to agree on the fate of the task. They have to either commit it (and each process make permanent its local results) or abort it. To that end, each process proposes a value *yes* or *no* (we usually say that it votes *yes* or *no*). The idea is that if all processes vote *yes*, they have to commit. Differently, if one process votes *no*, they all have to abort.

It is easy to see that the values proposed to the agreement (*yes* and *no*) have not an equal power with respect to the decided value COMMIT and ABORT. The problem is asymmetric in the sense that a single vote *no* decides on the fate of the task.

Definition   The crash of a process can prevent the other processes from knowing the value it proposes. Hence, the specification has to explicitly take into account process failures, i.e., not only in the termination property but also in the validity property. More precisely, the NBAC problem is defined by the following properties.

- Validity. A decided value is COMMIT or ABORT.
  - Justification. If a process decides COMMIT, then all processes have voted *yes*.
  - Obligation. If all processes vote *yes* and no process crashes, then ABORT cannot be decided.

- Agreement. No two processes decide differently.
- Termination. Every correct process decides.

The agreement and termination properties are similar to the ones of the previous agreement problems. In addition to defining the value domain of the decision (COMMIT or ABORT), the validity property relates the decided value not only to proposed values (votes) but also to the failure pattern. Basically, it states that, in "good circumstances", the decision has to be COMMIT. These circumstances are described by the obligation property, namely, only *yes* votes and no process crash.

It is important to notice that, if the obligation property was suppressed, it would be possible for the processes to always decide ABORT. Hence, this property implicitly states that the decision ABORT has to be justified, namely, either a process has voted *no*, or there is a process crash.

It is also important to notice that the specification does not prevent the correct processes from deciding COMMIT despite crashes (in that cases all faulty processes voted *yes* before crashing). This means that the decision COMMIT or ABORT is deterministically fixed in "good circumstances" and when a process votes *no*, and not deterministically fixed in the other cases (i.e., when all processes vote *yes* and there are crashes).

1.5   BIBLIOGRAPHIC NOTES

- The message-passing synchronous model is presented is several textbooks (e.,g., (3; 28; 49)).
- The consensus problem originates in the work of Lamport, Shostask and Pease (47; 64) where are defined the Byzantine failure model, the Byzantine generals problem and the interactive consistency problem. These papers establish lower bounds on the number of rounds to solve this problem in the context of synchronous systems prone to Byzantine failures and present corresponding algorithms. Variants of the problem are presented in (16; 45).
- The simultaneous consensus problem has been introduced in (17; 20). It has recently been investigated again in (54).
- The k-set agreement problem has been introduced by S. Chaudhuri (13). A survey of it appears in (71).
- Failure models are presented in several papers. The presentation adopted here is due to Hadzilacos and Toueg (37).
- The atomic commit problem has its origin in databases (30). Its non-blocking attribute has been first addressed in (77). More information can be found in (7). Relations between consensus and atomic commit are investigated in (32; 36). A study of atomic commit in the synchronous model is presented in (4).
- Results and algorithms on agreement problems in asynchronous systems prone to failures are presented found in the following books (3; 28; 35; 44; 49; 73).

PART II

Agreement in Presence of Crash Failures

CHAPTER 2

Consensus and Interactive Consistency in the Crash Failure Model

This chapter presents t-resilient consensus and interactive consistency algorithms for the synchronous round-based model introduced in the previous chapter ($1 \leq t < n$). It then presents a lower bound on the number of rounds that are necessary to solve these problems whatever the time instances at which the crash occurs.

2.1 CONSENSUS DESPITE CRASH FAILURES

This section presents two simple consensus algorithm for the synchronous crash failure model. The system parameter n denotes the number of processes while t denotes the maximum number of processes that may crash in a run.

2.1.1 A SIMPLE CONSENSUS ALGORITHM

A simple algorithm A process p_i invokes the operation propose (v_i) where v_i is the value it proposes. It terminates when it executes the statement return(v), and v is then the value it decides.

The principle of the algorithm is pretty simple. As at most t processes may crash (model assumption), any set of $t + 1$ processes contains at least one correct process. (If more than t processes crash, we are outside the model. In that case, there is no guarantee. More generally, if an algorithm is used in a more severe failure model than the one it is intended for, it is allowed to behave arbitrarily.) It follows that taking any set of $t + 1$ processes we can always rely on one of them to ensure that a single value is decided.

The corresponding algorithm is described in Figure 2.1. Each process manages a local variable est_i that contains its estimate of the decision value; est_i is consequently initialized to v_i (line 1). Then, the processes execute synchronously $t + 1$ rounds (line 2), each round being coordinated by one process, namely, round r is coordinated by process p_r. The coordinator of round r broadcasts its current estimate (message EST(), line 3). Let us notice that, as a round is coordinated by a single process, there is at most one value broadcast per round. During a round, a process p_i updates its estimates est_i if it receives the current estimate of the round coordinator (line 4). Finally, at the end of the last round, p_i decides (returns) the current value of its estimate est_i.

```
operation prope (v_i):
(1) est_i ← v_i;
(2) when r = 1, 2, ..., (t + 1) do
    begin synchronous round
(3)     if (i = r) then  broadcast  EST(est_i) end if;
(4)     if ( EST(v) received during round r) then est_i ← v end if;
(5)     if (r = t + 1) then  return(est_i) end if
    end synchronous round.
```

Figure 2.1: A simple (but unfair) t-resilient consensus algorithm (code for p_i)

Theorem 2.1   *Let $1 \leq t < n$. The algorithm described in Figure 2.1 solves the consensus problem in a synchronous system prone to up to t process crashes.* **Proof** The validity property (a decided value is a proposed value) is trivial. The termination property (every correct process decides) is an immediate consequence of the synchrony assumption: the system automatically progresses from a round to the next one (with the guarantee that the messages sent in a round are received in the very same round).

The agreement property (no two processes decide differently) is an immediate consequence of the following observation. Due to assumption on the maximum number t of processes that may crash, there is at least one round that is coordinated by a correct process. Let p_c be such a process. When $r = c$, p_c sends its current estimate $est_c = v$ to all the processes, and any process p_j that has not crashed updates est_j to v. It follows that all the processes that have not crashed by th end of round r, have their estimates equal to v, and consequently no other value can be decided. $\square_{Theorem\ 2.1}$

Time and message complexities   The algorithm requires $t + 1$ rounds. Moreover, at most one message is sent at each round. Let b the bit size of the proposed values. The bit complexity is consequently $(t + 1)b$.

Unfairness with respect to proposed values   Albeit correct, the previous algorithm has a drawback, namely, for any $j \in \{(t + 1), \dots, n\}$, there is no run in which the value proposed by p_j can be decided (but if the same value is proposed by a coordinator process). In that sense, the algorithm is unfair.

This unfairness can be eliminated by adding a preliminary round ($r = 0$) during which the processes exchange their values. This is done by inserting the statements " broadcast EST(est_i); est_i ← any estimate value received" between line 1 and 2). This makes the algorithm fair, but it is obtained at the additional cost of one round.

2.1.2   A FAIR CONSENSUS ALGORITHM

This section presents a fair consensus algorithm for the crash failure model that requires $t + 1$ rounds only. The input vector of a given a run is the size n vector such that, for any j, its j-th entry contains the value proposed by p_j. Of course, no process p_i knows initially this vector, it knows only the value it proposes to that consensus instance.

Principle of the algorithm   The idea is for a process to decide during the last round, a value according to a deterministic rule, among all values it has seen. An example of deterministic rule is to select the smallest value. This is the rule we consider here. This value is kept in the local variable est_i (that is initialized to v_i, the value proposed by p_i).

Let us observe that, if a process p_i does not crash and proposes the smallest input value, that value will be decided whatever the values proposed by the other processes. Hence, for any process p_i, there is (a) an input vector in which no two processes propose the same value, (b) a run and a failure pattern, such that the value decided by p_i is decided in that run. The algorithm is fair in that sense.

The algorithm is described in Figure 2.2. The processes execute $t + 1$ synchronous rounds (line 2). The idea is for a process p_i to broadcast during each round the smallest estimate value it has ever received. But a simple observation shows that this is required only if its estimate became smaller during the previous round (line 3). To that end, p_i manages a local variable denoted $prev\_est_i$ that contains the smallest value it has previously sent (line 5). That variable is initialized to the default value $\perp$ (a value that cannot be proposed to the consensus by the processes).

During a round r, the set $recval_i$ contains the estimate values received by p_i during round r (line 4). Due to the synchrony assumption, it contains all estimate values sent to p_i during round r. Before proceeding to the next round, p_i updates est_i (line 6). If r is the last round ($r = t + 1$), p_i decides by invoking return(est_i) (line 7).

```
operation propose (v_i):
(1) est_i ← v_i; prev_est_i ← ⊥;
(2) when r = 1, 2, . . . , (t + 1) do
    begin synchronous round
(3)     if (est_i ≠ prev_est_i) then broadcast EST(est_i) end if;
(4)     let recval_i = {values received during round r};
(5)     prev_est_i ← est_i;
(6)     est_i ← min(recval_i ∪ {est_i});
(7)     if (r = t + 1) then return(est_i) end if
    end synchronous round.
```

Figure 2.2: A simple fair t-resilient consensus algorithm (code for p_i)

Theorem 2.2   *Let $1 \le t < n$. The algorithm described in Figure 2.2 solves the consensus problem in a synchronous system prone to up to t process crashes.*

Proof   As in the previous algorithm, the validity and termination properties are trivial. Hence, we consider only the agreement property.

If a single process decides (we have then $t = n - 1$ and t processes crash), the agreement property is trivially satisfied. Hence, let us suppose that at least two processes decide, and let p_i and p_j be any two of them. Moreover, let us assume that p_i decide v, and p_j decide v'. We show that $v = v'$. Assuming process p_x has not crashed by the end of round r, let $est_x[r]$ be the value of est_x at the the end of round r.

As both p_i and p_j decide, they both execute $t + 1$ rounds. Let us consider p_i. It "learns" (receives for the first time) the value v at some round r (with $r = 0$ if $v = v_i$ the value proposed by p_i itself). As p_i decides $v = est_i[r]$ and est_i cannot increase, we have $est_i[r] = \cdots = est_i[t + 1]$. There are two cases.

- Case 1: $r < t + 1$ (r is not the last round, and consequently $r + 1$ does exist). In that case, p_i has broadcast $EST(v)$ during round $r + 1 \leq t + 1$. As p_j executes this round, it receives v and we have $est_j[r + 1] \leq v$. As est_j never increases, we have $est_j[t + 1] \leq v$.
- Case 2: $r = t + 1$. In that case, p_i learns v at round $t + 1$ and there are no more round to forward v to the other processes.

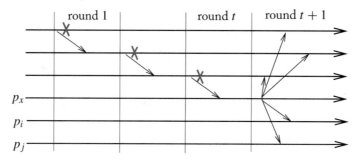

Figure 2.3: The second case of the agreement property (with $t = 3$ crashes)

As (a) a process broadcasts a value v at most once, and (b) p_i receives v for the time time at round $t + 1$, it follows that v has been forwarded (broadcast) along a chain of $t + 1$ distinct processes. Due to the model assumption, one of these $t + 1$ processes (say p_x) is correct. As it is correct, p_x has broadcast $EST(v)$ during a round r, $1 \leq r \leq t + 1$. Let us notice that p_x might be p_j. (See, Figure 2.3 where each arrow is associated with the message $EST(v)$ and $t = 3$. A cross indicates the crash of the corresponding process.) (Let us also observe that we necessarily have $r = t + 1$, otherwise p_i would have received $EST(v)$ before the last round.) It follows that all processes that execute round r are such that $est_j[r] \leq v$, and consequently $est_j[t + 1] \leq v$.

As $v = est_i[t + 1]$, it follows that we have $est_j[t + 1] \leq est_i[t + 1]$.

A symmetry argument where p_i and p_j are exchanged allows us to conclude that $est_j[t + 1] \leq est_i[t + 1]$. Hence, $est_j[t + 1] = est_i[t + 1]$, which concludes the proof of the theorem.

$\square_{Theorem\ 2.2}$

Time and message complexities   As the previous one, this algorithm requires $t + 1$ rounds.

During a round, a process send at most $n - 1$ messages (we do not count the message it sends to itself), and each message is made up of b bits. Moreover, due to the fact that a process sends an estimate value only it is smaller than the previous one, a process issues at most $\min(t + 1, |V|)$ broadcasts, where V is the set of values that can be proposed. It follows that the bit complexity of the algorithm is upper bounded by $n(n - 1)b \times \min(t + 1, |V|)$.

Interestingly, in the case of binary consensus ($V = \{0, 1\}$), we have $b = 1$ and $= |V| = 2$. The bit complexity is then $2n(n - 1)$.

2.2   INTERACTIVE CONSISTENCY DESPITE CRASH FAILURES

2.2.1   SIMULATING ATOMIC FAILURES

Atomic crash and perfect round-based model   The crash of a process p_i during a round r is *atomic* if either all or none of the messages it has sent are been received by their destination process.

A synchronous round-based system model in which (a) each process broadcasts a message at every round, and (b) all crashes are atomic, simplifies drastically the design of distributed algorithms. This is because it follows from the previous behavioral properties that all the processes that terminate a round r have received exactly the same messages during every round r', $1 \leq r' \leq r$. Such a model is called *perfect round-based* model.

From interactive consistency to the perfect round-based model   It is consequently worth designing an algorithm that simulates the perfect round-based model on top of the base round-based model. Among its many applications, this is exactly what is done by interactive consistency (IC).

The simulation is as follows. Assuming that each process p_i broadcasts a message during each round, let us call ρ the rounds in the perfect round-based model. Considering any round ρ, let m_i^ρ be the message broadcast by p_i during that round. The send and receive phases of a round ρ are implemented by an instance of the IC problem where m_i^ρ is the value proposed by process p_i to that IC instance. It follows from the IC specification that all the processes that terminate that IC instance obtain the very same vector $D[1..n]$ such that $D[j] \in \{m_j^\rho, \bot\}$ and is m_j^ρ if p_i has not crashed by the end of that IC instance.

As we are about to see, each round ρ of the perfect round-based model can be implemented with $t + 1$ rounds of the underlying base round-based model.

2.2.2   AN INTERACTIVE CONSISTENCY ALGORITHM

The interactive consistency algorithm that is presented in Figure 2.4 is based on the same principle as the algorithm described in Figure 2.2, namely at every round each process broadcasts what it has learnt during the previous round, which is here a set of values.

Given a process p_i, the local variable $view_i$ represents its current knowledge of the values proposed by the other processes, more precisely, $view_i[k] = v$ means that p_i knows that p_k has proposed value v, while $view_i[k] = \bot$ means that p_i does not know the value proposed by p_k. Initially, $view_i$ contains only $\bot$s, but its ith entry that contains v_i (line 1).

In order to forward the value of a process only once, the algorithm uses pairs (k, v) the meaning of which is "p_k has proposed value v". The local variable new_i is a (possibly empty) set of such pairs (k, v). At the beginning of a round r, new_i contains the new pairs that p_i has learned during that round (line 10). Hence, initially $new_i = \{(i, v_i)\}$ (line 1).

- Send phase. The behavior of a process p_i is simple. When it start a new round r, p_i broadcasts EST(new_i) if $new_i \neq \emptyset$ to inform the other processes of the pairs it has learnt during the previous round (line 3).

- Receive phase (lines 4-6). Then, p_i receives round r messages and saves their values in the local array $recfrom_i[1..n]$. Let us observe that it is possible that a process receives no message at some rounds.)

- Local computation phase (lines 7-13). After having reset new_i, p_i updates its array $view_i$ according to the pairs it has received. Moreover, it it has learnt (i.e., receives for the first time) a pair (k, v) during the current round, p_i adds it to new_i. Finally, if r is the last round, p_i returns $view_i$ as the vector it decides on.

```
operation  propose (v_i):
(1)  view_i ← [⊥, ..., ⊥]; view_i[i] ← v_i; new_i ← {(i, v_i)};
(2)  when r = 1, 2, ..., (t + 1) do
     begin synchronous round
(3)      if (new_i ≠ ∅) then  broadcast EST(new_i) end if;
(4)      foreach j such that (j ≠ i) do
(5)          if (new_j received from p_j) then recfrom_i[j] ← new_j else recfrom_i[j] ← ∅ end if;
(6)      end for;
(7)      new_i ← ∅;
(8)      for each j such that (j ≠ i) ∧ (recfrom_i[j] ≠ ∅) do
(9)          foreach (k, v) ∈ recfrom_i[j] do
(10)             if (view_i[k] = ⊥) then view_i[k] ← v; new_i ← new_i ∪ {(k, v)} end if
(11)         end for
(12)     end for;
(13)     if (r = t + 1) then  return(view_i) end if
     end synchronous round.
```

Figure 2.4: A t-resilient interactive consistency algorithm (code for p_i)

Proof of the algorithm   If would be possible to prove that the previous algorithm satisfies the agreement property of the IC problem using the same reasoning as in the proof of Theorem 2.2, i.e., considering the case where a process learns a pair (k, v) for the first time during the last round or a previous round. A different proof is given here. This proof is an immediate consequence of Lemma 2.3 that follows.

The interest of this lemma lies in the fact that it captures a fundamental property associated with the round-based synchronous model where, during each round r, each process (that has not crashed) forwards the values that it has learnt during round $r - 1$ (if any). The lemma captures the intuition that the "distance" separating the local views of the input vector (as perceived by each process) decreases as rounds go along. More precisely, given two vectors $view_i$ and $view_j$, let $dist(view_i, view_j)$ denote the Hamming distance separating these vectors, namely, $dist(view_i, view_j) = |\{x$ such that $view_i[x] \neq view_j[x]\}|$ (number of entries where the vectors differ).

Lemma 2.3   *Let $1 \leq t < n$, $1 \leq r < t + 1$, p_i and p_j be two processes not crashed at the end of round r, and $view_i^r$ and $view_j^r$ the value of $view_i$ and $view_j$ at the end of round r. We have $dist(view_i^r, view_j^r) \leq t - (r - 1)$.*

Proof Let $\delta(r)$ be the maximal Hamming distance between the vectors of any two processes not crashed by the end of round r. We have to show that $\delta(r) \leq t - (r - 1)$.

Claim C. Let r be a failure-free round and p_i and p_j any two processes not crashed by the end of round r. We have $\delta(r') = 0$ for $r \leq r' \leq t + 1$.

Proof of the claim. Let us first observe that, at each round r'' such that $1 \leq r'' \leq r$, each of p_i and p_j sends to the other every new value it has learnt during the round $r'' - 1$ (Observation $O1$). Moreover, as no process crashes during round r, p_i and p_j have received the same set of messages during that round (Observation $O2$). It follows from $O1$ and $O2$ that $view_i$ and $view_j$ are equal at the end of round r. As p_i and p_j are any pair of processes that terminate round r, it follows that $\delta(r) = 0$. Moreover, as from round r no process can learn new values, we trivially have $\delta(r') = 0$ for $r \leq r' \leq t + 1$. End   of proof of the claim.

The proof considers the failure pattern in the worst case scenario in which t processes crash. Let $c \geq 1$ be the number of processes that have crashed by the end of the first round. The worst situation is when, at the end of the first round, a process p_i has received all the proposed values (i.e., $view_i$ contains only non-$\perp$ values), while another process p_j has received only $n - c$ proposed values (i.e., $view_j$ has c entries equal to $\perp$). It follows that $\delta(1) \leq c$. From then on, no two vectors can differ in more than c entries, and, consequently, we have $\delta(r) \leq c$ for $1 \leq r \leq t + 1$. The rest of the proof is a case analysis, according to the value of r.

- The first case considers the rounds $1 \leq r \leq t + 1 - c$.

  As $r \leq t + 1 - c \equiv c \leq t - (r - 1)$, it follows from $\delta(r) \leq c$ for $1 \leq r \leq t + 1$, that $\delta(r) \leq c \leq t - (r - 1)$ for the rounds $1 \leq r \leq t + 1 - c$, which proves the lemma for these rounds.

- The second case considers the remaining rounds $t + 1 - c < r \leq t + 1$.

  By the end of the first round, c processes have crashed. The worst case scenario for the following rounds r, $1 \leq r \leq t + 1 - c$, is when there is a crash per round. Otherwise, due to Claim C, we would have $\delta(r') = 0$ from the first round r', $1 \le r' \le t + 1 - c$, during which there is no crash.

Table 2.1: Crash pattern

Round number r	1	2	...	r'	...	$t + 1 - c$
Number of crashes during r	c	1	...	1	...	1
Total number of crashes	c	$c + 1$	...	$c + (r' - 1)$	...	t

In that worst case, we can conclude that there is no more crash after the round $t + 1 - c$. This is because there are at most t crashes, c before the end of the first round and then one crash per round from round $r = 2$ until round $r = t + 1 - c$. This is depicted in Table 2.1. It then follows from Claim C that $\delta(r') = 0$ for $t + 1 - c < r' \le t + 1$, which concludes the proof of the lemma.

$$\square_{Lemma\ 2.3}$$

Theorem 2.4 *Let* $1 \le t < n$. *The algorithm described in Figure 2.4 solves the interactive problem in a synchronous system prone to up to t process crashes.*

Proof The termination property follows directly from the message synchrony assumption of the synchronous model: if a process does not crash, it necessarily progresses until round $t + 1$. The agreement property is an immediate consequence of Lemma 2.3: at round $t = t + 1$ we have $dist(view_i^{t+1}, view_j^{t+1}) = 0$.

The validity property states that the vector $view_i[1..n]$ decided by a process p_i is such that (a) $view_i[k] \in \{v_k, \bot\}$ where v_k is the value proposed by p_i, and $view_i[k] = v_k$ if p_k is correct. Let us assume that p_k is correct. It follows from the algorithm that p_k broadcasts EST($\{(k, v_k)\}$ during the first round. Due to the synchrony assumption and the reliability of the communication channels, process p_i receives this message (line 5). Then p_i updates accordingly $view_i[k]$ to v_k (line 10). Finally, let us observe that, due to the test of line 10, any entry $view_i[x]$ is set at most once. Consequently $view_i[k]$ remains equal to v_k forever, which concludes the proof of the validity property.

$$\square_{Theorem\ 2.4}$$

Time and message complexities As for the previous algorithms, this algorithm requires $t + 1$ rounds.

A pair (k, v) requires $b + \log_2 n$ bits (where b is the number of bits needed to encode a proposed value). As a process broadcasts a given pair (v, k) at most once, the bit complexity of the algorithm is upper bounded by $n^2(n - 1)(b + \log_2 n)$ bits (assuming a process does not physically send messages to itself).

From interactive consistency to consensus   The consensus problem can easily be solved as soon as one has an algorithm solving the IC problem. As the processes that decide in the IC problem decide the very same vector, they can use the same deterministic rule to extract a non-$\bot$ value from this vector (e.g., the first non-$\bot$ value or the greatest value, etc.). The only important point is that they all use the same deterministic rule.

2.2.3   A CONVERGENCE POINT OF VIEW

This section gives another view on the way the algorithm works. Let $VIEW^r[1..n]$ be the vector of proposed values collectively known by the set of processes that terminate round r. More explicitly, $VIEW^r[i] = v_i$ (the value proposed by p_i) if $\exists\, k$ such that $view_k^r[i] = v_i$, and $VIEW^r[i] = \bot$ otherwise. This means that $VIEW^r[1..n]$ is the "union" of the local vectors of the processes that terminate round r. It represents the knowledge on "which processes have proposed which values" that could have an external omniscient observer that would see all processes at the end of round r.

Definition 2.5 $(V1 \leq V2) \overset{def}{=} \forall x \in [1..n] : (V1[x] \neq \bot) \Rightarrow (V1[x] = V2[x]).$

The algorithm satisfies the following properties.

Property 2.6 $\forall r \in [0..t] : VIEW^{r+1} \leq VIEW^r.$

This property follows from the fact that crashes are stable (once it has crashed a process never recover). It states that global knowledge cannot increase.

Property 2.7 $\forall i \in [1..n] : \forall r \in [1..t+1] : view_i^r \leq view_i^{r+1}.$

This property follows from the fact that no value is ever withdrawn by a process p_i from its local array $view_i$. It states that local knowledge of a process can never decrease.
Let $view_i^r$ be the value of the local array $view_i$ (local knowledge of p_i) at the end of round r.

Property 2.8 $\forall i \in [1..n] : \forall r \in [1..t+1] : view_i^r \leq VIEW^r.$

This property states that, at the end of any round r, a process cannot know more than what is know by the whole set of processes still alive at the end of the round.

The interactive consistency algorithm, based on the fact that global knowledge cannot increase and local knowledge cannot decrease, is a distributed algorithm that directs the processes to converge to the same vector $VIEW^{t+1}$.

2.3   LOWER BOUND ON THE NUMBER OF ROUNDS

This section shows that, when considering the synchronous round-based model, any consensus algorithm that copes with t process crashes requires at least $t + 1$ rounds. This means that there is no algorithm that always solves consensus in at most t rounds ("always" means "whatever the failure pattern defined as the subset of processes that crash and the time instants at which they crash").

As any algorithm that solves the IC problem can be used to solve the consensus problem, it follows that $t + 1$ is also a lower bound on the number of rounds for the IC problem. Moreover, as the consensus and IC algorithms that have been presented in this chapter do not direct the processes to execute more than $t + 1$ rounds, it follows that they are optimal with respect to the number of rounds.

2.3.1   PRELIMINARIES

Assumptions

- The round-based model considered is such that, in every round, each process sends a message to all processes.

  It is easy to see this assumption does not limit the generality of the result. This is because it is always possible to modify a round-based algorithm in order to obtain an equivalent algorithm using such a sending pattern. If during a round, a process sends a message m to a subset of the processes, only that message can carry the set of its destination processes, and when a process p_j receives m, it discards it if is is not one of the destination processes.

- The lower bound proof considers the following assumptions. It is easy to see that, as the previous one, none of them limits the generality of the result.

    - The proof considers binary consensus.
    - The proof assumes that at least two processes do not crash, i.e., $t < n - 1$.
    - The proof assumes that there is one crash per round.
    - The proof considers the non-uniform version of consensus that is weaker than consensus (it requires only that no two correct processes decide different values).

Global state, valence, and k-round execution

- Considering the execution of a synchronous round-based algorithm A (also called a run), the *global state at the end round r* is made up of the state of each process at the end of that round (if a process has crashed, its local state indicates the round at which it has crashed).

  Let us notice that the global state at the end of a round is the same as the global state at the beginning of the next round. Only these global states need to be considered. (A global state is sometimes called *configuration*.)

  Given an initial global state and a failure pattern, the execution of an algorithm A gives rise to a sequence of global states.

- Let S be a global state obtained during the execution of a binary consensus algorithm A.

- S is 0-*valent* (resp., 1-*valent*), if whatever the following global states produced by A, the value 0 (resp., 1) only can be decided.
- S is *univalent* if it is 0-valent or 1-valent.
- S is *bivalent* if it not univalent.

- A *k-round execution* E_k of an algorithm A is a an execution of A up to the end of round k.

  Let S_k be the corresponding global state. E_k is 0-valent, 1-valent, univalent or bivalent if S_k is 0-valent, 1-valent, univalent or bivalent, respectively.

2.3.2   THE $(t + 1)$ LOWER BOUND

Theorem 2.9   *Let $t < n - 1$, and let us assume that, at most, one process crashes in each round. There is no algorithm that solves binary consensus in such a synchronous round-based model.*

Proof   The proof is by contradiction. It supposes that there is an algorithm A that solves binary consensus in t rounds, in presence of t process crashes (one per round). The proof follows from the two following lemmas that are proved in the next section.

- Lemma 2.10 shows that the $(t - 1)$-round execution E_{t-1} of any round of A is is univalent.
- Lemma 2.12 shows that A has a $(t - 1)$-round execution E_{t-1} that is bivalent.

These two lemmas contradict each other, thereby proving the impossibility for A to terminate in t rounds. Hence the $t + 1$ lower bound. $\square_{Theorem\ 2.9}$

2.3.3   PROOF OF THE LEMMAS

Lemma 2.10   *Any $(t - 1)$-round execution E_{t-1} of A is univalent.*

Proof The proof is by contradiction. Let us assume that A has a bivalent $(t - 1)$-round execution E_{t-1}. Let us consider the following three one-round extensions of E_{t-1} (Figure 2.5).

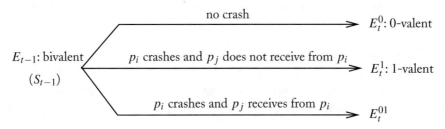

Figure 2.5: Three possible one-round extensions from E_{t-1}

- Let E_t^0 be the t-round execution obtained by extending E_{t-1} by one round in which no process crashes. As (by assumption) A terminates in t rounds, the correct processes decide by the end of round t of E_t^0. Let us suppose that they decide the value 0.

- As E_{t-1} is bivalent (contradiction assumption), it follows that it has a one-round extension E_t^1 in which the correct processes decide 1.

    Let us observe that in round t of E_t^1 exactly one process (say p_i) crashes. (At least one process crashes because otherwise E_t^0 and E_t^1 would be identical, and, at most, one process crashes because there is at most one crash per round.)

    Moreover, p_i must crash before sending its round t message to at least one correct process p_j; otherwise, p_j would be would be unable to distinguish E_t^0 and E_t^1 and would consequently decide the same value in both executions.

- Let us now consider the one-round extension E_t^{01} that is identical to E_t^1 except that p_i sends its round t message to p_j. (This means the only difference between E_t^{01} and E_t^1 lies in the round t message from p_i to p_j that p_j receives in E_t^{01} and does not in E_t^1.)

Let p_k be a correct process different from p_j (such a process exists because $t < n - 1$). We have then the following.

1. The correct process p_j cannot distinguish E_t^0 and E_t^{01}. This is because from its local state in S_{t-1} (its local state at the end of execution E_{t-1}), process p_j has received the same messages during the last round in both E_t^0 and E_t^{01}. Hence, it has to decide the same value in both executions. As it decides 0 in E_t^0, it has to decide 0 in E_t^{01}.

2. The correct process p_k cannot distinguish E_t^1 and E_t^{01}. This is because (as previously for p_j) from its local state in S_{t-1}, it has received the same messages during the last round in both E_t^1 and E_t^{01}. Hence, it has to decide the same value in both executions. As it decides 1 in E_t^1, it has to decide 1 in E_t^{01}.

It follows that while both p_j and p_k are correct in E_t^{01}, they decide differently, which contradicts the consensus agreement property, and concludes the proof of the lemma. $\square_{Lemma\ 2.10}$

Lemma 2.11   *The algorithm A has a bivalent initial global state (or equivalently a bivalent 0-round execution).*

Proof The proof is by contradiction. Assuming that there is no bivalent initial global state, let $\mathcal{S}_0$ the set of all 0-valent initial global states and $\mathcal{S}_1$ be the set of all 1-valent initial global states. As only 0 (resp., 1) can be decided when all processes propose 0 (resp., 1) the set $\mathcal{S}_0$ (resp., $\mathcal{S}_1$) is not empty. As these sets are not empty there must be two global states $S[0] \in \mathcal{S}_0$ and $S[1]1 \in \mathcal{S}_1$ that differ only in the value proposed by one process (say p_i).

Let us consider an execution E of A from $S[0]$ in which p_i crashes before taking any step. As $S[0]$ is 0-valent, it follows that the processes decides 0. But, as p_i does not participate in E, exactly the same execution can be produced from $S[1]$, and in that case, the processes have to decide 1. But, in the execution E, no process can distinguish if the initial global state is $S[0]$ or $S[1]$. Consequently, they have to decide the same value if E is executed from $S[0]$ or $S[1]$, contradicting the fact that $S[0]$ is 0-valent while $S[1]$ is 1-valent. $\square_{Lemma}$ 2.11

Lemma 2.12   *The algorithm A has a bivalent $(t-1)$-round execution.*

Proof The proof shows that for each $k, 0 \leq k \leq t-1$, there is a bivalent k-round execution E_k. It is based on an induction on k. The base case $k = 0$ is exactly what is proved by Lemma 2.11, namely, there is bivalent initial global state S_0. The corresponding 0-round execution (in which no process has yet executed a step) is denoted E_0. So, let us consider the following induction assumption: for each $k, 0 \leq k < t-1$, there is a bivalent k-round execution E_k.

To show that E_k can be extended by one round into a bivalent $(k+1)$-round execution E_{k+1}, the reasoning is by contradiction. Let us assume that every one-round extension of E_k is univalent. Let E^1_{k+1} be the one-round extension of E_k in which no process crashes during that round. Without loss of generality, let us assume that E^1_{k+1} is 1-valent. As E_k is bivalent, and all its one-round extensions are univalent, it has a one-round extension E^0_{k+1} that is 0-valent. (See Figure 2.6.)

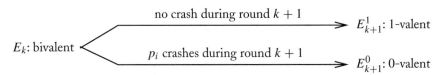

Figure 2.6: Extending the k-round execution E_k

As (a) E^1_{k+1} and E^0_{k+1} are one-round extensions of the same k-round execution E_k, (b) they have the different valence, (c) no process crashes during the round $k+1$ of E^1_{k+1}, it follows that E^0_{k+1} is such that there is exactly one process (say p_i) that crashes during round $k+1$ ("exactly one" is because at most one process crashes per round), and fails to send its round $k+1$ message to some processes, say the processes $q_1, \ldots, q_m$ with $0 \leq m \leq n$ ($m = 0$ corresponds to the case where p_i crashes after it has sent its round $k+1$ message to every process).

Starting from E^0_{k+1}, let us define a sequence of $(k+1)$-round extensions of E_k such that (see Table 2.2):

- $E_{k+1}[0]$ is E^0_{k+1} (hence, $E_{k+1}[0]$ is 0-valent),
- $\forall j, 0 < j \leq m, E_{k+1}[j]$ is identical to $E_{k+1}[j-1]$ except that p_i crashes after it has sent its round $k+1$ message to q_j. It is follows from this definition that p_i has sent its round $k+1$ message to the processes $q_1, \ldots, q_j$.

As by assumption, all one-round extensions of E_k are univalent, $E_{k+1}[0]$, etc., until $E_{k+1}[m]$ are univalent.

Table 2.2: Missing messages due to the crash of p_i	
$(k + 1)$-round execution	round $k + 1$ message from p_i not sent to the processes
$E_{k+1}[0] \overset{\text{def}}{=} E_{k+1}[0]$	$q_1, q_2, \ldots, q_j, q_{j+1}, \ldots, q_m$
$E_{k+1}[1]$	$q_2, \ldots, q_j, q_{j+1}, \ldots, q_m$
$E_{k+1}[j - 1]$	$q_j, q_{j+1}, \ldots, q_m$
$E_{k+1}[j]$	$q_{j+1}, \ldots, q_m$
$E_{k+1}[m - 1]$	q_m
$E_{k+1}[m]$	$\emptyset$

Claim C. $\forall\, j, 0 \leq j \leq m$, $E_{k+1}[j]$ is 0-valent.

Proof of the claim. The proof is by induction. As $E_{k+1}[0]$ is 0-valent, the claim follows for $j = 0$. Hence, let us assume that all $(k + 1)$-round executions $E_{k+1}[\ell]$, $0 \leq \ell < j$ are 0-valent, while $E_{k+1}[j]$ is 1-valent. We show that it is not possible.

Let us extend (see Figure 2.7) the 0-valent execution $E_{k+1}[j - 1]$ into the execution E^0_{k+2} and the 1-valent execution $E_{k+1}[j]$ into the execution E^1_{k+2} by crashing in both executions process q_j at the very beginning of round $k + 2$ (if it has not crashed before). It follows there is no round after round $k + 1$ in which q_j sends a message. Let us notice that, as $k < t - 1$, round $k + 2$ exists.

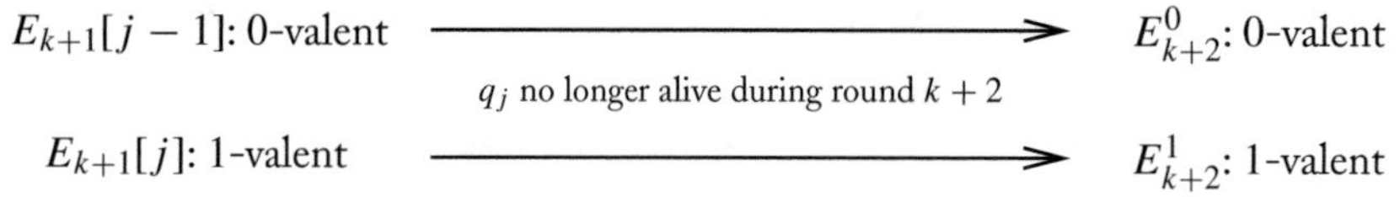

$E_{k+1}[j - 1]$: 0-valent $\quad\longrightarrow\quad$ E^0_{k+2}: 0-valent

q_j no longer alive during round $k + 2$

$E_{k+1}[j]$: 1-valent $\quad\longrightarrow\quad$ E^1_{k+2}: 1-valent

Figure 2.7: Extending two $(k + 1)$-round executions

Let us observe that no process that has not crashed by the end of round $k + 2$ can distinguish E^0_{k+2} from E^1_{k+2} (any such process has the same local state in both executions). Hence, E^0_{k+2} and E^1_{k+2} are identical for the processes that terminate round $k + 2$. Hence, these processes have to decide both 0 (because E^0_{k+2} is 0-valent), and 1 (because E^1_{k+2} is 1-valent), which is clearly impossible. End   of proof of the claim.

It follows from the claim that $E_{k+1}[m]$ is 0-valent. Let us now consider E^1_{k+1} that is 1-valent. The only difference between these two $(k + 1)$-round executions is that p_i crashes at the end of the round $(k + 1)$ in $E_{k+1}[m]$, and does not crash during the round $(k + 1)$ in E^1_{k+1}. Let us construct the two following $(k + 2)$-round executions (see Figure 2.8).

- Let F^1_{k+2} be the one-round extension of E^1_{k+1} where p_i crashes when round $k + 2$ starts and then no process crashes. Let us notice that F^1_{k+2} is 1-valent.

- Let F^0_{k+2} be the one-round extension of $E_{k+1}[m]$ where no more process crashes. Let us notice that F^0_{k+2} is 0-valent.

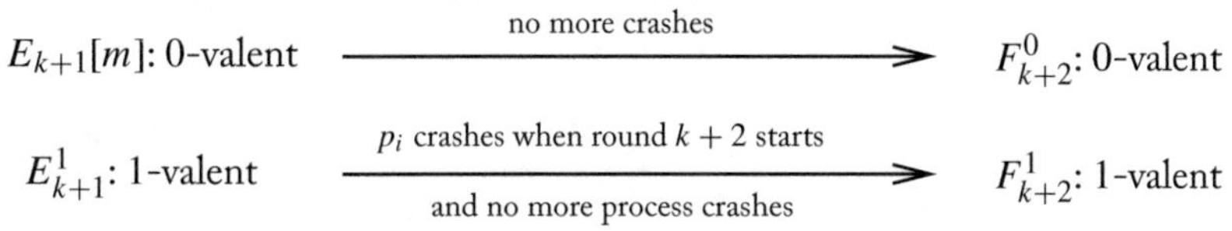

$E_{k+1}[m]$: 0-valent $\xrightarrow{\text{no more crashes}}$ F_{k+2}^0: 0-valent

E_{k+1}^1: 1-valent $\xrightarrow[\text{and no more process crashes}]{p_i \text{ crashes when round } k+2 \text{ starts}}$ F_{k+2}^1: 1-valent

Figure 2.8: Extending again two $(k+1)$-round executions

Let us observe on the one hand that a correct process has to decide 1 from the $(k+2)$-round execution F_{k+2}^1, and 0 from the $(k+2)$-round execution F_{k+2}^0. On another hand, no process executing round $k+2$ can distinguish if the execution is F_{k+2}^1 or F_{k+2}^0, hence it has to decide both 0 and 1 which is impossible. A contradiction which concludes the proof of the lemma. $\square_{Lemma\ 2.12}$

2.4   BIBLIOGRAPHIC NOTES

- The algorithms presented in this chapter are all based on variants of the extinction/propagation strategy, namely, during every round each process propagates the new values it has learnt during the previous round. Similar algorithms are described in (3; 28; 44; 49; 70).

- The notions of atomic failure and perfect synchronized model is due Delporte, Fauconnier, Guerraoui and Pochon (15).

- The $t+1$ lower bound for consensus and interactive consistency has first been proved for the Byzantine failure model in the early eighties (18; 22; 46). Proofs customized for the crash model have appeared later (e.g., in (2; 17; 20; 49; 52)). The proof presented in this chapter is due Aguilera and Toueg (2).

- The notion of valence is due to Fischer, Lynch and Paterson (23).

CHAPTER 3

Expedite Decision in the Crash Failure Model

The last section of the previous chapter has shown that there is no synchronous round-based consensus (or interactive consistency) algorithm that can cope with t process crashes and allows the processes to always decide in less than $t + 1$ rounds (i.e., whatever the failure pattern).

This chapter examines first the case where less than t processes crash in a run. It shows that the number of rounds can then be lowered to $\min(f + 2, t + 1)$ where f is the actual number of crashes, i.e., $0 \le f \le t$.

It then proposes two ways to circumvent the previous lower bound. The first is data oriented. It consists in restricting the allowable sets of input vectors. This is the *condition* approach. The second consists in enriching the round-based synchronous model with an additional device that provides each process with information on failures. This is the *fast failure detector* approach.

3.1 EARLY DECIDING AND STOPPING IN INTERACTIVE CONSISTENCY

Without loss of generality this section considers the interactive consistency problem. The results apply trivially to consensus.

3.1.1 EARLY DECIDING AND EARLY STOPPING

As just indicated, while $t + 1$ rounds are necessary in worst case scenarios, it might be supposed that in executions where the number f of process crashes is small compared to the model upper bound t, the number of rounds could be correspondingly small. This section shows that this is indeed the case. It presents a synchronous round-based algorithm in which the processes decide in at most $\min(f + 2, t + 1)$ rounds. Moreover, when a process decides, it stops its execution, which means that a process has not to send messages after it has decided.

3.1.2 A PREDICATE TO EARLY DECIDE

From late decision to early decision   Let us consider the non-early deciding interactive consistency algorithm described in Chapter 2. The aim is to modify it in order to obtain an early-deciding algorithm. This non-early deciding algorithm allows a process p_i not to send a message in a round r when p_i has not received new pairs (k, v) during the previous round $r - 1$. As we have seen, this does not prevent the processes that terminate round $t + 1$ to have the very same vector of proposed values at the end of that round.

These "missing" messages can create a problem when we want that a process (say p_i) decides "as early as possible". This is because if p_i does not receive a message from process p_j during a round r, it cannot differentiate the case where p_j has crashed from the case where p_j has nothing new to forward. To solve this problem, a process is required to follow the following behavioral rules:

- A process broadcasts a message at every round until it decides or crashes.

- Any message indicates if its sender was about to decide after having broadcast it.

These simple rules reduce the uncertainty on the state of p_j as perceived by p_i. Let r be the first round during which p_i does not receive a message from p_j. It follows from the previous sending rules that this message is missing either because p_j has decided during round $r - 1$, or because it has crashed during round r. Moreover, let us observe that, if p_j has decided, it has sent to p_i all the pairs (k, v) it has previously received during rounds 1 to $r - 1$.

A predicate for early decision   It remains to state a predicate that allows a process p_i to early decide by itself (i.e., before knowing that another process has decided). Hence, assuming that no process has decided up to round $r - 1$, let us consider the following definitions:

- $UP[r]$ is the set of processes that start round r.

- $R_i[r]$ is the set of processes from which p_i has received messages during round r, and let $R_i[0]$ be the full set of n processes.

Let us notice that, while no process p_i knows the value of $UP[r]$, it can determine the values of $R_i[r]$ and $R_i[r - 1]$. The following relation is an immediate consequence of (a) the previous definitions, (b) the previous sending rules and (c) the fact that crashes are stable (no process recovers):

$$\forall\, r' \in [1..r]: \quad R_i[r] \subseteq UP[r] \subseteq R_i[r - 1].$$

Let us consider the particular case where, for p_i, two consecutive rounds $r - 1$ and r are such that $R_i[r] = R_i[r - 1]$. It follows from the previous relation that $R_i[r] = UP[r] = R_i[r - 1]$, which means that p_i has received during round r a message exactly from every process that was alive at the beginning of round r. This is illustrated in Figure 3.1 where p_a crashes during round $r - 1$ and p_b crashes during round r (this is indicated with crosses on p_a and p_b process axes). As far as messages are concerned, only the round $r - 1$ message from p_a to p_b and rounds $r - 1$ and r messages received by p_d are indicated on the Figure.

It follows that $R_i[r] = R_i[r - 1]$ is the predicate we are looking for. It means that p_i has received (during the rounds 1 to r all the pairs (k, v) known by the processes that are alive at the beginning of r. Said another way, all the other pairs (ℓ, w) are lost forever, and, consequently, no process can learn them in a future round. Process p_i can consequently decide the current value of its local vector $view_i$.

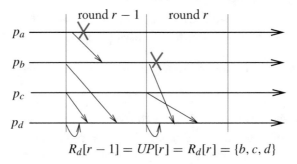

$$R_d[r-1] = UP[r] = R_d[r] = \{b, c, d\}$$

Figure 3.1: Early decision predicate

Inform the other processes before deciding   It is not because the predicate $R_i[r] = R_i[r-1]$ is satisfied at process p_i, that $R_j[r] = R_j[r-1]$ is necessarily satisfied at another process p_j. As an example, when we consider the end of round r in Figure 3.1, p_d can be the only process to know some pair (k, v) that has been forwarded only to p_a, that forwarded it only to p_b that in turn forwarded it only to p_d. In that case, if p_d decided during round r and stops executing just after deciding, it would decide a different vector from the vector decided by other processes. This issue can be easily solved by directing p_i to execute the additional $(r+1)$-th round during which it forwards the new pairs (k, v) it has learnt during round r. It also indicate in the corresponding message that its local early decision predicate was satisfied during round r. In that way, a process p_j that receives this message learns that it knows the vector decided by p_i. Hence, p_j learns that it can decide in the next round $r+2$, i.e., after having forwarded all the pairs (k, v) it has learned during round $r+1$ from p_i.

3.1.3   AN EARLY DECIDING ALGORITHM

The early deciding algorithm based on the previous design principles is described in Figure 3.2. As indicated, this algorithm is obtained from the non-early deciding interactive consistency algorithm described in the previous chapter. In order to make its understanding easier, the lines with exactly the same statements are numbered the same way. The new lines are numbered N1 to N4, and the two lines that are modified is indicated with a prime (').

Local data structures   In addition to the vector $view_i[1..n]$ and the set variable new_i, a process manages three additional local variables, two Booleans and an array of integers.

- $nbr_i[0..n]$ is an array of integers comprised between 1 and n, such that $nbr_i[r]$ is the number of processes from which p_i has received a message during round r, i.e., $nbr_i[r] = |R_i[r]|$. By definition $nbr_i[0] = n$.

  As crashes are stable, the early decision predicate $R_i[r-1] = R_i[r]$ is re-stated $nbr_i[r-1] = nbr_i[r]$. (As only $nbr_i[r-1]$ and $nbr_i[r]$ are needed the array $nbr_i[0..n]$ can be trivially replaced by two variables. This is not done here for clarity of the exposition.)

- $early_i$ is a Boolean initialized to *false*. It is set to *true* when the local early decision predicate becomes satisfied, or when p_i learns that another process is about to decide.

- $decide_i$ is a Boolean set to true when p_i receives a message from a process p_j indicating that $early_j$ is satisfied.

Process behavior   The lines that are modified with respect to the non-early deciding algorithm are line 1' and 3'. The first concerns the initialization. The second concerns the addition of the current value of the Boolean $early_i$ to the message that process p_i broadcasts at every round.

As far as the new lines are concerned, we have the following. Line N2 gives its value to $nbr_i[r]$. At line N3, p_i sets $decide_i$ to *true* if and only if it has received a round r message from a process p_j indicating that p_j is about to decide (i.e., $early_j$ is equal to *true*).

For the lines N1 and N4 let us first consider line N4. At that line, p_i sets $early_i$ to *true* if, during the current round, its local early decision predicate has become true or p_i has received a round r message with $early_j = true$. Said, another way, $early_i$ is set to *true* as soon as p_i learns (directly from its local predicate, or indirectly from another process) that it can early decide.

Let r be the first round at which $early_i$ becomes true. During round $r + 1$, p_i broadcasts EST(new_i, *true*) thereby indicating that it is about to early decide during that round. It then early decides at line N1.

```
operation propose (v_i):
(1')    view_i ← [⊥, ..., ⊥]; view_i[i] ← v_i; new_i ← {(i, v_i)}; nbr_i[0] ← n; early_i ← false;
(2)     when r = 1, 2, ..., (t + 1) do
        begin synchronous round
(3')        broadcast EST(new_i, early_i) end if;
(4)         for each j such that (j ≠ i) do
(5)             if (new_j received from p_j) then recfrom_i[j] ← new_j else recfrom_i[j] ← ∅ end if;
(6)         end for;
(N1)        if (early_i) then return(view_i) if;
(N2)        nbr_i[r] ← number of processes from which round r messages have been received;
(N3)        decide_i ← ⋁(early_j received during round r);
(7)         new_i ← ∅;
(8)         for each j such that (j ≠ i) ∧ (recfrom_i[j] ≠ ∅) do
(9)             foreach (k, v) ∈ recfrom_i[j] do
(10)                if (view_i[k] = ⊥) then view_i[k] ← v; new_i ← new_i ∪ {(k, v)} end if
(11)            end for
(12)        end for;
(N4)        if ((nbr_i[r − 1] = nbr_i[r]) ∨ decide_i) then early_i ← true end if;
(13)        if (r = t + 1) then return(view_i) end if
        end synchronous round.
```

Figure 3.2: An early-deciding t-resilient interactive consistency algorithm (code for p_i)

3.1.4   CORRECTNESS PROOF

Let var_i^r denote the value of the local variable var_i at the end of round r. The sentence "p_i knows the pair (k, v)" is a shortcut to say "$view_i[k] = v$". Process p_i has "learnt" that pair at round 0 if $i = k$, or at round $r > 0$ during which it receives for the first time a set new_j such that $(k, v) \in new_j$.

Lemma 3.1   *If a process p_i decides at line N1 of round r, it knows all the pairs (k, v) known by the processes that where not crashed at the beginning of round $r - 1$, and no more pair can be learnt by a process in a round $r' \geq r$.*

Proof If p_i decides at round r, it previously set $early_i$ to the value *true* at line N4 of round $r - 1$. There are two cases.

- Case 1. At line N4 of round $r - 1$, we have $nbr_i[r - 2] = nbr_i[r - 1]$. In that case, at every round r', $1 \leq r' \leq r - 1$, p_i has received a message from each process in $R_i[r - 1]$. Consequently, it knows all the pairs known by the processes in $R_i[r - 1]$. Moreover, as $nbr_i[r - 2] = nbr_i[r - 1]$, the set $R_i[r - 1]$ is exactly the set of processes alive at the beginning of $r - 1$. Hence, p_i knows all the pairs (k, v) known by the processes that where not crashed at the beginning of round $r - 1$, and no more pair can ever be known by a process, which completes the proof of the lemma for this case.

- Case 2. At line N4 of round $r - 1$, we have $decide_i = true$. In that case, there is a round $r' < r$ and a chain of distinct processes $p_{j1}, \ldots, p_{jx}$ ending at p_i such that (a) $nbr_{j1}[r' - 1] = nbr_{j1}[r']$, and (b) p_{j1} sent $\text{EST}(-, true)$ to p_{j2} during round $r' + 1$, that in turn sent $\text{EST}(-, true)$ to p_{j3} during round $r' + 2$, etc., until p_{jx} that sent $\text{EST}(-, true)$ to p_i during round $r - 1$, and p_i set consequently $decide_i$ to *true* when it received that message.

  It follows from Case 1 that, at the end of round r', p_{j1} knew all the pairs known by the processes that where not crashed at the beginning of round r'. Hence, p_i knows all these pairs (at least from the chain of $\text{EST}(-, true)$ messages starting at p_{j1} end ending at p_i). Consequently, p_i knows all the pairs (k, v) known by the processes that where not crashed at the beginning of round r'. As no pair can be learnt by a process in a later round, p_i knows all the pairs (k, v) known by the processes that where not crashed at the beginning of round $r - 1$, which completes the proof of the lemma.

$\square_{Lemma\ 3.1}$

Lemma 3.2   *No two processes decide different vectors.*

Proof It no process early decides at line N1, the proof is exactly the same as the proof of the base non-early deciding algorithm (see Chapter 2).

Let us consider the case where two processes p_i and p_j that decide at line N1 the vectors $view_i^r$ and $view_j^{r'}$, respectively. The fact that $view_i^r = view_j^{r'}$ follows from Lemma 3.1.

Let us finally consider a process p_i that decides at line N1 while another process decides at line 13. In that case, process p_i decides during round r or $t + 1$. If p_i had decided during a round $r < t$, it would have sent EST$(-, true)$ to p_j during that round and p_j would have then set $decide_j$ to $true$, and decided during $r + 1 \leq t$. Due to Lemma 3.1, when p_i decides at $r = t$ or $t + 1$, it knows all the pairs that can be known at the beginning of round $r - 1$. Moreover, from round 1 to round r, it has transmitted these pairs to p_j. It follows that $view_i^r = view_j^{t+1}$, $\square_{Lemma\ 3.2}$

Theorem 3.3   *Let $1 \leq t < n$. The algorithm described in Figure 3.2 solves the interactive consistency problem in a synchronous system prone to up to t process crash failures.*

Proof The termination property is a direct consequence of the synchrony assumption of the model: a correct process executes at most $t + 1$ rounds. The agreement property follows from Lemma 3.2. The proof of the validity property is the same as for the non-early deciding algorithm (the correct processes exchange the proposed value during the first round and consequently belong to the vectors of the correct processes). $\square_{Theorem\ 3.3}$

Theorem 3.4   *Let f denote the number of crashes in a given execution ($0 \leq f \leq t$). No process executes more than $\min(f + 2, t + 1)$ rounds.*

Proof As already said, the fact that a process executes at most $t + 1$ rounds follows from the text of the algorithm and the synchrony assumption. For the $f + 2$ rounds bound, let us consider two cases.
- Case 1. There is a process p_i that decides at line N1 of round $d \leq f + 1$. In that case, just before deciding at line N1 during round $f + 1$, p_i has broadcast EST$(-, true)$ at line 3'. It follows that each process p_j that terminates round $f + 1$ receives the message EST$(-, true)$ sent by p_i, and consequently updates $early_j$ to $true$ during round $f + 1$ (lines N3 and N4). It follows that, if p_j does not crash by the end of $f + 2$, it decides at line N1 of that round, which proves the theorem for this case.
- Case 2. No process has decided by round $d = f + 1$. Let p_i be any process that terminates that round. As p_i has not decided by the end of round $f + 1$, we have $nbr_i[r' - 1] \neq nbr[r']$ for any round r', $1 \leq r' \leq f$. As there are exactly f crashes, it follows that we have:
  - $nbr_i[0] = n$, $nbr_i[1] = n - 1$, $nbr_i[2] = n - 2$, etc., $nbr_i[f - 1] = n - (f - 1)$ and $nbr_i[f] = n - f$ (there is one crash per round, and the process that crashes does not send a message to p_i), and
  - $nbr_i[f + 1] = n - f$.

Consequently $nbr_i[f] - nbr_i[f + 1] = 0$. Hence, p_i sets $early_i$ to $true$ at line N4 of round $f + 1$, and if it does not crash during round $f + 2$, it decides at line N1 of that round. Let us finally observe that, as p_i is any process that terminates round $f + 1$, the reasoning applies to all processes that execute round $f + 2$, which completes the proof of the theorem. $\square_{Theorem\ 3.4}$

3.1.5 ON EARLY DECISION PREDICATES

Let $P1(i, r)$ denote the early decision predicate used in the the previous algorithm ($nbr_i[r] - nbr_i[i, 1] = 0$).

Another early detection predicate Let $faulty_i[r] = n - nbr_i[r]$, i.e., the number of processes that p_i perceives as crashed. The predicate $P2(i, r) \equiv (faulty_i[r] < r)$ is another correct early decision predicate that can be used instead of $P1(i, r)$. This is because $P2(i, r)$ is satisfied at the first round r such that this round number is higher than the number of processes currently perceived as crashed by p_i. Said differently, from p_i point of view, there are currently less crashed processes than the number of rounds it has executed, i.e., for p_i there is a round r', $1 \leq r' \leq r$, without crashes. Hence, at the end of that round, the vector $view_i$ contains the values v of all the pairs (k, v) that were still known at the beginning of r', which means that no more pair can be known by any process in the future.

Comparing the predicates Hence the question: while both $P1(i, r)$ and $P2(i, r)$ ensure that the processes decide in at most $\min(f + 2, t + 1)$ rounds in the worst cases, is one predicate better than the other? We show here that $P1(i, r)$ is better than $P2(i, r)$. To that end, we prove the following theorem.

Theorem 3.5 *(a) Given an execution, let $r \geq 2$ be the first round at which $P2(i, r)$ is satisfied. We have $P2(i, r) \Rightarrow P1(i, r)$.*
(b) Given an execution, let $r \geq 2$ be the first round at which $P1(i, r)$ is satisfied. There are failure patterns for which $\neg(P1(i, r) \Rightarrow P2(i, r))$.

Proof Let us first prove item (a). As r is the first round during which $P2(i, r) \equiv (faulty_i[r] < r)$ is satisfied, $P2(i, r - 1)$ is false, i.e., $faulty_i[r - 1] \geq r - 1$. It follows from $faulty_i[r] < r$ and $faulty_i[r - 1] \geq r - 1$ that $faulty_i[r] - faulty_i[r - 1] < 1$, i.e., $(n - nbr_i[r]) - (n - nbr_i[r - 1]) < 1$. Combined to the fact that $nb_i[r] \geq nb_i[r]$, we obtain $nb_i[r] - nb_i[r - 1] = 0$, which concludes the proof of item (a).

Let us now prove item (b). To that end, we exhibit a counter-example. Let consider a run in which $2 \leq x \leq t$ processes have crashed before taking any step, and then no more process crashes.

The predicate $P2(i, r) \equiv (faulty_i[r] < r)$ becomes true for the first time at round $x + 1$. Let us now look at the predicate $P1(i, r) \equiv (nb_i[r] - nb_i[r - 1] = 0)$. We have, $nb_i[1] = nb_i[2] = n - x$. Consequently, $P1(i, 2)$ is satisfied. As $x \geq 2$, it follows that $\neg P2(i, 2) \wedge P1(i, 2)$, which concludes the proof of item (b).
$\square_{Theorem\ 3.5}$

Discussion The previous theorem shows that while both predicates $P1(i, r)$ and $P2(i, er)$ allow the processes to decide and stop by round $r = \min(f + 2, t + 1)$, the predicate $P1(i, r) \equiv (nbr_i[r] - nbr_i[r - 1] = 0)$ is better than the predicate $P2(i, r) \equiv (faulty_i[r] = n - nbr_i[r])$, in the sense

```
operation propose (v_i)
(1)   est_i ← v_i; nb_i[0] ← n; early_i ← false;
(2)   when r = 1, 2, ..., t + 1 do
      begin synchronous round
(3)         broadcast EST(est_i, early_i)
(4)         if (early_i) then return (est_i) end if;
(5)         let nb_i[r] = number of messages received by p_i during r;
(6)         let decide_i ← ⋁(early_j values received during current round r);
(7)         est_i ← min({est_j values received during current round r});
(8)         if ((nb_i[r − 1] = nb_i[r]) ∨ decide_i) then early_i ← true end if
(9)         if (r = t + 1) then return(est_i) end if
      end synchronous round.
```

Figure 3.3: Early stopping synchronous consensus (code for $p_i, t < n$)

that there are failure patterns for which $P1(i, r)$ allows the processes to terminate before the round $r = \min(f + 2, t + 1)$.

This is due to the fact that $P1(i, r)$ takes into consideration the actual failure pattern, namely, a process computes the number of process crashes it perceives during a round (the value of this number is $nbr_i[r] − nbr_i[r − 1]$). Differently, the predicate $P2(i, r)$ is based only on the number of processes perceived as crashed by p_i since the beginning of the execution. This means that, whatever the actual failure pattern, $P2(i, r)$ always considers the worst case in which there is one crash per round. Differently, when using $P1(i, r)$, the fact that crashes occur in the very same round is taken into account and used to allow for a faster decision.

3.1.6   EARLY-DECIDING AND STOPPING CONSENSUS

The algorithm described in Figure 3.3 describes an early-deciding and stopping consensus algorithm. This algorithm, where a process decides the smallest value it has ever seen is directly obtained from the interactive consistency early-deciding algorithm described in Figure 3.2. Its proof is left to the reader.

3.2   THE SYNCHRONOUS CONDITION-BASED APPROACH

3.2.1   THE CONDITION-BASED APPROACH IN SYNCHRONOUS SYSTEMS

An input vector $I[1..n]$ is a vector with one entry per process, such that $I[i]$ contains th value v_i proposed by process p_i. Let us remember that, in a synchronous system, both consensus and interactive consistency can be solved whatever the actual input vector and the value of the model parameter t.

The underlying idea   The idea that underlies the synchronous condition-based approach is motivated by the following question: is it possible to characterize sets of input vectors for which the processes always decide in less than $t + 1$ rounds whatever the failure pattern? This section shows that the answer to this question is "yes". To that end, it first defines the notion of legal condition and then presents a corresponding condition-based algorithm.

A hierarchy of conditions   A condition is a set of input vectors. Let $C[x]$ be the set (also called class) of conditions that allows consensus to be solved in at most $f_t(x)$ rounds, where $f_t(x) \leq t + 1$ and $f_t(x + 1) < f_t(x)$. The parameter x is called the *degree* of the class, and (by a slight abuse of language) we also say that it is the degree of conditions that are in $C[x]$ and not in $C[y]$ where $y > x$.

As we will see later, the classes $\{C[x]\}_{0 \leq x \leq t}$ define the following hierarchy (Figure 3.4)

$$C[t] \subset C[t - 1] \subset \cdots \subset C[x] \subset \cdots \subset C[1] \subset C[0],$$

where $C[0]$ contains the condition including all possible input vectors.

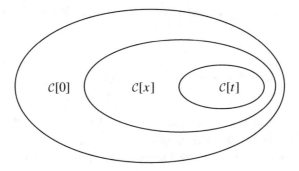

Figure 3.4: Hierarchy of classes of conditions

As we are about to see, there is a consensus algorithm that, when instantiated with a condition $C \in C[x]$, allows the processes to decide in at most $f_t(x) = t + 1 - x$ rounds whatever (a) the actual input vector $I \in C$, and (b) the failure pattern.

This means that, if the condition C the algorithm is instantiated with belongs to $C[t]$, the processes decide in one round (which is clearly optimal, when the decided value is not fixed a priori). At the other extreme, if the condition C the algorithm is instantiated with is the condition including all possible input vectors, the processes decide in at most $t + 1$ rounds. Hence, there is a tradeoff between the number of input vectors of a condition C (as measured by its degree x) and the maximal number of rounds needed to decide.

A relation with error-correcting codes   One way to address an agreement problem such as consensus is to consider that an input vector encodes a value, namely the value that has to be decided from that vector (i.e., an input vector is then seen as a codeword). Given an upper bound d on the number of rounds we want to execute, the condition-based approach allows us to characterize which are the sets of input vectors (codewords) that allow consensus to be solved in at most d rounds (where $d = t + 1 - x$). The condition-based approach thereby establishes a strong relation between agreement problems and error correcting codes.

3.2.2 A PREDICATE FOR EARLY DECISION

Legality   Not any set C of input vectors allows to decide in less that $t + 1$ rounds whatever the pattern of up to t process crashes, and the input vector $I \in C$. The notion of legality is introduced to capture the conditions that allow consensus to be solve in $t + 1 - x$ rounds.
- Let $\mathcal{V}$ denote the set of values that can be proposed.
- Let $\#_a(I)$ denote the number of occurrences of the value a in the vector I.
- Let $dist(I1, I2)$ denote the Hamming distance between the vectors $I1$ and $I2$ (number of entries in which they differ).

Definition 3.6   A condition C is *x-legal* if there exists a function $h : C \mapsto \mathcal{V}$ with the following properties:

- $\forall I \in C : \#_{h(I)}(I) > x$,
- $\forall I1, I2 \in C : \big(h(I1) \neq h(I2)\big) \Rightarrow \big(dist(I1, I2) > x\big)$.

The intuition that underlies this definition is the following. For each of its input vectors I, a condition C allows a proposed value to be selected in order to be the value decided by the processes. That value is extracted from an input vector by the function $h()$, namely $h(I)$ is the value decided from input vector I.

To that end, $h()$ and all vectors I of C have to satisfy some constraints. The first constraint states that the value that the processes have to decide from I (this value is $h(I)$) has to be present enough in vector I. "Enough" means "more than x times". This is captured by the first constraint defining x-legality: $\forall I \in C : \#_{h(I)}(I) > x$.

The second constraint states that if different values are decided from different vectors $I1, I2 \in C$, then $I1$ and $I2$ must be "far apart enough" one from the other. This is to prevent processes that would obtain different views of the input vector from deciding differently. This is captured by the second constraint defining x-legality: $\forall I1, I2 \in C : \big(h(I1) \neq h(I2)\big) \Rightarrow \big(dist(I1, I2) > x\big)$.

The set of all x-legal conditions defines the class $\mathcal{C}[x]$. Hence, a set C of input vectors for which there is no function $h()$ as defined previously does not define a legal condition, and, consequently, $C \notin \mathcal{C}[x]$.

Section 3.2.3 will describe a consensus algorithm that, when instantiated with the function $h()$ of a condition $C \in \mathcal{C}[x]$, allows the processes to decide in at most $t + 1 - x$ rounds whatever the input vector $I \in C$.

Examples of legal conditions   Assuming that the values that can be proposed can be totally ordered, a natural example of an x-legal condition is the one that favors the largest value present in an input vector. Let us call C_{max}^x this condition for a given degree x. Moreover, let max$[I]$ denote the greatest value in the input vector I. C_{max}^x is defined as follows

$$C_{max}^x \overset{def}{=} \{I \mid \#_a(I) > x \text{ where } a = max(I)\}.$$

Theorem 3.7   *The condition C_{max}^x is x-legal.*

Proof Let us take max(I) as the decision function $h()$. Due to the definition of C_{max}^x, the function max$()$ trivially satisfies the first item of the definition of x-legality. Hence, we have only to show that $\forall\ I1, I2 \in C_{max}^x$ we have max$((I1) \neq$ max$(I2) \Rightarrow dist(I1, I2) > x$.

   Let $a =$ max$(I1)$ and $b =$ max$(I2)$. As a and b are different, one is greater than the other. Let us assume without loss of generality that $a > b$. As $b =$ max$(I2)$, we conclude that a does not appear in $I2$. As a appear more than x times in $I1$, it immediately follows that $dist(I1, I2) > x$, which concludes the proof of the theorem. $\square_{Theorem\ 3.7}$

   Another natural example of an x-legal condition is the condition denoted C_{min}^x that favors the smallest value present in an input vector.

   Another one is the condition that favors the value that is the most frequent in an input vector. Let first(I) and second(I) be the values that appear the most frequent and the second most frequent in the input vector I. (If two values are equally most frequent, we have first(I)=second(I), and a vector I made up of a single value is such that first$(I) = n$ and second$(I) = 0$.) The condition C_{mf}^x defined as follows

$$C_{mf}^x \overset{def}{=} \{I \mid \#_a(I) - \#_b(I) > x \text{ where } a = \text{first}(I) \text{ and } b = \text{second}(I)\}$$

is x-legal. The associated function $h()$ is the function first$()$.

Maximal legal conditions   An x-legal condition C is maximal if adding a vector to C makes it not x-legal. More formally, C is maximal if $C \cup \{I\}$ is not x-legal when $I \notin C$. The conditions C_{max}^x and C_{min}^x are maximal x-legal conditions, while C_{mf}^x is x-legal but not maximal.

The hierarchy of legal conditions   It is easy to see that C_{max}^{x+1} contains C_{max}^x while C_{max}^x does not contain C_{max}^{x+1}. Hence, $C_{max}^t \subset C_{max}^{t-1} \cdots \subset C_{max}^x \cdots \subset C_{max}^0$. As $\forall\ x, 0 \leq x \leq t, C_{max}^x \in \mathcal{C}[x]$, it follows (as previously announced) that the classes $\{\mathcal{C}[x]\}_{0 \leq x \leq t}$ define a strict hierarchy.

Definition 3.8   Let I be an input vector of an x-legal condition C. A *view J* of I (denoted $J \leq I$) is a vector that is identical to I except for at most x entries that can be equal to $\perp$.

   From an operational point of view, a view captures the non-$\perp$ entries of an input vector that a process obtains by receiving messages.

Lemma 3.9   *Let C be an x-legal condition and $I1$ and $I2$ two input vectors of C. If there is a view J such that $J \leq I1$ and $J \leq I2$, we have $h(I1) = h(I2)$.*

Proof Let us assume by contradiction that there is an x-legal condition C that has two vectors $I1$ and $I2$ such that (a) there is a view $J \leq I1$ and $J \leq I1$, and (b) $h(I1) \neq h(I2)$.

As $J \leq I1$ and $J \leq I2$, we have $dist(J, I1) \leq x$ and $dist(J, I2) \leq x$. From these inequalities, the fact that J has at most x entries equal to $\perp$, and the fact that the entries of J that differ in $I1$ or $I2$ are only its entries equal to $\perp$, it follows that $dist(I1, I2) \leq x$.

On another side, as $h(I1) \neq h(I2)$, it follows from the second item of the definition of x-legality of C, that $dist(I1, I2) > x$, which contradicts the previous observation, and concludes the proof. $\square_{Lemma\ 3.9}$

The previous lemma allows the definition of the selection function $h()$ associated with an x-legal condition C to be extended to views as follows.

Definition 3.10   If I is an input vector of an x-legal condition C, and J is a view of I, then the function $h()$ is extended as follows $h(J) = h(I)$.

3.2.3   A SYNCHRONOUS CONDITION-BASED CONSENSUS ALGORITHM

A condition-based consensus algorithm is presented in Figure 3.5. The parameter x is the degree of the condition C the algorithm is instantiated with. The function $h()$ is the selection function associated with this x-legal condition.

Local variables   In addition to the local variable $view_i$ (whose meaning is similar to the one of the same variable used in the previous algorithm), a process p_i manages two local variables, both initialized to the default value $\perp$. This default value is assumed to be smaller than any value than can be proposed by a process.

- The aim of v_cond_i is to keep (once known) the value $h(I)$ decided from the input vector I.
- The aim of v_tmf_i is to contain the value that will be decided when (as we will see below) it is not possible to use the function $h()$ to decide a value from the input vector. (v_tmf stands for *too many failures*.)

Process behavior   The behavior of p_i depends on the round.

- During the first round, a process p_i broadcasts the value it proposes (message $EST1(v_i)$ sent at line 3), and builds its local view of the input vector during the receive phase (line 4). Then, p_i counts the number of entries of its view that are equal to $\perp$. There are two cases.
  - If $\#_{\perp}(view_i) \leq x$ (line 5), p_i knows enough entries of the input vector in order to use the selection function $h()$ associated with the x-legal condition the algorithm is instantiated with. In that case, p_i computes $h(view_i)$ and saves it in v_cond_i.
  - If $\#_{\perp}(view_i) > x$ (line 6), there are too many failures for $h()$ to be used. This is because in order to be recognized before being decided a value has to be present at least once in a local view of the input vector. Hence, when more than x entries of the local view of

p_i are equal to $\perp$, $h()$ is meaningless. In that case, p_i behaves as in a classical consensus algorithm. It computes the greatest proposed value it knows and saves it in v_tmf_i.

The case of an x-legal condition such that $x = t$ is particular. This is because if $x = t$, we necessarily have $\#_\perp(view_j) \leq x$ at any process that does not crash by the end of the first round. Consequently, no process p_j needs more rounds to know the value decided from the condition. It follows that any p_j can safely decide $h(view_j)$ during the first round (line 8).

- During the rounds 2 until $t + 1 - x$, p_i first broadcasts its current state (message EST2(v_cond_i, v_tmf_i), line 10). Then, it early decides the value of v_cond_i if it is not equal to $\perp$ (line 11). Let us observe that, in that case, v_cond_i was different from $\perp$ at the end of the previous round, and consequently, its value is carried by the message EST2() that p_i has just sent.

If $v\_cond_i = \perp$, p_i updates it to the value decided from the condition if it has received such a value from another process (line 12). It also updates the value of v_tmf_i in case no value can be computed from the condition (line 13).

Finally, if $r = t + 1 - x$, p_i decides (line 15). The decided value is the non-$\perp$ value kept in v_cond_i if there is one. Otherwise, it is the value kept in v_tmf_i.

```
operation proposeₓ (vᵢ):
(1)    viewᵢ ← [⊥,...,⊥]; viewᵢ[i] ← vᵢ; v_cond ← ⊥; v_tmfᵢ ← ⊥;
(2)    when r = 1 do
       begin synchronous round
(3)        broadcast EST1(vᵢ);
(4)        for each vⱼ received do viewᵢ[j] ← vⱼ end for;
(5)        case (#⊥(viewᵢ) ≤ x) then v_condᵢ ← h(viewᵢ)
(6)             (#⊥(viewᵢ) > x) then v_tmfᵢ ← max(all values vⱼ received)
(7)        end case;
(8)        if (x = t) then return(v_condᵢ) end if
       end synchronous round;
(9)    when r = 2, ..., t + 1 − x do
       begin synchronous round
(10)       broadcast EST2(v_condᵢ, v_tmfᵢ);
(11)       if (v_condᵢ ≠ ⊥) then return(v_condᵢ) end if;
(12)       if (v_condⱼ ≠ ⊥ received during round r) then v_condᵢ ← v_condⱼ end if;
(13)       v_tmfᵢ ← max(all v_tmfⱼ values received during r);
(14)       if (r = t + 1 − x) then
(15)           if (v_condᵢ ≠ ⊥) then return(v_condᵢ) else return(v_tmfᵢ) end if;
(16)       end if
       end synchronous round.
```

Figure 3.5: A t-resilient condition-based algorithm (code for p_i)

3.2.4   PROOF OF THE ALGORITHM

Theorem 3.11   *let C be an x-legal condition the algorithm described in Figure 3.5 is instantiated with. This algorithm solves the consensus problem for any input vector $I \in C$ in a round-based synchronous model where up to t processes may crash. Moreover, no process executes more than $t + 1 - x$ rounds.*

Proof   The fact that no process executes more than $t + 1 - x$ rounds follows directly from the synchrony assumption and the text of the algorithm (line 8 for $x = t$, and line 14- 16 for $x \leq t$).

For the validity and agreement properties of consensus, let us first consider the case $x = t$. All the processes that execute line 8 have then previously executed the assignment $v\_cond_i \leftarrow h(view_i)$ at line 5. It then follows from Definition 3.10 (that extends the definition of $h()$ to views) that, for any process p_i, we have $v\_cond_i = h(view_i) = h(I)$, which (due the definition of $h()$) is a value that appears more than x times in I, i.e., at least once in any of its views perceived by the processes. Hence, the algorithm satisfies both the validity and agreement properties of consensus.

Let us now consider the validity property for the x-legal conditions such that $x < t$. Any process p_i that terminates the first round is such that $(v\_cond_i \neq \bot) \vee (v\_tmf_i \neq \bot)$. Moreover, (for the same reasons as in the case $t = x$) if $v\_cond_i \neq \bot$, it is a value of I. Similarly, if $v\_tmf_i \neq \bot$, it is a value of I.

It follows from the text of the algorithm that, if v_cond_i is assigned at line 12, it takes the value of another non-$\bot$ v_cond_j variable, from which we conclude that any non-$\bot$ v_cond_i variable contains a value selected by $h()$ which (due to the definition of $h()$) is a value of the input vector. It follows that if process p_i decides the value v_cond_i, it decides a value of the input vector I.

If a process p_i decides the value of v_tmf_i, it does it at lines 15. In that case, we have $v\_cond_i = \bot$, from which we conclude that p_i has executed line 6 where v_tmf_i is assigned a proposed value. It then follows from line 13 (and the fact that $\bot$ is smaller than any proposed value) that v_tmf_i always contains a proposed value. Hence, if p_i decides it, it decides a proposed value.

Let us now address the agreement property when $t < x$. We consider two cases.

- A process decides at line 11. Let r be the first round at which a process (say p_i) decides at line 11 of that round. Hence, p_i decides $v\_cond_i = v \neq \bot$.

  - Let us first consider the case of another process p_j that decides line 11 of round r. Hence, p_j decides $v\_cond_i = v' \neq \bot$.

    It follows from the text of the algorithm that there are processes p_k and p_ℓ that have computed $v\_cond_k = h(view_k) = v$ and $v\_cond_\ell = h(view_\ell) = v'$ during the first round, and then these values have been propagated to p_i and p_j directly or via other processes (lines 10 and line 12). (Let us observe that p_k and p_ℓ can be the same process, or can even be p_i or p_j.)

It follows from Lemma 3.9 and Definition 3.10 that $h(view_y) = h(view_z)$ for any pair of processes p_x and p_y that execute line 5. Hence, we have $v = v'$ from which we conclude that no two processes that decides at line 11 during r decide differently.

- Let us now consider the case of a process p_k that decides during a round $r' > r$. Let us observe that, at the beginning of round r, we necessarily have $v\_cond_k = \bot$ (otherwise, p_k would have decided at line 11 of round r). let us also observe that any process p_i that decides at line 11 of round r has broadcast $EST2(v, -)$ before deciding. It follows that any process p_k that proceeds to round $r + 1$ is such that $v\_cond_k = v$ at the end of r (line 12). It follows from the text of the algorithm that p_k will decide $v\_cond_k = v$ during round $r + 1$ (if it does not crash). Consequently, no value different from v can be decided.

- No process decides at line 11. In that case, the processes terminate at line 15 of round $r = t + 1 - x$. We show that all the processes p_i that execute line 15 of round $r = t + 1 - x$ (a) have the same value in v_cond_i and the same value in v_tmf_i and (b) at least one of the value v_tmf_i is not equal to $\bot$, which proves the agreement property for that case.

Let P be the set of processes that execute line 15 of round $r = t + 1 - x$. (This set is not empty; otherwise, decision would occur only at line 11.) Let us first observe that as no process p_i of P decides at line 11 during a round r, each of them has necessarily executed line 6 during the first round (otherwise, we would have $v\_cond_i \neq \bot$ at the end of the first round and p_i would have decided at line 11 of the second round).

We conclude from the previous observation that, at the end of the first round, $\#_\bot(view_i) > x$ and $v\_tmf_i \neq \bot$ for each process p_i of P. It then follows from line 13 that these variables remain forever different from $\bot$. It also follows from $\#_\bot(view_i) > x$ that at least $x + 1$ processes have crashed during the first round. This means that at most $t - (x + 1)$ processes can crash from round 2 until round $t + 1 - x$, i.e., during $t - x$ rounds.

As $t - (x + 1)$ processes can crash during $t - x$ rounds, there is necessarily a round r', $2 \leq r' \leq t + 1 - x$, with no crash. Moreover, all the processes that execute round r' exchange their values v_cond_i and v_tmf_i (line 10), and (the values v_tmf_i sent by the processes of P are not equal to $\bot$. It follows that all the processes that execute round r' have the the same value in v_cond_i (this value can be $\bot$), and in v_tmf_i (and this value cannot be $\bot$), which concludes the proof of the agreement property.

$\square_{Theorem\ 3.11}$

The next corollary follows from the proof of the previous theorem.

Corollary 3.12   *If at most $f \leq x$ processes crash, no process decides after the second round.*

3.3   USING FAST FAILURE DETECTORS

3.3.1   THE CLASS OF FAST PERFECT FAILURE DETECTORS

What is a failure detector   A failure detector is a device that provides each process with information on failures. According to the quality of this information, several classes of failure detectors can be defined.

Duration of a round   To simplify the presentation, let us assume (without loss of generality) that the synchronous model is such that local computation takes no time while message transfer delays are upper bounded by duration D (a message sent at time τ is received by time $\tau + D$). The assumption that local computation takes no time is without loss of generality as processing times can be included in D. This means that the duration of a round is D time units.

The class of fast perfect failure detectors   A *fast perfect failure detector* is a distributed object that provides each process p_i with a set denoted $suspected_i$. This set contains process identities, and p_i can only read it. If $j \in suspected_i$ we say "p_i suspects p_j" or "p_j is suspected by p_i".

   This object satisfies the following properties that involve a duration d, called *maximal detection time*, and is such that $d << D$ (hence the attribute *fast* of the failure detector class).

- Strong accuracy. No process p_j is suspected by another process p_i before p_j crashes.

- Detection timeliness. If a process p_j crashes at time τ, then from time $\tau + d$, every non-crashed process suspects it forever.

   The first property states that if $j \in suspected_i$, then p_j has crashed. The second property states that a process p_i is informed of the crash of a process p_j at most d time units after the crash occurred. Let nevertheless observe that, if a process p_j crashes at some time τ, it is possible that some processes are informed at time $\tau + d'$, while other processes are informed at time $\tau + d''$, etc., with $0 \le d' < d'' < d$. The failure detector is *perfect* because it never makes mistakes: any crashed process is suspected, and only crashed processes are suspected.

   A fast failure detector can be implemented with specialized hardware.

3.3.2   ADAPTING THE SYNCHRONOUS MODEL TO BENEFIT FROM A FAST FAILURE DETECTOR

Instead of round numbers, the behavior of a process is described with respect to date occurrences. To that end, the synchronous system provides the processes with a read-only global clock variable denoted clock. It is assumed that clock= 0 when the algorithm starts.

   The dates are defined from the durations d (as defined by the failure detector) and D (as defined by the synchrony assumption). Hence, they are meaningful both from the application point of view (D) and the failure detector point of view (d). A particular algorithm defines which are the dates that are relevant for it.

3.3.3   A SIMPLE CONSENSUS ALGORITHM BASED ON A FAST FAILURE DETECTOR

As previously, t denotes the maximal number of process crashes that the failure detector-based synchronous algorithm has to cope with. Such an algorithm, described in Figure 3.6, allows the processes to decide at time $t \times d + D$. This is is better than its counterpart in a pure synchronous system which requires $t + 1$ rounds, i.e., $(t + 1)D$ times units.

Relevant dates   The algorithm considers two types of round, rounds of duration D time units as defined by the synchronous system, and rounds (called FD-rounds) of duration d (maximal detection time) related to the underlying failure detector. According to these rounds, the dates that are relevant for a process p_i are $(i - 1)d$ for sending a message and $t \times d + D$ for deciding.

Description of the algorithm   The principles on which the algorithm relies are pretty simple. Each FD-round is coordinated by a process that is the only process allowed to send a message during that FD-round. Process p_1 is the coordinator of the first FD-round, process p_2 the coordinator of the second FD-round, etc. More precisely, at the beginning of the FD-round $(i - 1)d$ process p_i is required to broadcast the pair (est_i, i) (where est_i is its current estimate of the decision value) if and only if it suspects all the processes that were assumed to broadcast during the previous FD-rounds (i.e., if it suspects the processes p_1 to p_{i-1}). Let us observe that, if p_1 does not crash its broadcast predicate is trivially satisfied when the algorithm starts (i.e., when CLOCK=0).

   If any, the message broadcast by a process p_i is sent at time $(i - 1)d$ and received by time $(i - 1)d + D$. If p_i crashes during the broadcast, an arbitrary subset of processes receive its message, and if p_i crashes at time τ, a process p_j starts suspecting p_i forever at any time between τ and $\tau + d$. When a process p_i receives a message, it stores the pair contained in the message into a set denoted $view_i$. If a message it received by a process p_i when a relevant date occurs for it (i.e., when CLOCK=$(i - 1)d$ or $t \times d + D$), that process first process the message received (which by assumption takes no time), and then executes the statement associated with the corresponding date.

   Finally, at time $t \times d + D$, any alive process p_i decides and stops. The value it decides is the value it has received that has been sent by the process with the highest identity.

Remark   As at most t processes crash, the processes p_{t+2}, ..., p_n can never be round coordinator, and consequently their value can never be decided (except when that value is also proposed by process p_x with $1 \leq x \leq t + 1$). The algorithm is consequently unfair in the sense given in Chapter 2.

Theorem 3.13   *Let $1 \leq t < n$. The fast failure detector–based synchronous algorithm described in Figure 3.6 solves the consensus problem despite up to t process crashes. Moreover, the decision is obtained in $t \times d + D$ time units.*

Proof   The termination property follows from the synchrony assumptions of the synchronous system and the underlying failure detector: when the clock is equal to $t \times d + D$, all alive processes decide. Moreover, when a process p_i decides, $view_i$ is not empty (because there is at least one

```
operation propose(v_i)
    init est_i ← v_i; view_i ← ∅.

    when CLOCK = (i − 1)d do
        if ({1, 2, . . . , i − 1} ⊆ suspected_i) then broadcast EST(est_i, i) end if.

    when EST(est, j) is received: view_i ← view_i ∪ {(est, j)}.

    when CLOCK = t × d + D do
        let (v, k) be the pair in view_i with the greatest process identity;
        return(v).
```

Figure 3.6: Synchronous consensus with a fast failure detector (code for p_i)

correct process among the $t + 1$ coordinators) and contains only proposed values. Hence, the validity property.

To prove the consensus agreement property, we first introduce a definition and then prove a claim from which agreement is derived.

Definition A FD-round k is *eligible* if, at time $(k − 1)d$, the processes p_1, ..., $p_{k−1}$ are crashed and p_k either is crashed or suspect them. *End of definition.*

Let us observe that, if FD-round $t + 1$ is eligible, then process p_{t+1} must be alive at time $td + D$. This is because at most t processes can crash, and, as FD-round $t + 1$ is eligible, the processes p_1 to p_t have crashed. Let us also observe that no FD-round $k > t + 1$ can be eligible. Finally, let us notice that, due to the definition of eligibility, a process p_i can send a message in FD-round i only if that FD-round is eligible.

Claim For $1 \leq k \leq t + 1$, if FD-round k is eligible, then either p_k sends EST(est_i, v) to all or round $k + 1$ is eligible.

Proof of the claim If FD-round k is eligible and p_k does not send EST(est_i, v) to all, then p_k crashes by time $(k − 1)d$. In that case, due to detection timeliness of th failure detector, it will be suspected by all alive processes by time $(k − 1)d + d = k × d$, and then FD-round $k + 1$ is eligible. *End of proof of the claim.*

Let us now prove the agreement property. Let r be the largest eligible FD-round. It follows from the previous discussion that $r \leq t + 1$. It then follows from the claim that process p_r sends EST(est_r, v) to all without crashing (otherwise, r would not be the largest eligible FD-round). Moreover, no process with a larger identity ever sends a message (this is because for p_j to send a message, the FD-round j has to be eligible, and r is the largest eligible round). It follows that all processes that decide at time $t × d + D$, decide the value est_r they have received, which concludes the proof of the theorem.
□ $_{Theorem}$ 3.13

3.3.4 AN EARLY-DECIDING AND STOPPING ALGORITHM

Decide in $f \times d + D$ time units   This section presents a fast failure detector-based synchronous consensus algorithm in which any process (that does not crash) decides by $D + fd$ time units where f is the actual number of process crashes in the considered run, $0 \le f \le t$. This is better than $\min(f + 2, t + 1)D$ time units, which is the bound attained by the early-deciding algorithm presented in Section 3.1.

To simplify the presentation, it is assumed that D is an integral multiple of d.

A fast failure detector-based algorithm   The algorithm is described in Figure 3.8. Each process p_i manages two local variables. est_i represents its estimate of the decision value. Initially, $est_i = v_i$ the value proposed by p_i. But for its initial value that is 0, max_id_i contains a process identity.

This algorithm is an extension of the previous failure detector-based algorithm. It has consequently the same coordinator-based sequential nature. More precisely, it also considers periods of length d, each coordinated by a process: process p_i is the only process that can send a message at the beginning of the period $[(i - 1)d, i \times d)$. Hence, as before, the first period is coordinated by p_1, the second by p_2, etc. Hence, the dates that are defined relevant for that algorithm are: $D, d + D$, $2d + D, ..., t \times d + D$, for all processes, plus the date the $(i - 1)d$ for every process p_i. These dates are represented on Figure 3.7.

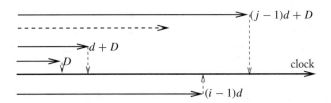

Figure 3.7: Relevant dates for process p_i

The statements executed by p_i when CLOCK$= (i - 1)d$ are the same as in Figure 3.6: if p_i suspects all the processes with a smaller identity, it sends the pair (est_i, i) to all processes.

The statements executed by a process p_i when it receives a message or when CLOCK$= (j - 1)d + D$ are different from the ones in the previous algorithm. When process p_i receives a pair (est, j), it updates its own estimate est_i if the identity j of the sender process is larger than max_id_i (that has been initialized to a value smaller than any process identity). Hence, but for its initial value, the successive values of est_i are coming from processes with increasing identities.

Finally, at every date $(j - 1)d + D$, $1 \le j \le t + 1$, p_i checks a predicate to see if it can decide. This predicate is on the current output of the failure detector. More precisely, p_i decides if it does not suspect the process p_j as defined from the current value of the clock. If the predicate is false, p_i has received the message (if any) sent by p_j. (This is because the difference between its sending time and the current time is D. Moreover, if p_j has not sent a message, it is because it was not suspecting at least one of its predecessors p_1 to p_{j-1}.) Hence, if $j \notin suspected_i$, p_i decides the current value of est_i and consequently executes $return(est_i)$.

```
operation propose(v_i)
    init est_i ← v_i; max_id_i ← 0.

    when CLOCK = (i − 1)d do
        if ({1, 2, ..., i − 1} ⊆ suspected_i) then broadcast EST(est_i, i) end if.

    when EST(est, j) is received:
        if (j > max_id_i) then est_i ← est; max_i ← j end if.

    when CLOCK = (j − 1)d + D for every 1 ≤ j ≤ t + 1 do
        if (j ∉ suspected_i) then return(est_i) end if;
```

Figure 3.8: Early-deciding synchronous consensus with a fast failure detector (code for p_i)

It is easy to see that the processes decide by D time units when the process p_1 does not crash (in that case they decide the value v_1 proposed by p_1). If p_1 crashes while p_2 does not, they decide by time $d + D$. According to the failure pattern, the decided value that is decided is then the value v_1 proposed by p_1 or the value v_2 proposed by p_2 (it is v_1 if p_2 has received v_1 by d time units), etc.

Theorem 3.14   *Let $1 \le t < n$. The fast failure detector-based synchronous algorithm described in Figure 3.8 solves the consensus problem despite up to t process crashes. Moreover, the decision is obtained in $f \times d + D$ time units where f is the actual number of process crashes.*

Proof Let us first observe that no process p_i decides after $d \times f + D$ times units. Indeed, as f processes crash and $f \le t$, there is at least one process p_j such that $1 \le j \le t + 1$ and the predicate $j \notin suspected_i$ is consequently satisfied at the latest when when CLOCK $= (j − 1)d + D$. The termination property follows from that observation. Moreover, validity property is trivial (for any p_i, est_i is initialized to v_i and then possibly updated only with another estimate value). . Hence, let us focus on the consensus agreement property.

Definition A FD-round k is *active* if, at time $(k − 1)d$, p_k is not crashed and suspects the processes $p_1, ..., p_{k-1}$. *End of definition*. (It follows that an active FD-round is also eligible, while an eligible FD-round is not necessarily active).

The timing pattern used in the proof is described in Figure 3.9.

- Let us consider the first process (say p_i) that decides. Let v be the value it decides. Process p_i has decided v at some time $T = (j − 1)d + D$ for some j. It follows from the failure detector-based decision predicate that, at time T, process p_i was not suspecting p_j. It follows from the detection timeliness property of the failure detector that no process suspected p_j at least up to time $T − d$ (Observation O1).

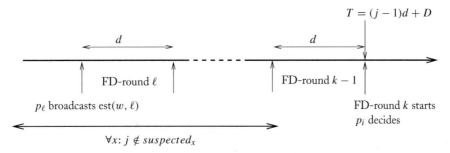

Figure 3.9: The pattern used in the proof of the agreement property

- Due to simplifying assumption that D is an integral multiple of d, it follows that there is an FD-round k that starts at time T. Moreover, (due to O1) no process has suspected p_j at the beginning of every FD-round $x < k$ (Observation O2).

- Due to the definition of "active FD-round" and O2, it follows that none of the rounds from $j + 1$ until $k - 1$ is active (Observation O3).

- On another side, as p_j is alive at time $T - d$ (see O1), and $T - d = (j - 1)d + D - d > (j - 1)d$, process p_j is alive at time $(j - 1)d$ (Observation O4).

- It follows that there is at least one active FD-round among the FD-rounds 1 to j. The only way for none of these FD-rounds be active is that for any x in $\{1, \ldots, j\}$ process p_x crashes at time $(x - 1)d$, and we know from O4 that this is false at least for p_j. Hence, there is a largest active FD-round -say ℓ- in the FD-rounds from 1 to j (Observation O5).

- It follows from the text of the algorithm and the definition of an active FD-round that p_ℓ (that exists due to O5) broadcast EST(w, ℓ) at the beginning of FD-round ℓ, and that message is received by all by time $(\ell - 1)d + D < T$ (Observation O6).

- It follows from the choice of ℓ and observation O3 that there is no active FD-rounds among the FD-rounds from $\ell + 1$ to $k - 1$. Consequently, none of the processes $p_{\ell+1}$ to p_{k-1} sends messages (Observation O7).

- It follows from O6 that, at time T, all processes have received EST(w, ℓ) and changed their est_i variable to w. Moreover, due to O7 est_i is not overwritten. Hence, at time T, no estimate value of an alive process is different from w. It follows that, whatever the messages sent after T, all estimates remain equal to w. Hence, $v = w$, and no decided value can be different from w.

$\square_{Theorem\ 3.14}$

On th failure detector behavior   Let us observe that when a process p_i decides, it stops its execution as far consensus is concerned but it continues executing the program it is involved in. If process p_i crashes later (i.e., outside th consensus algorithm), the failure detector detects its crash, and this detection does not alter the correction of the consensus algorithm. Differently, if p_i terminates, the failure detector has not to consider its normal termination as a crash (such a false detection could make incorrect the consensus algorithm). The failure detector detects crash failures and only crash failures. A normal termination is not a failure.

3.4   BIBLIOGRAPHIC NOTES

- Early deciding agreement has first been investigated by Dolev, Reischuk and Strong in (17).
- The predicate for early interactive consistency used in Section 3.1.2 and the corresponding early deciding and stopping algorithm are from (70).
- The early-decision lower bound on the number of rounds for consensus is $f + 2$ when $f < t - 1$ and $f + 1$ when $f \geq t - 1$ (e.g., (12; 43)). By an abuse of notation, this lower bound is usually denoted $\min(f + 2, t + 1)$ (the special case is when $f = t - 1$).
- The condition-based approach has been introduced by Mostefaoui, Rajsbaum and Raynal in (56) where it is shown that x-legality is a necessary and sufficient property to solve consensus in an asynchronous system prone to up to x process crashes.
- The condition-based approach has been extended to synchronous system by the same authors in (57) where is presented the hierarchy of conditions for synchronous systems.

  This paper presents also an early-deciding condition-based consensus algorithm that does not require that the input vector always belongs to the x-legal condition C it is instantiated with. This algorithm directs the processes to decide in at most $\min(f + 2, t + 1 - x)$ rounds in all the executions whose input vector I belongs to C, and in at most $\min(f + 2, t + 1)$ rounds if $I \notin C$.

- The condition-based approach has been extended to the interactive consistency problem in (58).
- The relation between agreement problems and error-correcting codes is due to Friedman, Mostefaoui, Rajsbaum and Raynal (24). More developments on the condition-based approach can be found in (41; 42; 59; 60; 81).
- Failure detectors have been introduced by Chandra, Hadzilacos and Toueg in (10; 11) where they are used to circumvent the impossibility to solve consensus in asynchronous systems prone to process crash failures (23). Introductory surveys to failure detectors can be found in (33; 72).
- Fast failure detectors have been introduced by Aguilera, Le Lann and Toueg in (1) where are given the algorithms that have been presented.

Simultaneous Consensus Despite Crash Failures

This chapter addresses the simultaneous consensus problem is presence of crash failures. Let us remember that this problem is the basic consensus problem with an additional agreement property related to the time (round) at which processes are allowed to decide, namely, no two processes decide at different rounds. Hence, simultaneous consensus provides each process with a strong global knowledge. Not only a process that decides a value v during round r knows that no other value can ever be decided by another process, but it also knows that no other process decides at a different round.

4.1   WHY IT IS DIFFICULT TO DECIDE SIMULTANEOUSLY BEFORE $t + 1$ ROUNDS

Using a non-early deciding algorithm   The previous chapter has presented a non-early consensus algorithm in which the processes decide during the round $t + 1$, hence this algorithm satisfies the required simultaneity property.

Let us also notice that the condition-based algorithm that has been presented in the previous chapter can be easily modified in order that each process decides during round $t + 1 - x$ where x is the legality degree of the condition the algorithm is instantiated with (such an algorithm is presented in Section 4.4.1).

Decide before $t + 1$ rounds   The aim is to design a simultaneous consensus algorithm in which the processes decide simultaneously before round $t + 1$. This means that we want an early-deciding simultaneous consensus algorithm. The problem is not as easy as it could seem at first glance. As we will see, differently from the base early-deciding problem, the worst case in when no process crashes!

To better understand the intuition that underlies the solution, let us consider the particular failure pattern in which t processes have crashed before the execution starts. As t is the upper bound on the number of crashes, it follows that the $n - t$ remaining processes define a failure-free system. During the first round, each non-crashed process can learn that, from then on, it is in a failure-free system, and, consequently, the $n - t$ correct processes can exchange their view of the system during the first round and discover during the second round that each had the same view at the end of the first round. Hence, at the end of the second round, each process can safely decide.

More generally, what makes things easier is when many crashes occur at the beginning of the computation. Roughly speaking this is because a crash is stable (once crashed a process remains crashed forever), while the property "a process is not crashed" is not a stable property. This instability property and the occurrence of only a few crashes, makes agreement on an early round for a simultaneous decision more difficult to obtain.

Early decision vs simultaneity   When looking for early decision only, a process strives for discovering a round r without crashes. When this occurs, it knows that no more value can be learnt, and (as we have seen in the previous chapter) it can safely decide (after having propagated during round $r + 1$ what it learnt during round r).

When looking for simultaneous agreement, the processes have to agree on how many crashes have occurred in order to be able to decide simultaneously before the last round (round $t + 1$). When y processes crash "simultaneously" during a round r, in the sense that the processes that terminate this round detect these crashes, the "simultaneity" of these crashes allows the saving of $y - 1$ rounds, i.e., the processes can safely decide during round $t + 1 - (y - 1)$. This is the basic principle on which relies the implementation of the early-deciding simultaneous agreement. The worst cases are when there are no crashes (as already said) and when there is one crash per round. In these cases, no round can be saved and simultaneous decision cannot occur before the last round.

4.2   PRELIMINARY DEFINITIONS

4.2.1   FAILURE PATTERN, FAILURE DISCOVERY, AND WASTE

Failure pattern   Up to now, the notion of a failure pattern was used in an informal way and has not been given a precise definition. Such a definition is now needed.

A *failure pattern* F is a list of at most t triples (j, k_j, b_j) where j is a process identity, k_j a round number and b_j a set of processes. Such a triple states that process p_j crashes in round k_j (hence, it sends no message after that round), and b_j is the set of processes that do not receive the message sent by p_j during round k_j. It is supposed that the list defining a failure pattern is well-defined, i.e., for any j, there is at most one triple $(j, -, -)$.

Failure discovery   The failure of a process p_j is *discovered* (for the first time) in round r if r is the first round such that (a) there a process p_i that does not receive a round r message from p_j and (b) p_i completes round r without crashing.

The notion of waste   The discussion at the end the previous section suggests that determining the smallest round at which the processes can simultaneously decide should take into account the pairs (round number, number of processes perceived as crashed at that round). This intuition is formalized as follows.

- Let $C[r, F]$ (abbreviated $C[r]$ when the pattern F is left implicit) be the number of processes perceived as crashed by (at least) one of the processes that does not crash before the end of round r.

- For any round r, let $d_r = \max(0, |C[r]| - r)$. As we will see, d_r represents the number of rounds that could be saved with respect to the worst case ($t + 1$ rounds), thanks to the crashes that occurred and were seen by at least one process that terminate round r.

- Given a failure pattern F, let $D(F) = \max_{r \geq 0}(d_r)$. According to the definition of d_r, this value represents the best saving in terms of rounds that can obtained with failure pattern F. When there is no ambiguity, $D(F)$ is denoted D.

D and d_r depends on the failure pattern. The quantity D is called the *waste* inherent in the failure pattern F. This is because it represents the number of rounds that an adversary has "lost" in its quest to delay the simultaneous decision as long as possible. As we will see, the algorithm presented in Section 4.3 computes (in some way) the values d_r, and is consequently able to direct the processes to simultaneously decide during round $t + 1 - D$.

4.2.2   NOTION OF CLEAN ROUND AND HORIZON

In order to design an algorithm that allows the processes to simultaneously decide during round $t + 1 - D$, a few more important notions have to be defined.

Notion of clean round   A round r is *clean* if no process is discovered faulty for the first time in that round, i.e., $C[r - 1] = C[r]$. This means that a process that crashes during a clean round r has sent its round r message to all the processes that proceed to round $r + 1$. Hence, the notion of clean round is not associated directly with crashes but with their discovery by processes.

Let us recall that in the synchronous model considered, a process never sends different messages to distinct processes in the same round. We also consider here that a process sends a message at every round until it crashes or decides. The following property is an immediate consequence of these assumptions and the definition of a clean round.

Property 4.1   If round r is clean, then all the processes that proceed to round $r + 1$ received, during round r, messages from the same set of processes (and this set includes at least all of them).

Let us observe that a clean round is not necessarily a failure-free round. It is possible that a process p_i crashes in a clean round r but no process active at the end of r has noticed its crash (p_i has crashed after its sending phase and before the end of round r, or more generally p_i has crashed during r after sending its round r message at least to the processes that terminate round r). Similarly, a failure-free round is not necessarily clean. As an example, a failure-free round $r + 1$ that follows a clean round r during which a crash occurred is not clean. This is depicted on Figure 4.1 where round $r - 1$ is clean, while round r is failure-free but not clean (because p_i is discovered faulty for the first time in round r).

Notion of horizon   Given a process p_i and a round $r \geq 1$, let x be the greatest number of process crashes that occurred between round 1 and round $r - 1$ (included) and are known by p_i (to have

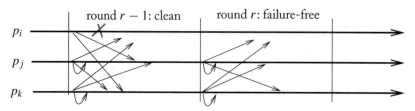

round $r-1$: clean   round r: failure-free

Figure 4.1: Clean round vs failure-free round

crashed in the first $r-1$ rounds) by the end of round r. By definition, we always have $x=0$ for $r=1$.

The value $h_i(r) = r + t - x$ is called the *horizon* of p_i at round r. We have $h_i(1) = t+1$. As an example, if three processes crash by the end of the first round and p_i discovers their crash during the second round (it has received messages from them during the first round but not during the second round), we have $h_i(2) = 2 + t - 3 = t - 1$.

As we will see, the horizon notion (of a process p_i at round r) is a key notion to determine the smallest round at the end of which the same value can be simultaneously decided. The following simple theorem (that will be exploited by the algorithm described in Section 4.3) explains why this notion is crucial.

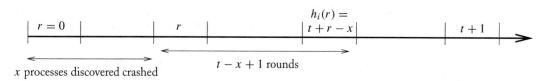

Figure 4.2: Existence of a clean round

Theorem 4.2 *Let x be defined as indicated above, and p_i a process that terminates round r. There is a clean round y such that $r \leq y \leq h_i(r) = r + t - x$.*

Proof Let us first observe that, as at least x processes have been discovered faulty by the end of round $r-1$, at most $t-x$ processes can be discovered faulty between round r (included) and round $r+t-x$ (included) (see Figure 4.2). But there are $t-x+1$ rounds from r to $r+t-x$, from which we conclude that at least one of these rounds is clean. $\square_{Theorem\ 4.2}$

4.3 AN OPTIMAL SIMULTANEOUS CONSENSUS ALGORITHM

4.3.1 AN OPTIMAL ALGORITHM

Local variables Each process p_i manages the following local variables. Some variables are presented as belonging to an array. This is only for notational convenience, as such array variables can be implemented as simple variables.

- est_i contains, at the end of r, p_i's current estimate of the decision value. Its initial value is v_i, the value proposed by p_i.

- $f_i[r]$ denotes the set of processes from which p_i has not received a message during the round r. (So, this variable is the best current estimate that p_i can have of the processes that have crashed.)
  Let $\overline{f_i[r]} = \Pi \setminus f_i[r]$ (i.e., the set of processes from which p_i has received a round r message).

- $f_i'[r-1]$ is a value computed by p_i during the round r, but that refers to crashes that occurred up to the round $r-1$ (included), hence the notation. It is the value $\bigcup_{p_j \in \overline{f_i[r]}} f_j[r-1]$, which means that $f_i'[r-1]$ is the set of processes that were known as crashed at the end of the round $r-1$ by at least one of the processes from which p_i has received a round r message. This value is computed by p_i during the round r. As process p_i receives its own messages, we have $f_i[r-1] \subseteq f_i'[r-1]$.

- $bh_i[r]$ represents the best (smallest) horizon value known by p_i at round r. It is p_i's best estimate of the smallest round for a simultaneous decision. Initially, $bh_i[0] = h_i(0) = t+1$.

$$h_i(r) = t + r - |f_i'[r-1]|$$
$$h_i(r) = t + 1 - \big(|f_i'[r-1]| - (r-1)\big) \text{ (stated wrt } r-1)$$

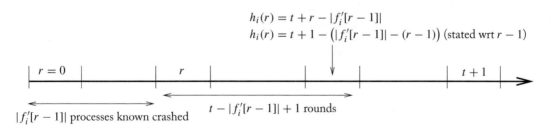

Figure 4.3: Computing the current horizon value

Process behavior Each process p_i not crashed at the beginning of r sends to all the processes a message containing its current estimate of the decision value (est_i), and the set $f_i[r-1]$ of processes it currently knows as faulty. After it has received the round r messages, p_i computes the new value of est_i and the value of $bh_i[r]$. The new value of est_i is the smallest of the estimates values it has seen so far. As far as the value of $bh_i[r]$ is concerned, we have the following.

- The computation of $bh_i[r]$ has to take into account $h_i(r)$. This is required to benefit from Theorem 4.2 that states that there is a clean round y such that $r \leq y \leq h_i(r)$. When this clean round will be executed, any two processes p_i and p_j that execute it will have $est_i = est_j$, and (as they will receive messages from the same set of processes, see Property 4.1) will be such that $f_i'[r-1] = f_j'[r-1]$. It follows that, we will have $h_i(y) = h_j(y)$, thereby creating correct "seeds" for determining the smallest round for a simultaneous decision. This allows the processes to determine rounds at which they can simultaneously decide.

- As we are looking for the first round where a simultaneous decision is possible, $bh_i[r]$ has to be set to $\min\big(h_i(0), h_i(1), \ldots, h_i(r)\big)$, i.e., $bh_i[r] = \min\big(bh_i[r-1], h_i(r)\big)$.

Finally, according to the previous discussion, the algorithm directs a process p_i to decide at the end of the first round r that is equal to the best horizon currently known by p_i, i.e., when $r = bh_i[r]$.

As far $h_i(r)$ is concerned, we have $h_i(r) = t + r - |f_i'[r-1]|$. The resulting algorithm is presented in Figure 4.4 where $h_i(r)$ is expressed as a function of $r-1$ to emphasize the fact that it could be computed at the end of the round $r-1$ by an external omniscient observer. This formulation is described in Figure 4.3 that is the same as Figure 4.2 where x is replaced by its value as known by p_i, namely, $x = |f_i'[r-1]|$.

```
operation  propose (v_i):
(1)      est_i ← v_i; bh_i[0] ← t + 1; f_i[0] ← ∅;
(2)      when r = 1, 2, ... do
         begin synchronous round
(3)              broadcast EST(est_i, f_i[r − 1]);
(4)              let f_i'[r − 1] = union of the f_j[r − 1] sets received during r;
(5)              let f_i[r] = set of processes from which p_i has not received a message during r;
(6)              est_i  ← min( all the est_j received during r);
(7)              let h_i(r) = (r − 1) + (t + 1 − |f_i'[r − 1]|);
(8)              bh_i[r] ← min (bh_i[r − 1], h_i(r));
(9)              if r = bh_i[r] then  return(est_i) end if
         end synchronous round.
```

Figure 4.4: Optimal simultaneous decision despite up to t crash failures (code for p_i)

4.3.2   PROOF OF THE ALGORITHM

Lemma 4.3   Validity property. *A decided value is a proposed value.*

Proof The proof is an immediate consequence of the initialization of the est_i local variables (line 1), the reliability of the channels, and the min() operation used at line 6. $\square_{Lemma\ 4.3}$

Lemma 4.4   *Let p_i be a correct process. $\forall r \geq 0$ we have $h_i(r) \geq r$.*

Proof Since the processes in the set $f_i'[r-1]$ are processes that have crashed by the end of the round $r-1$, it follows that $t - |f_i'[r-1]| \geq 0$. Consequently, $h_i(r) = r + t - |f_i'[r-1]| \geq r$.

$\square$ *Lemma 4.4*

Notation: Considering an arbitrary execution, let p_i be a process that is correct in that execution.
- Let $BH_i = \min_{r \geq 0} h_i(r)$. BH_i is the smallest value ever attained by the function $h_i(r)$, i.e., the smallest horizon value determined by p_i.
- Let $L_i = \max(\{r \mid h_i(r) = BH_i\})$. L_i is the last round whose horizon value is BH_i.

It follows from these definitions that if $L' > L_i$ then $h_i(L') > h_i(L_i)$.

Lemma 4.5   *Let $t < n$. The round L_i is a clean round (i.e., no process is discovered faulty for the first time in that round).*

Proof Assume, by way of contradiction, that L_i is not clean (recall that p_i is a correct process). This means there is a process p_z that is seen faulty for the first time in round L_i by some process p_y. Notice that $p_z \notin f_i'[L_i - 1]$ since p_z was not discovered faulty in the previous rounds. There are two cases.
- Case 1: p_i receives a message from p_y in round $L_i + 1$.
  (This case includes the case where p_i and p_y are the same process). As p_y does not receive a message from p_z during L_i, and a crash is stable, we have $p_z \in f_y[L_i]$. Moreover, due to the case assumption, and the fact that the round $L_i + 1$ message from p_y to p_i carries $f_y[L_i]$, it follows that $f_i'[L_i]$ contains $f_i'[L_i - 1] \cup \{p_z\}$. Consequently, $|f_i'[L_i]| > |f_i'[L_i - 1]|$. It follows that $h_i(L_i + 1) \leq h_i(L_i)$, contradicting the definition of L_i.
- Case 2: p_i does not receive a message from p_y in round $L_i + 1$.
  In that case, both p_z and p_y are seen faulty for the first time by p_i during the round $L_i + 1$. So, $f_i[L_i + 1]$ contains $f_i'[L_i - 1] \cup \{p_y, p_z\}$. Since $f_i'[L_i + 1]$ (computed by p_i during the round $L_i + 2$) contains $f_i[L_i + 1]$, we have $|f_i'[L_i + 1]| \geq |f_i'[L_i - 1]| + 2$. Thus, we have

$$
\begin{aligned}
h_i(L_i + 2) &= (L_i + 2) + t - |f_i'[L_i + 1]|, \\
&\leq (L_i + 2) + t - (|f_i'[L_i - 1]| + 2), \\
&= L_i + t - |f_i'[L_i - 1]|, \\
&= h_i(L_i),
\end{aligned}
$$

which again contradicts the definition of L_i.

$\square$ *Lemma 4.5*

Lemma 4.6   *Let $t < n$. Every correct process decides. Moreover, all processes that decide do so in the same round and decide on the same value.*

Proof

Termination property.   Let us consider a correct process p_i. Notice that, due to the initialization and line 8 we have $\forall r : bh_i[r] \leq t + 1$, from which we conclude $BH_i \leq t + 1$. So, to prove that p_i decides we have to show that p_i does not miss the test $r = BH_i$ at line 9. This could happen if the first round ℓ such that $bh_i[\ell - 1] > BH_i$ and $bh_i[\ell] = BH_i$ is such that $\ell > BH_i$. We prove that this cannot happen.

Let us observe that, due to Lemma 4.4, we have $h_i(\ell) \geq \ell$. It then follows from $bh_i[\ell - 1] > BH_i$, $h_i(\ell) \geq \ell$, $bh_i[\ell] = BH_i$, and line 8, that $BH_i = bh_i[\ell] = \min(bh_i[\ell - 1], h_i(\ell)) = h_i(\ell) \geq \ell$, i.e., $BH_i \geq \ell$, which establishes the result. It follows that p_i decides no later than round $t + 1$.

Simultaneous decision for the correct processes.   We first show that no two correct processes p_i and p_j decide at distinct rounds. Due to the algorithm, if p_i and p_j decide, they decide at round BH_i and BH_j, respectively. We show that $BH_i = BH_j$. Due to Lemma 4.5, the round L_i is clean. Hence, during the round L_i, p_j receives the same messages that p_i receives (Property 4.1). Thus $f_i'[L_i - 1] = f_j'[L_i - 1]$ and consequently, $h_i(L_i) = h_j(L_i)$. Then, we have

$$
\begin{array}{ll}
BH_j \leq bh_j[L_i] & \text{(Due the definition of } BH_j\text{),} \\
bh_j[L_i] \leq h_j(L_i) & \text{(Due to line 09),} \\
bh_j[L_i] \leq h_i(L_i) & \text{(Due to } h_i(L_i) = h_j(L_i)\text{),} \\
h_i(L_i) = BH_i & \text{(Due to the definition of } L_i\text{),}
\end{array}
$$

from which we conclude $BH_j \leq BH_i$. By symmetry the same reasoning yields $BH_i \leq BH_j$, from which it follows that $BH_i = BH_j$. This proves that no two correct processes decide at distinct rounds.

Simultaneous decision for the faulty processes. BH being the round at which the correct processes decide, let us now consider the case of a faulty process p_j. As p_j behaves as a correct process until it crashes, and as the correct processes decide in the same round BH, it follows that no faulty process decides before BH, and if p_j executes line 9 of round BH, it does decide as if it was a correct process.

Data agreement property.   The fact that no two processes decide different values comes from the existence of the clean round L_i that appears before a process decision. During that round, all the processes that are alive at the end of this round have received the same set of estimate values (Property 4.1), and selected the smallest of them. It follows that, from the end of that round, there is a single estimate value in the system, which proves the data agreement property. $\square_{Lemma\ 4.6}$

Definition 4.7   We now formally define S and C, which have been previously introduced more informally. Given an execution of propose, let F be the failure pattern that occurs in that execution.

- $S[r] = S[r, F]$ is the set of processes that complete round r according to F.
- $C[r] = C[r, F] = \bigcup_{p_i \in S[r]} f_i[r]$, i.e., the set of the processes that are known to have crashed by at least one of the processes that survives round r. Observe that $f_i'[r] \subseteq C[r]$, for any $p_i \in S[r]$.

Let us recall that $d_r = \max(0, |C[r]| - r)$, for every round r, and the "waste" $D = \max_{r \geq 0}(d_r)$ (number of rounds the adversary has lost in his quest to delay decision for as long as possible.) Let us observe that as no process can be discovered faulty before the first round, we have $C[0] = 0$. More generally, we assume $C[r] = 0$ for all $r \leq 0$ (the fictitious round 0 is used for ease of exposition). Notice also that $D \geq 0$, since $C[0] = 0$ and $D \geq d_0 = C[0] - 0 = 0$.

Theorem 4.8   *Let $t < n$. The algorithm described in Figure 4.4 solves the consensus problem with simultaneous decision. In a run with failure pattern F, decision is reached in round $t + 1 - D$ where $D = D(F)$ is the waste inherent in F.*

Proof The proof of the validity, termination, simultaneous decision and data agreement properties follow from the Lemmas 4.3 and 4.6. We now show that the decision is obtained in round $t + 1 - D$. Let us consider an arbitrary run of the algorithm. It follows from Lemma 4.6 that $BH_i = BH_j$ for any pair of processes p_i and p_j that decide. Let BH denote this round. The proof of the claim amounts to showing that $BH \leq t + 1 - D$ and $BH \geq t + 1 - D$.

Let p_i be a process that decides and R the last round such that $|C[R]| - R = D$ (i.e., $|C[R + x]| - (R + x) < D = |C[R]| - R$, for any $x > 0$). Let us observe that, due to the lines 7-9 of the algorithm, BH is attained at the round numbers that make the function $h_i()$ minimal. Moreover, it follows from the definition of D and R that $|C[R + 1]| \leq |C[R]|$. Since $C[R] \subseteq C[R + 1]$, it follows that $C[R] = C[R + 1]$, i.e., no new process failure is discovered in round $R + 1$, so the round $R + 1$ is clean and we have $|f_i'[R]| = |C[R]|$. Due to line 7 of the round $R + 1$, we have $h_i(R + 1) = R + t + 1 - |f_i'[R]| = (t + 1) - (|f_i'[R]| - R) = t + 1 - D$, from which we conclude $BH \leq t + 1 - D$.

For the other direction, let us recall that, due to Lemma 4.5, the round $L_i > 0$ is clean. It follows that $f_i'[L_i - 1] = C[L_i - 1]$, since any p_i hears in round L_i from all processes that survived round $L_i - 1$. Therefore, $BH = t + 1 - (|f_i'[L_i - 1]| - (L_i - 1)) = t + 1 - (|C[L_i - 1]| - (L_i - 1)) = t + 1 - d_{(L_i-1)} \geq t + 1 - D$, which completes the proof of the theorem. $\square_{Theorem\ 4.8}$

Remark   As indicated in the bibliographic notes at the end of this chapter, the value $t + 1 - D$ is a lower bound for simultaneous decision. It is important to remark that the algorithm presented in Figure 4.4 requires $t + 1 - D$ rounds in each and every execution. This comes from the fact that D is defined from the failure pattern (that states, not only the round at which processes crash but also which processes do not receive messages when a process crashes).

This contrasts with early-deciding consensus algorithms where, while $\min(f + 2, t + 1)$ is a lower bound on the number of rounds, not all executions requires $\min(f + 2, t + 1)$ rounds. Only worst case executions require this number of rounds.

4.4   CONDITION-BASED SIMULTANEITY

This section addresses the case where the set of input vectors is restricted, namely, the input vector is assumed to belong to an x-legal condition C.

4.4.1 CONDITION-BASED SIMULTANEOUS CONSENSUS ALGORITHM

When the input vector always belongs to an x-legal condition C, it is possible (as indicated in the first section of this chapter) to modify the condition-based consensus algorithm described in the previous chapter in order to obtain a condition-based simultaneous consensus algorithm in which the decision occurs only at round $t + 1 - x$. This is obtained by delaying decision until round $t + x - 1$. The modification are the following ones:

- As a condition-based consensus algorithm terminates in one round when $x = t$ and we are interested in combining it with an algorithm that terminates in 2 rounds in the best case, we assume that $x < t$ and eliminates, consequently, the statement "**if** $(x = t)$ **then** return(est_i) **end if**" that appears at the end of the first round.

- The second modification consists in the the suppression of the early decision line at the beginning of a round when $v\_cond_i \neq \bot$.

  The resulting algorithm is described in Figure 4.5.

```
operation  propose_x (v_i):
(1)    view_i ← [⊥, ..., ⊥]; view_i[i] ← v_i; v_cond ← ⊥; v_tmf_i ← ⊥;
(2)    when r = 1 do
       begin synchronous round
(3)        broadcast EST1(v_i);
(4)        for each v_j received do view_i[j] ← v_j end for;
(5)        case (#_⊥(view_i) ≤ x) then v_cond_i ← h(view_i)
(6)             (#_⊥(view_i) > x) then v_tmf_i ← max(all values v_j received)
(7)        end case;
       end synchronous round;
(8)    when r = 2, ..., t + 1 − x do
       begin synchronous round
(9)        broadcast EST2(v_cond_i, v_tmf_i);
(10)       if (v_cond_j ≠ ⊥ received during round r) then v_cond_i ← v_cond_j end if;
(11)       v_tmf_i ← max(all v_tmf_j values received during r);
(12)       if (r = t + 1 − x) then
(13)           if (v_cond_i ≠ ⊥) then return(v_cond_i) else return(v_tmf_i) end if;
(14)       end if
       end synchronous round.
```

Figure 4.5: A t-resilient condition-based simultaneous algorithm (code for p_i)

4.4.2 OPTIMAL CONDITION-BASED SIMULTANEOUS CONSENSUS

A condition-based simultaneous consensus algorithm can be obtained from the two base algorithms described in Figures 4.4 and 4.5. Their combination consists in executing both algorithms in parallel as follows:

1. The r-th round, $1 \leq r \leq t + 1 - x$, of the combined algorithm is a simple merge of the r-th round of both algorithms. This means that the message sent by p_i at round r now piggybacks v_cond_i, $vtmf_i$, est_i and $f_i[r-1]$.

2. Line 9 of the algorithm in Figure 4.4 and lines 12-13 of the algorithm in Figure 4.5 are replaced by the following lines:

$$\textbf{if } (r = bh_i[r]) \ \vee \ (r = t + 1 - x) \textbf{ then}$$
$$\quad \textbf{if } (r = bh_i[r]) \textbf{ then } \text{return } (est_i)$$
$$\quad\quad\quad\quad \textbf{else } \textbf{if } (v\_cond_i \neq \bot) \textbf{ then } \text{return } (v\_cond_i)$$
$$\quad\quad\quad\quad\quad\quad\quad\quad \textbf{else } \text{return } (v\_tmf_i) \textbf{ end if}$$
$$\textbf{end if}$$

The following theorem is an immediate consequence of the combination of Theorem 3.11 (Chapter 3) and Theorem 4.8. More precisely, if the algorithm described in Figure 4.4 terminates first (case $r = bh_i[r] < t + 1 - x$), or both terminate at the same round (case $r = bh_i[r] = t + 1 - x$), that algorithm imposes the common early decision round, namely $bh_i[r]$. Otherwise, the condition-based algorithm imposes $t + 1 - x$ as the common early decision round.

Theorem 4.9   *Let $x < t < n$. The algorithm obtained by the combined execution (as described in the previous items) of the algorithms described in Figures 4.4 and 4.5 solves the condition-based simultaneous consensus problem. In a run with failure pattern F, decision is reached in round $t + 1 - \max(D, x)$.*

4.5   BIBLIOGRAPHIC NOTES

- The notion of simultaneous consensus has been introduced by Dolev, Reischuk and Strong (17) and Dwork and Moses (20) in the early nineties.

- The notion of simultaneous decision is strongly related to the notion of *common knowledge* and how common knowledge can be gained during a synchronous execution. This notion is deeply investigated in (38; 51; 55). The book by Fagin, Halpern, Moses and Vardi (21) is entirely devoted to knowledge-based reasonning.

- The notions of waste and clean round are due to Dwork and Moses (20). The notion of horizon is due to Mizrahi and Moses (50).

- The simultaneous decision consensus algorithm that has been presented is due to Moses and Raynal (54). It is a variant that revisits an algorithm introduced in (20).

- The fact that $t + 1 - D$ is a lower bound on the number of rounds for simultaneous consensus is due to Dwork and Moses (20). A simpler proof appears in (54).

- The use of the condition-based approach to solve simultaneous consensus is due to Moses and Raynal (53) where it is shown that $t + 1 - \max(x, D)$ is a lower bound for that problem. This means that, contrarily to what could be hoped, when considering condition-based consensus with simultaneous decision, we can benefit from the best of both actual worlds: either the failure world (case $t + 1 - D$) or the condition world (case $t + 1 - x$), but we cannot benefit from the sum of savings offered by both. Only one discount applies.

CHAPTER 5

From Consensus to k-Set Agreement

This chapter is devoted to the k-set agreement problem in presence of up to t process crashes. This problem is a weakening of consensus, namely, each process that does not crash is required to decide a but up to k different values can be decided (each being a proposed value). Hence, consensus is 1-set agreement.

If $k > t$, more values can be decided than the maximal number of crashes. In that case, the k-set agreement problem can be trivially solved. For example, $k + 1$ processes broadcast their initial values and a process decides the first value it receives. (If we are interested in a fair solution -i.e., the set of values that can be decided in not restricted to the values proposed by a given subset of processes- the processes can first execute a preliminary round during which they shuffle their values.) Hence, it is assumed that $k \leq t$.

This chapter presents first a simple synchronous algorithm in which the processes decide in at most $\lfloor \frac{t}{k} \rfloor + 1$. It then considers early decision and presents an algorithm in which a process decides in at most $\min \left(\lfloor \frac{t}{t} \rfloor + 2, \lfloor \frac{t}{k} \rfloor + 1 \right)$. It can be seen that, when $k = 1$, these values are lower bounds on the number of rounds for consensus. Finally, considering the case of a synchronous system enriched with additional base objects, each solving the ℓ-set agreement problem among m processes (with $\ell \leq k$ and $m < n$), this chapter presents a corresponding k-set agreement algorithm, proves it correct, and shows that $\lfloor \frac{t}{k} \rfloor + 1$ is a lower bound on the number of rounds for k-set agreement.

5.1 A SIMPLE k-SET AGREEMENT PROBLEM

A simple algorithm A very simple algorithm that solves k-set agreement problem in the base synchronous model made up of n processes, where up to $t < n$ of them may crash, is presented in Figure 5.1. This algorithm assumes that the values proposed by processes are totally ordered.

A process p_i decides the smallest value it has ever seen, after having executed $\lfloor \frac{t}{k} \rfloor + 1$ rounds. The aim of this sequence of rounds is to ensure that, when they have been executed, it remains at most k values in the system. From an operational point of view, during each round a process p_i first broadcasts its current estimate est_i (this estimate is initialized to v_i, the value it proposes). Then, after it has received the estimates of the processes that are alive during that round, p_i updates est_i to the smallest of them.

```
operation propose (v_i):
(1)  est_i ← v_i;
(2)  when r = 1, 2, ..., ⌊t/k⌋ + 1 do
     begin synchronous round
(3)      broadcast EST(est_i);
(4)      est_i ← min(est_j values received during r);
(5)      if (r = ⌊t/k⌋ + 1) then return(est_i) end if
     end synchronous round.
```

Figure 5.1: A simple t-resilient $k$set agreement algorithm (code for p_i)

Theorem 5.1   *The algorithm described in Figure 5.1 solves the k-set agreement problem in a synchronous system prone to t process crashes. It requires $\lfloor \frac{t}{k} \rfloor + 1$ for the processes to decide.*

Proof   The validity property and the fact that no process executes more than $\lfloor \frac{t}{k} \rfloor + 1$ rounds are trivial. As far as the agreement property is concerned, let $t = \alpha \times k + \beta$, where $\alpha = \lfloor \frac{t}{k} \rfloor$ and $\beta = (t \bmod k)$. We show that at round $r = \alpha + 1$ there are at most $\beta + 1$ different estimates values in the system. As $\beta = t \bmod k < k$, it follows that at most k different values can be decided.

Let us first observe that if y processes crash by the end of a round r, there are at most $y + 1$ different estimates values at the end of r. This is because the processes that do not crash exchange their estimates, and, consequently, they all know their smallest estimate value w at the end of round r. Moreover, it is possible that, at the beginning of r, the estimates $w_1, w_2, ..., w_y$ of the y processes that crash during r are all different and smaller than w, .g., $w_1 < w_2 < \cdots < w_y < w$. As each value w_x ($1 \leq x \leq y$) can be received by only one process that terminates round r, it follows that the processes that terminate round r have at most $y + 1$ different estimate values at the end of round r.

The worst case scenario is when there are at least k process crashes at every round from round 1 to round $\alpha = \lfloor \frac{t}{k} \rfloor$. Then, due the previous observation, it is then possible to have at least $k + 1$ different estimate values at the end of each of these rounds.

Let us consider the last round $r = \alpha + 1$. During that round, at most $\beta = (t \bmod k) < k$ processes can crash. It follows from the previous observation (taking $y = \beta$) that there are at most $\beta + 1 \leq k$ different estimate values at the end of round $r = \alpha + 1$, which concludes the proof of the agreement property.
□ $_{Theorem\ 5.1}$

Running time: k-set agreement with respect to consensus   When comparing k-set agreement and consensus (1-set agreement), the important point is that allowing up to k different values to be decided instead of a single one divides the number of rounds (running time) by k.

Reduce the number of messages   In the algorithm described in Figure 5.1, each process broadcasts its current estimate at every round, even if this estimate has not been modified in the previous round. As we have seen for the consensus problem, it is possible to improve this algorithm is order a process broadcasts its current estimate during a round r only when it has modified it during round $r - 1$. This allows to save messages and reduces consequently the message cost of the corresponding execution.

5.2 EARLY-DECIDING AND STOPPING k-SET AGREEMENT

This section presents an early-deciding and stopping k-set agreement algorithm. Assuming that at most f processes crash in a given execution, $0 \leq f \leq t$, no process executes more than min $\left(\lfloor \frac{t}{t} \rfloor + 2, \lfloor \frac{t}{k} \rfloor + 1 \right)$.

This algorithm is a generalization of the early-deciding and stopping consensus algorithm described in Section 3.1 of Chapter 3. The local variables are exactly the same. The only modification is the maximal number of rounds that is now $\lfloor \frac{t}{k} \rfloor + 1$ instead of $t + 1$.

To make this chapter easier to read and as most as possible self-contained, some notions and principles introduced in Chapter 3 are stated again.

5.2.1 AN EARLY-DECIDING AND STOPPING ALGORITHM

As previously stated the value decided by a process p_i is the smallest value it has even seen, and the broadcasts are used to allow processes to improve their knowledge of the smallest values which are still present in the system. The algorithm is described in Figure 5.2.

Definitions: Reminder   Let us recall that $UP[r]$ denotes the set of processes that have not crashed by the end of round $r - 1$. (It is possible for a process of $UP[r]$ to crash just after starting round r.) Moreover, as defined in Chapter 3, $R_i[r]$ is the set of processes from which p_i has received a message during round r.

Although p_i has no means to known the exact value of $UP[r]$ in the general case, as process crashes are stable we always have $R_i[r] \subseteq UP[r] \subseteq R_i[r - 1]$. More, in the particular case where $R_i[r - 1] = R_i[r]$, p_i has received a message from each process $p_j \in UP[r]$, i.e., from all the processes that were active at the beginning of r. It can then correctly conclude that it knows the smallest value among the values still present in the system at the beginning of r.

Description of the algorithm   Let us observe that, as the failure model is the crash model and a process p_i sends at most one message per round to each other process, we can use instead of $R_i[r]$ a local variable $nbr_i[r]$ counting the number of processes from which p_i has received a message during r. The predicate $R_i[r - 1] = R_i[r]$ then becomes $nbr_i[r - 1] - nbr_i[r] = 0$.

As we are interested in solving k-set agreement, it is not necessary for p_i to know the smallest value present in the system, it is sufficient for it to known one amongst the k smallest values present in the system. This knowledge can be obtained by weakening the locally evaluable predicate $nbr_i[r - 1] - nbr_i[r] = 0$ into $nbr_i[r - 1] - nbr_i[r] < k$. This weakening is due to the following observation (Figure 5.3). When $nbr_i[r - 1] - nbr_i[r] < k$, p_i knows that it misses values from at most $k - 1$ processes in the system. In the worst case, these $k - 1$ missing values are smaller than

---

operation propose (v_i)
(1) $est_i \leftarrow v_i; nbr_i[0] \leftarrow n; early_i \leftarrow false;$
(2)   **when** $r = 1, 2, \dots, \lfloor \frac{t}{k} \rfloor + 1$ **do**
        begin synchronous round
(3)   broadcast EST$(est_i, early_i)$
(4)   **if** $early_i$ **then** return(est_i) **end if**;
(5)   **let** $nbr_i[r]$ = number of messages received by p_i during r;
(6)   **let** $decide_i \leftarrow \bigvee(early_j$ values received during current round $r)$;
(7) $est_i \leftarrow \min(\{est_j$ values received during current round $r\})$;
(8)   **if** $((nbr_i[r-1] - nbr_i[r] < k) \vee decide_i)$ **then** $early_i \leftarrow$ true **end if**
(9)   **if** $(r = \lfloor \frac{t}{k} \rfloor + 1)$ **then** return(est_i) **end if**
        end synchronous round.

Figure 5.2: Early stopping synchronous k-set agreement: (code for $p_i, t < n$)

the value of est_i at the end of r, from which we conclude that, at the end of r, the value of its current estimate est_i is one of the k smallest values present in the system.

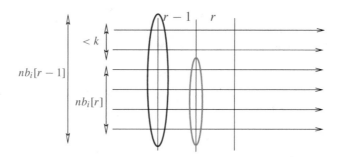

Figure 5.3: Comparing $nbr_i[r]$ vs $nbr_i[r-1]$

Unfortunately, the local predicate $nbr_i[r-1] - nbr_i[r] < k$ is not powerful enough to allow p_i to conclude that the other processes know it has one of the k smallest values. Consequently, p_i cannot decide and stop immediately. To be more explicit, let us consider the case where p_i has (not any of the k smallest values but) the smallest value v in the system, is the only process that knows v, decides it at the end of r and then crashes by the end of r. The other processes can then decide k other values as v is no longer is the system from round $r + 1$. An easy way to fix this problem consists in requiring p_i to proceed to $r + 1$ before deciding (this is similar to the way used to guarantee uniform agreement in consensus protocols). When $nbr_i[r-1] - nbr_i[r] < k$ becomes true, p_i sets a boolean $(early_i)$ to true and proceeds to the next round $r + 1$. As, before deciding at line 4 of $r + 1$, p_i has first sent the pair $(est_i, early_i)$ to all processes, any process p_j active during $r + 1$ not only knows v but, as $early_i$ is true, knows also that v is one of k smallest values present in the system during $r + 1$.

5.2.2   PROOF OF THE ALGORITHM

Lemma 5.2   [Validity] *A decided value is a proposed value.*

Proof The proof of the validity consists in showing that an est_i local variable always contains a proposed variable. This is initially true (round $r = 0$). Then, a simple induction reasoning proves the property: assuming the property is true at a round $r \geq 1$, it follows from the protocol code (lines 4 and 7), and the fact that a process receives at least the value it has sent, that the property remains true at round $r + 1$. $\square_{Lemma\ 5.2}$

Lemma 5.3   [Termination] *Every correct process decides.*

Proof The proof is an immediate consequence of the fact that a process executes at most $\lfloor t/k \rfloor + 1$ rounds and the computation model is the synchronous round-based computation model. $\square_{Lemma\ 5.3}$

Lemma 5.4   [Agreement] *No more than k different values are decided.*

Proof Let $EST[0]$ be the set of proposed values, and $EST[r]$ the set of est_i values of the processes that decide during r or proceed to $r + 1$ ($r \geq 1$). We first state and prove three claims.

Claim C1. $\forall r \geq 0$: $EST[r + 1] \subseteq EST[r]$.
Proof of the claim. The claim follows directly from the fact that, during a round, the new value of an est_i variable computed by a process is the smallest of the est_j values it has received. So values can only disappear, due to the minimum function used at line 7 or to process crashes. *End of the proof of the claim C1.*

Claim C2. Let p_i be a process such that $early_i$ is set to true at the end of r. Then est_i is one of the k smallest values in $EST[r]$.
Proof of the claim. Let v be the value of est_i at the end of r ($v \in EST[r]$). If $early_i$ is set to true at the end of r, $nbr_i[r - 1] - nbr_i[r] < k$ is satisfied or p_i has received a message carrying a pair $(v1, true)$, and $v1$ has been taken into account when computing the new value of est_i at line 7 during round r, i.e., $v \leq v1$. So, there is a chain of processes $j = j_a, j_{a-1}, \ldots, j_0 = i$ that has carried the boolean value *true* to p_i. This chain is such that $a \geq 0, nb_j[r - a - 1] - nb_j[r - a] < k$ is satisfied, and any value v' sent by a process participating in this chain is such that $v \leq v'$ (as each process in the chain computes the minimum of the values it has received). In particular, we have $v \leq v''$ where v'' is the value sent by the first process in the chain. (The case $a = 0$ corresponds to the "one process" chain case where the local predicate is satisfied at p_i.) Due to claim C1, $EST[r] \subseteq EST[r - a]$. Consequently, if v'' is one of the k smallest values of $EST[r - a]$, $v \leq v''$ implies v is one of the k smallest values of $EST[r]$.

So, taking $r - a = r'$, we have to show that $nb_j[r' - 1] - nb_j[r'] < k$ implies that the value v'' of est_j at the end of r', is one of the k smallest values of $EST[r']$. As the crashes are stable, $nb_j[r' - 1] - nb_j[r'] < k$, allows concluding that p_j has received a message from all but at most $k - 1$ processes that where not crashed at the beginning of r'. As p_j computes the minimum of all the values it has received, and misses at most $k - 1$ values of $EST[r']$, this means that the value v'' computed by p_j at the end of r' is one of the k smallest values present in $EST[r']$. *End of the proof of the claim C2.*

Claim C3. Let p_i be process that decides at line 4 or 9 during the round r. Its boolean flag $early_i$ is then equal to *true*.
The claim is trivially true if p_i decides at line 4. If p_i decides at line 9, it decides during the last round, namely $r = \lfloor t/k \rfloor + 1$. Let us consider two cases.

- At round r, p_i receives from a process p_j a message such as $early_j = true$. In that case, p_i sets $early_i$ to *true* at line 8, and the claim follows.

- In the other case, no process p_j has decided at a round $r' < r$ (otherwise, p_i would have received from p_j a message such that $early_j = true$). Let $t = k\,x + y$ with $y < k$ (hence, $x = \lfloor t/k \rfloor = r - 1$). As $nbr_i[r' - 1] - nbr_i[r'] < k$ was not satisfied at each round r' such that $1 \le r' \le x = r - 1$, we have $nbr_i[x] \le n - kx$. Moreover, as p_i has not received from any p_j a message such that $early_j$ is equal to *true*, if, during r, p_i does not receive a message from p_j it is because p_j has crashed. So, as at most t processes crash, we have $nbr_i[x + 1] \ge n - t = n - (k\,x + y)$. It follows that $nbr_i[x] - nbr_i[x + 1] \le y < k$. the claim follows.

End of the proof of the claim C3.

To prove the lemma, we now consider two cases according to the line during which a process decides.

- No process decides at line 4. This means that a process p_i that decides, decides at line 9 during the last round. Due to the claim C3, such a p_i has then its flag $early_i$ equal to *true*. Due to the claim C2, it decides one of the k smallest values in $EST[\lfloor t/k \rfloor + 1]$.

- A process decides at line 4. Let r be the first round during which a process p_i decides at that line and v be the value it decides. Since p_i decides at r:

  - p_i set its boolean flag $early_i$ to *true* at the end of $r - 1$. Its estimate $est_i = v$ is consequently one of the k smallest values in $EST[r - 1]$ (Claim C2). It follows that two processes that decide during r decide values that are among the the k smallest values in $EST[r - 1]$.

  - p_i has sent to all the processes (line 3) the pair $(v, true)$ before deciding at line 4 during r. This implies that a (non-crashed) process p_j that does not decide during round r receives v during r and uses it to compute its new value of est_j. Due to the minimum function used at line 7, it follows that, from now on, we will always have $est_j \le v$.

Let us assume that p_j does not crash. If it decides, it decides at $r' > r$, and then it necessarily decides a value $v' \leq v$. As $EST[r'] \subseteq EST[r-1]$ (claim $C1$), we have $v' \in EST[r-1]$. Combining $v' \leq v$, $v' \in EST[r-1]$, and the fact that v is one of the k smallest values in $EST[r-1]$, it follows that the value v' decided by p_j is one of the k smallest values in $EST[r-1]$.

$\square_{Lemma\ 5.4}$

Theorem 5.5   *The algorithm described in Figure 5.2 solves the k-set agreement problem in a synchronous system prone to up to t process crashes.*

Proof The proof follows from Lemmas 5.2, 5.3, and 5.4. $\square_{Theorem\ 5.5}$

Theorem 5.6   *Let us assume that at most f processes crash, $0 \leq f \leq t$. No process halts after the round* $\min(\lfloor f/k \rfloor + 2, \lfloor t/k \rfloor + 1)$.

Proof Let us first observe that a process decides and halts at the same round; this occurs when it executes return (est_i) at line 4 at line 8. As observed in Lemma 5.3, the fact that no process decides after $\lfloor t/k \rfloor + 1$ rounds is an immediate consequence of the code of the protocol and the round-based synchronous model. So, considering that $0 \leq f \leq t$ processes crash, we show that no process decides after the round $\lfloor f/k \rfloor + 2$. Let $f = xk + y$ (with $y < k$). This means that $x = \lfloor f/k \rfloor$.

The worst case scenario is when, for any process p_i that evaluates the local decision predicate $nbr_i[r-1] - nbr_i[r] < k$, this predicate is false as many times as possible. Due to the pigeonhole principle, this occurs when exactly k processes crash during each round. This means that we have $nbr_i[1] = n - k, \cdots, nbr_i[x] = n - kx$ and $nbr_i[x+1] = n - f = n - (kx + y)$, from which we conclude that $r = x + 1$ is the first round such that $nbr_i[r-1] - nbr_i[r] = y < k$. It follows that the processes p_i that execute the round $x + 1$ set their $early_i$ boolean to *true*. Consequently, the processes that proceed to $x + 2$ decide at line 4 during that round. As $x = \lfloor f/k \rfloor$, they decide at round $\lfloor f/k \rfloor + 2$. $\square_{Theorem\ 5.6}$

5.2.3   REMARK ON THE EARLY DECISION PREDICATE

A similar discussion has already appeared in Chapter 3 when discussing early decision predicate for interactive consistency. This discussion is generalized here to encompass k-set agreement.

Instead of using the local predicate $nbr_i[r-1] - nbr_i[r] < k$, an early stopping algorithm could be based on the local predicate $faulty_i[r] < k\,r$ where $faulty_i[r] = n - nbr_i[r]$ (the number of processes perceived as faulty by p_i). While both predicates can be used to ensure early stopping, we show here that $nbr_i[r-1] - nbr_i[r] < k$ is a more efficient predicate than $faulty_i[r] < k\,r$ (more efficient in the sense that it can allow for earlier termination). To that end it, we show the following:

- (i) Let r be the first round during which the local predicate $faulty_i[r] < k\, r$ is satisfied. The predicate $nbr_i[r-1] - nbr_i[r] < k$ is then also satisfied.

- (ii) Let r be the first round during which the local predicate $nbr_i[r-1] - nbr_i[r] < k$ is satisfied. It is possible that $faulty_i[r] < k\, r$ be not satisfied.

We first show (i). As r is the first round during which $faulty_i[r] < k\, r$ is satisfied, we have $faulty_i[r-1] \geq k\,(r-1)$. So, we have $faulty_i[r] - faulty_i[r-1] < k\,r - k\,(r-1) = k$. Replacing the sets $faulty_i[r]$ and $faulty_i[r-1]$ by their definitions, we obtain $(n - nbr_i[r]) - (n - nbr_i[r-1]) < k$, i.e., $(nbr_i[r-1] - nbr_i[r]) < k$.

A simple counter-example is sufficient to show (ii). Let us consider a run where $f1 > ak$ ($a > 2$) processes crash initially (i.e., before the protocol starts), and $f2 < k$ processes crash thereafter. We have $n - f1 \geq nbr_i[1] \geq nbr_i[2] \geq n - (f1 + f2)$, which implies that $(nbr_i[r-1] - nbr_i[r]) < k$ is satisfied at round $r = 2$. On an other side, $faulty_i[2] \geq f1 = ak > 2k$, from which we conclude that $faulty_i[r] < r\, k$ is not satisfied at $r = 2$.

This discussion shows that, while the early decision lower bound can be obtained with any of these predicates, the predicate $nbr_i[r-1] - nbr_i[r] < k$ is more efficient in the sense it takes into consideration the actual failure pattern (a process counts the number of failures it perceives during a round, and not only from the beginning of the run). Differently, the predicate $faulty_i[r] < r\, k$ considers only the actual number of failures and not their pattern (it basically always considers the worst case where there are k crashes per round, whatever their actual occurrence pattern).

5.3 AN ENRICHED SYNCHRONOUS SYSTEM TO EXPEDITE k-SET AGREEMENT

This section considers that the base synchronous system is enriched with objects that solves the ℓ-set agreement among m processes (for free). It presents and proves correct a k-set synchronous algorithm in such an enriched synchronous system. It then considers this enriched system to prove that $\lfloor \frac{t}{k} \rfloor + 1$ is a lower bound on the number of round to solve k-set agreement in the base synchronous model.

5.3.1 ENRICHING THE MODEL WITH ADDITIONAL OBJECTS

$[m, \ell]$-*set agreement object*   An $[m, \ell]$-set agreement object is an object that allows m processes to solve ℓ-set agreement despite any number of crashes. Such an object is denoted $[m, \ell]$-SA. Moreover, these objects are given for free, i.e., it is assumed that there are cost-free.

The problem   The problem we are interested in is then the following: how to use $[m, \ell]$-set agreement object in order to build an $[n, k]$-set agreement object; i.e., solve k-set agreement among n processes. This is depicted in Figure 5.4.

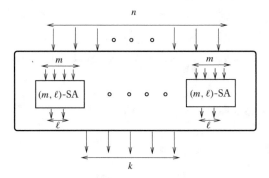

Figure 5.4: From $[m, \ell]$-set agreement objects to k-set agreement (1)

Let us observe that if m, n, ℓ and k are such that $n \leq a \times m$ and $k \geq a \times \ell$, it is possible to solve the k-set agreement problem only with $[m, \ell]$-SA objects, without exchanging any values i.e., in 0 round, whatever the value of t. This is obtained (see Figure 5.5) by partitioning the n processes into a subsets of at most m processes, each subset using an underlying $[m, \ell]$-SA object to allow its processes to decide on at most ℓ different values. Hence, the interesting cases are when the values of m, n, ℓ and k do not allow a trivial partitioning such as the previous one.

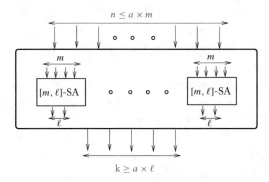

Figure 5.5: From $[m, \ell]$-set agreement objects to k-set agreement (2)

Another way to present the previous problem is as follows: how many crashes can be tolerated when one wants to build a $[10, 3]$-SA object from $[2, 1]$-SA objects in at most one round? Or in at most two rounds? Or in at most three rounds? As we are about to see, less than 6 crashes can be tolerated if termination in one round is required, and up to 11 processes can crash if decision is allowed in two rounds. As $n = 10$, this means that 3-set agreement is obtained in two rounds whatever the number of process crashes.

Thus, the issue addressed in this section is the computational power of $[m, \ell]$-SA objects when one wants to solve k-set agreement among n processes.

5.3.2 A GENERAL $[m, \ell]$-SA-BASED k-SET AGREEMENT ALGORITHM

This section presents a simple algorithm that, when at most t processes may crash, builds an $[n, k]\_SA$ object if the system provides the n processes with round-based synchrony and $[m, \ell]\_SA$ base objects.

Notation

- $\alpha = \lfloor \frac{k}{\ell} \rfloor$ and $\beta = k \bmod \ell$ (i.e., $k = \alpha\ell + \beta$),
- $\Delta = \alpha\, m + \beta = m \lfloor \frac{k}{\ell} \rfloor + (k \bmod \ell)$.
- $R_t = \lfloor \frac{t}{\Delta} \rfloor + 1 = \lfloor \frac{t}{m \lfloor \frac{k}{\ell} \rfloor + (k \bmod \ell)} \rfloor + 1$.

The algorithm The algorithm is pretty simple. It is described in Figure 5.6. A process p_i invokes the operation propose(v_i) where v_i is the value it proposes. That value is initially stored in the local variable est_i (line 1), which afterwards will contain the current estimate of p_i's decision value (line 10). The process terminates when it executes the return(est_i) statement.

Each process executes R_t rounds (line 2). During any round r, only Δ processes are allowed to send their current estimates. These processes are called the *senders* of round r. When $r = 1$, they are the processes $p_1, \ldots, p_\Delta$, during the second round the processes $p_{\Delta+1}, \ldots, p_{2\Delta}$, and so on (lines 3-4).

The Δ senders of a round r are partitioned into $\lceil \frac{\Delta}{m} \rceil$ subsets of m processes (the last subset containing possibly less than m processes), and each subset uses an $[m, \ell]\_SA$ object to narrow the set of its current estimates (lines 5-6). After this "narrowing", each sender process sends its new current estimate to all the processes. A process p_i accesses an $[m, \ell]\_SA$ object by invoking the operation propose(est_i). The $\lceil \frac{\Delta}{m} \rceil$ $[m, \ell]\_SA$ objects used during a round r are in the array $SA[r, 0..\lceil \frac{\Delta}{m} \rceil - 1]$ Actually, only $R_t \lfloor \frac{\Delta}{m} \rfloor$. base $[m, \ell]\_SA$ objects are needed. This follows from the following observation: during each round r, if $\beta \neq 0$, the "last" β sender processes do not need to use such an $[m, \ell]\_SA$ object because $\beta \leq \ell$. (Let us recall that $0 \leq \beta < \ell$ and Δ is defined as $\alpha\, m + \beta$.) Finally, when during a round, a process p_i receives estimates, it updates est_i accordingly (line 9).

It is important to see that, if at least one sender process does not crash during a round, at most $k = \alpha\ell + \beta$ estimates are sent during that round, which means that k-set agreement is guaranteed as soon as there is a round during which an active process does not crash.

5.3.3 PROOF OF THE ALGORITHM

Lemma 5.7 *Let $nc[r]$ be the number of processes that crash during the round r. There is a round r such that $r \leq R_t$ and $nc[r] < \Delta$.*

Proof Let $t = \alpha'\Delta + \beta'$ with $\alpha' = \lfloor \frac{t}{\Delta} \rfloor$ and $\beta' = t \bmod \Delta$. The proof is by contradiction. Let us assume that, $\forall\, r \leq R_t$, we have $nc[r] \geq \Delta$. We then have:

$$\sum_{r=1}^{R_t} nc[r] \geq \Delta \times R_t = \Delta\big(\lfloor \frac{t}{\Delta} \rfloor + 1\big) = \Delta\big(\alpha' + \lfloor \frac{\beta'}{\Delta} \rfloor + 1\big) = \Delta \times \alpha' + \Delta > t.$$

```
operation propose(v_i)
(1)   est_i ← v_i;
(2)   for r = 1, 2, ..., R_t do % r: round number %
      begin synchronous round
(3)       first_sender ← (r − 1)Δ + 1; last_sender ← rΔ;
(4)       if first_sender ≤ i ≤ last_sender then % p_i is "sender" at round r %
(5)           let y be such that first_sender + ym ≤ i < last_sender + (y + 1)m;
              % y is the index of the [m, ℓ]_SA object used by p_i %
(6)           est_i ← SA[r, y].propose(est_i);
(7)           for each j ∈ {1, ..., n} do send (est_i) to p_j end do
(8)       end if;
(9)       est_i ← any est value received if any, unchanged otherwise
(10)      if (r = R_t) then return(est_i) end if
      end synchronous round.
```

Figure 5.6: $[n, k]$_SA object from $[m, \ell]$_SA objects in a synchronous system (code for p_i)

Consequently, there are more than t processes that crash: a contradiction. $\square_{Lemma\ 5.7}$

Lemma 5.8   *At any round r, at most k different estimate values are sent by the processes.*

Proof Let us recall that $k = \alpha\,\ell + \beta$ (Euclidean division of k by ℓ) and $\Delta = \alpha\,m + \beta = m\lfloor\frac{k}{\ell}\rfloor + (k \bmod \ell)$.

Due to the lines 4-5, at most Δ processes are senders at each round r. These Δ sender processes are partitioned into $\alpha = \lfloor\frac{\Delta}{m}\rfloor$ sets of exactly m processes plus a set of β processes. As each underlying $[m, \ell]$_SA object used during the round r outputs at most ℓ estimates values from among the (at most) m values it is proposed, it follows that at most $\alpha\ell + \beta = k$ estimate values can be output by these objects, which proves the lemma. $\square_{Lemma\ 5.8}$

Lemma 5.9   [Agreement] *At most k different values are decided by the processes.*

Proof At any round the number of senders is at most Δ (lines 4-5). Moreover, due to Lemma 5.7, there is at least one round $r \le R_t$ during which a correct process is a sender. If follows from Lemma 5.8, line 8 and line 10, that, at the end of such a round r, the estimates of the processes contain at most k distinct values. $\square_{Lemma\ 5.9}$

Theorem 5.10   *The algorithm described in Figure 5.6 is a t-resilient algorithm that solves the k-set agreement algorithm in a synchronous system enriched with $[m, \ell]$-SA objects. Moreover, no process executes more than $\left\lfloor \dfrac{t}{m\lfloor\frac{k}{\ell}\rfloor+(k \bmod \ell)} \right\rfloor + 1$ rounds.*

Proof The termination property follows directly from the synchrony of the model: a process that does not crash executes R_t rounds. The validity property follows directly from the initialization of the estimate values est_i, the correctness of the underlying $[m, \ell]$_SA objects (line 7), and the fact that the algorithm exchanges only est_i values. Finally, the agreement property is Lemma 5.9.

$\square_{Theorem\ 5.10}$

5.3.4   LOWER BOUND

This section proves that the previous algorithm is optimal with respect to the number of rounds. This proof is based on (1) a deep connection relating synchronous efficiency and asynchronous computability in presence of failures and (2) an impossibility result in asynchronous set agreement.

A side effect of this result is that $\lfloor \frac{t}{k} \rfloor + 1$ is the lower bound on the number of rounds for the k-set agreement problem in a round-based synchronous system.

Notation   This section uses the following notations.

- Let $\mathcal{S}_{n,t}[\emptyset]$ denotes the classical round-based synchronous system model made up of n processes, where up to t processes may crash.

- Let $\mathcal{S}_{n,t}[m, \ell]$ denote the previous system model enriched with $[m, \ell]$_SA objects.

- Let $\mathcal{AS}_{n,t}[\emptyset]$ denotes the classical asynchronous system model (n processes, up to processes t may crash, no synchrony assumption).

- Let $\mathcal{AS}_{n,t}[m, \ell]$ denote the asynchronous system model $\mathcal{AS}_{n,t}[\emptyset]$ enriched with $[m, \ell]$_SA objects. (From a computability point of view, $\mathcal{AS}_{n,t}[\emptyset]$ is weaker than $\mathcal{AS}_{n,t}[m, \ell]$.)

Two important theorems   The following theorems are central in proving that R_t is a lower bound.
- Gafni's theorem. This theorem establishes a deep connection relating synchronous efficiency and asynchronous computability in presence of process crashes.

Theorem 5.11   *Let $n > t \geq k > 0$. It is possible to simulate in $\mathcal{AS}_{n,k}[\emptyset]$ the first $\lfloor \frac{t}{k} \rfloor$ rounds of any algorithm designed for the $\mathcal{S}_{n,t}[\emptyset]$ system model.* The next corollary is a simple extension of

Gafni's theorem suited to our needs.

Corollary 5.12   *Let $n > t \geq k > 0$. It is possible to simulate in $\mathcal{AS}_{n,k}[m, \ell]$ the first $\lfloor \frac{t}{k} \rfloor$ rounds of any algorithm designed for $\mathcal{S}_{n,t}[m, \ell]$ system model.*

- Herlihy-Rajsbaum's theorem. This theorem states an impossibility result when one wants to solve asynchronous K-set agreement among n processes from $[m, \ell]$-SA base objects.

Theorem 5.13   *Let $J_{m,\ell}$ be the function $u \to \ell \lfloor \frac{u}{m} \rfloor + \min(\ell, u \bmod m) - 1$. There is no algorithm that solves the K-set agreement problem, with $K = J_{m,\ell}(t + 1)$, in $\mathcal{AS}_{n,t}[m, \ell]$.*

The synchronous lower bound proved below is a reduction to the asynchronous lower bound (impossibility) as defined in Herlihy-Rajsbaum's theorem. This reduction is based on Gafni's simulation of rounds of a synchronous system by an asynchronous system. From a methodological point of view, this establishes a synchronous lower bound from an asynchronous impossibility result.

The lower bound   **Theorem 5.14**   *Let $1 \leq \ell \leq m < n$ and $1 \leq k \leq t < n$. Any algorithm that solves the k-set agreement problem in $\mathcal{S}_{n,t}[m, \ell]$ has at least one run in which at least one process does not decide before the round $R_t = \lfloor \frac{t}{m \lfloor \frac{k}{\ell} \rfloor + (k \bmod \ell)} \rfloor + 1$.*

Proof The proof is by contradiction. Let us assume that there is an algorithm A that solves the k-set agreement problem in at most $R < R_t$ rounds in $\mathcal{S}_{n,t}[m, \ell]$ (this means that any process decides by at most R rounds, or crashes before). We consider two cases.

- $k < \ell$. We have then $R < R_t = \lfloor \frac{t}{k} \rfloor + 1$.

  1. As $k < \ell$, the ℓ-set agreement can be solved in $\mathcal{AS}_{n,k}[\emptyset]$. It follows that as far as set agreement is concerned, $\mathcal{AS}_{n,k}[\emptyset]$ and $\mathcal{AS}_{n,k}[m, \ell]$ have the same computational power.

  2. It follows from the corollary of Gafni's theorem that there is, in $\mathcal{AS}_{n,k}[m, \ell]$, a simulation of the first $\lfloor \frac{t}{k} \rfloor$ rounds of any algorithm designed for the $\mathcal{S}_{n,t}[m, \ell]$ system model. It is consequently possible to simulate in $\mathcal{AS}_{n,k}[m, \ell]$ the $R < R_t = \lfloor \frac{t}{k} \rfloor + 1$ rounds of the algorithm A. It follows that the k-set agreement problem can be solved in in $\mathcal{AS}_{n,k}[m, \ell]$.

  3. Combining the two previous items, we obtain an algorithm that solves the k-set agreement problem in $\mathcal{AS}_{n,k}[\emptyset]$. This contradicts the impossibility to solve the k-set agreement problem in $\mathcal{AS}_{n,k}[\emptyset]$. This proves the theorem for the case $k < \ell$.

- $k \geq \ell$. Let us recall the definition $\Delta = m \lfloor \frac{k}{\ell} \rfloor + (k \bmod \ell) = \alpha \, m + \beta$.

  1. It follows from the corollary of Gafni's theorem that at least $\lfloor \frac{t}{\Delta} \rfloor$ rounds of any algorithm designed for the $\mathcal{S}_{n,t}[m, \ell]$ system model can be simulated in $\mathcal{AS}_{n,\Delta}[m, \ell]$.

     So, as the algorithm A solves the k-set agreement problem in $\mathcal{S}_{n,t}[m, \ell]$, in at most $R < R_t = \lfloor \frac{t}{\Delta} \rfloor + 1$, combining the simulation with algorithm A, we obtain an algorithm that solves the k-set agreement problem in $\mathcal{AS}_{n,\Delta}[m, \ell]$.

  2. Considering the argument used in Herlihy-Rajsbaum's theorem, we have the following:

$$
\begin{aligned}
J_{m,\ell}(\Delta + 1) &= \ell \lfloor \frac{\Delta + 1}{m} \rfloor + \min\left(\ell, (\Delta + 1) \bmod m\right) - 1, \\
&= \ell \lfloor \frac{\alpha \, m + \beta + 1}{m} \rfloor + \min\left(\ell, (\alpha \, m + \beta + 1) \bmod m\right) - 1, \\
&= \ell \, (\alpha + \lfloor \frac{\beta + 1}{m} \rfloor) + \min\left(\ell, (\beta + 1) \bmod m\right) - 1.
\end{aligned}
$$

Let us observe that $\ell \leq m$. Moreover, as $\beta = k \bmod \ell$, we also have $\beta < \ell$. To summarize: $\beta < \ell \leq m$. There are two cases to consider.

(a) $m = \beta + 1$. Observe that this implies that $\ell = m$ and $\ell - 1 = \beta$.

$$
\begin{aligned}
J_{m,\ell}(\Delta + 1) &= \ell\,(\alpha + 1) + \min\left(\ell, m \bmod m\right) - 1, \\
&= \ell\,\alpha + \ell - 1 = \ell\,\alpha + \beta = k.
\end{aligned}
$$

(b) $m > \beta + 1$:

$$
\begin{aligned}
J_{m,\ell}(\Delta + 1) &= \ell\,\alpha + \min\left(\ell, (\beta + 1) \bmod m\right) - 1, \\
&= \ell\,\alpha + \beta + 1 - 1 = k.
\end{aligned}
$$

In both cases, $J_{m,\ell}(\Delta + 1) = k$. It follows from Herlihy-Rajsbaum's theorem that there is no algorithm that solves the $J_{m,\ell}(\Delta + 1)$-set agreement problem (i.e., the k-set agreement problem) in $\mathcal{AS}_{n,\Delta}[m, \ell]$.

3. The two previous items contradict each other, thereby proving the theorem for the case $k \geq \ell$.

$$\square_{Theorem\ 5.14}$$

Corollary 5.15 $\lfloor \frac{t}{k} \rfloor + 1$ *is a lower bound on the number of rounds for k-set agreement in a round-based synchronous system.*

Proof The corollary follows directly from Theorem 5.14 and the fact that a classical round-based synchronous system corresponds to the case with the $[m, \ell]$-SA objects have no power, i.e., $m = \ell$.

$$\square_{Corollary\ 5.15}$$

Corollary 5.16   *When $k < \ell$, the underlying $[m, \ell]$_SA objects are useless.*

Proof The corollary follows from the fact that $k < \ell \Rightarrow R_t = \lfloor \frac{t}{k} \rfloor + 1$, that is the lower bound in the base round-based synchronous model (as shown by the previous corollary). $\square_{Corollary\ 5.16}$

This corollary means that no k-set agreement algorithm can benefit from $[m, \ell]$_SA objects when $k < \ell$.

5.4   BIBLIOGRAPHIC NOTES

- The k-set agreement problem has been introduced by S. Chaudhuri to investigate how the number k of choices allowed to the processes is related to the maximal number t of processes that can crash in a run (13). A short introduction to this problem (both in synchronous and asynchronous systems) appears in (71).

- While the k-set agreement problem be solved in synchronous systems whatever the value of $t < n$, it is impossible to solve in pure asynchronous systems when $k \leq t$ (9; 40; 76).

- Non-early deciding synchronous k-set algorithms are described in (3; 49; 74).

- The early-deciding and stopping algorithm described in Figure 5.2 and its proof are from (67).

- The k-set agreement algorithm based on underlying (m, ℓ)-set agreement objects and its proof are from (61). That paper presents also a corresponding early-deciding and stopping algorithm where no process decides after the round $\min\left(\lfloor\frac{f}{\Delta}\rfloor + 2, \lfloor\frac{t}{\Delta}\rfloor + 1\right)$, where $\Delta = m\lfloor\frac{k}{\ell}\rfloor + (k \bmod \ell)$.

- A proof that $\lfloor\frac{t}{k}\rfloor + 1$ is a lower bound on the number of rounds for the k-set agreement problem can be found in (14). Topology-based proofs for this bound can be found in (26; 34). The general and simple proof given in the last section (based on underlying ℓ-set agreement objects) is due to Mostefaoui, Raynal and Travers (61).

- The proof of Gafni's theorem can be found in (25). The proof of Herlihy-Rajsbaum's theorem can be found in (39).

- The condition-based approach has been extended in (8) to address the k-set agreement problem. When $k = 1$, this extension boils down to the x-legal conditions introduced in (56).

CHAPTER 6

Non-Blocking Atomic Commit in Presence of Crash Failures

This chapter is on the non-blocking atomic commit problem. The reader is referred to the first chapter for its definition. The main difference with the consensus problem lies in the fact that the two values that can be proposed (COMMIT and ABORT) are not "equal": the decision cannot be COMMIT as soon as one process votes *no*. Moreover, in presence of failures, the decision can be ABORT even when all processes vote *yes*.

6.1 A SIMPLE NON-BLOCKING ATOMIC COMMIT ALGORITHM

6.1.1 NBAC: SHORT REMINDER

The *non-blocking atomic commit* problem (NBAC) has been defined in the first chapter. It is an agreement problem in which only two values can be proposed. These values, called votes, are usually denoted *yes* (or 1) and *no* (or 0).

The aim of an NBAC instance is to allow the n processes to commit on their current local states. To that end, good circumstances in which the processes do have to commit and bad circumstances in which they have to abort the local computations they want to commit are defined.

- The *good* circumstances are when all processes vote *yes* and there is no failure. In that case, all processes agree on the fact that their computation can progress and each can then safely commit its local computation. The decision COMMIT is coded 1.

- The *bad* circumstances are when one (or more) process votes *no*. In that case, whatever the failure pattern, the only possible decision is ABORT. This is because, something went wrong at some process and that process cannot commit its local computation. In that case, the local computations executed by the processes cannot be committed and have to be aborted. The decision ABORT is coded 0.

- For the other cases, namely, all processes vote *yes* and there are crashes, the decision can be commit or abort. As seen in the NBAC specification given in Chapter 1, the processes that do not crash can decide either commit or abort. The only requirement is then that they have to decide the same way.

6.1.2   A SIMPLE ALGORITHM

A simple way to solve the NBAC problem in a round-based synchronous system is to reduce it to the consensus problem. Such a reduction consists in adding a preliminary round to a consensus algorithm.

Let $votes_i$ be the vote of process p_i where $vote_i \in \{0; 1\}$, and nbac˙propose $(vote_i)$ the operation it invokes. During the additional preliminary round, the processes exchange their votes, and each process computes a value v_i in order to propose it to an underlying consensus instance. If p_i receives a votes yes from every process, then $v_i = 1$. Otherwise, $v_i = 0$ (in that case, during the preliminary round, p_i receives less than n votes or one vote is vote no).

The corresponding algorithm is described in Figure 6.1. This algorithm uses a multiset denoted rec_votes_i. As far as a set is concerned, a value belongs or does not belong to a set. While similarly to a set, a value belongs or not to a multiset; differently from a set, a value can belong several times to a multiset. Hence, the multiset $rec\_votes_i = \{yes, yes, no\}$ has two elements, yes that is present twice and no that is present only once, and the size of the multiset is $|rec\_votes_i| = 3$.

```
operation  nbac˙propose (vote_i):
      begin synchronous round % preliminary round %
         broadcast EST(vote_i);
         let rec_votes_i = multiset of votes received during this preliminary round;
         if (|rec_votes_i| = n) ∧ (no ∉ rec_votes_i) then v_i ← 1 else v_i ← 0 end if
      end synchronous round; % preliminary round %
      dec_i ← propose (v_i); % underlying consensus instance %
      return(dec_i).
```

Figure 6.1: A consensus-based NBAC algorithm (code for p_i)

It is easy to see that this algorithm is correct. Due to the underlying consensus algorithm, no two processes decide differently. If all processes votes yes and there is no crash, each process receives the n votes yes and proposes $v_i = 1$ to the underlying consensus. Consequently, the only value that can be decided by that consensus instance is 1, i.e., COMMIT. If one process votes no then, whether there are crashes or not, no process can propose 1 to the underlying consensus, and consequently only 0, i.e., ABORT, can be decided by the underlying consensus instance. Let us observe that, in both previous cases, the decision is independent of the number of processes that crash during the execution on the underlying consensus instance.

It is easy to see that, when no process votes no and processes crash during the preliminary round, the value decided by the correct process can be COMMIT (1) or ABORT (0). That value depends on the messages sent by the faulty processes that are received by the correct processes.

6.2   FAST COMMIT AND FAST ABORT

6.2.1   LOOKING FOR EFFICIENT ALGORITHMS

The time complexity of the previous algorithm is one round plus the cost of the underlying consensus algorithm, i.e., $1 + \min(f + 2, t + 1)$ (where, as previously, f is the actual number of process crashes). Hence the natural question: is it possible to design NBAC algorithms in which processes decide earlier?

Fast abort and fast commit   The previous question is motivated by the fact that the values *yes* and *no* that can be proposed have not the same power with respect to the values COMMIT and ABORT that can be decided.

A single vote *no* entails the decision ABORT, whatever the votes of the other processes and the failure pattern. This means that if a process receives a vote *no* during the first round, it knows that the decision is ABORT whatever the other votes. It consequently decides ABORT by the end of the first round. On another side, the big majority of the cases are "good circumstances": there is no crash and every process votes *yes*. Hence, the idea to design an efficient NBAC algorithm for these cases, i.e., an algorithm in which no process executes more than two rounds when circumstances are good. These observations motivate the following definitions.

Definition 6.1   An NBAC algorithm satisfies the *fast abort* property, if no process decides after the first round in all executions in which at least one process votes *no*.

Definition 6.2   An NBAC algorithm satisfies the *fast commit* property, if no process decides after the second round in all crash-free executions in which all processes vote *yes*.

6.2.2   AN IMPOSSIBILITY THEOREM

This section shows that the *fast commit* property and the *fast abort* property are antagonistic: there is no algorithm that can simultaneously satisfy both.

Be as general as possible   In order the impossibility result be as general as possible, we consider NBAC algorithms such that:

- Until it stops or crashes, a process broadcasts a message to all processes at every round.
- Dissociate decide and stop. The atomic statement return(v) previously used to simultaneously decide and stop is now decomposed into two atomic statements denoted decide(v) and return(). The former allows the invoking process to decide v, while the latter stops its participation in the algorithm. Hence, an NBAC algorithm is not required to force a process to stop when it decides. According to its code, a process can continue executing the algorithm after it has decided.

Theorem 6.3   *Let t be such that $3 \leq t < n$. There is no deterministic NBAC algorithm that satisfies both the fast commit property and the fast abort property.*

Proof The proof is by contradiction. Let us assume that there is an NBAC round-based synchronous algorithm A that satisfies both the fast commit and fast abort deciding properties. The proof consists in building two executions (denoted $E3$ and $E5$ in the following) (a) that cannot be distinguished by some processes and (b) are such that COMMIT has to be decided in one of them while ABORT has to be decided in the other one.

To ease its understanding the proof uses figures. Moreover, 1 is used as synonym of both *yes* and COMMIT, while 0 is used as synonym of both *no* and ABORT. The vote of a process is indicated on its axis just before the first round. The notation $dec(x)$ that appears on a process axis at the end of some rounds means that the corresponding process decides x at the end of that round. As indicated previously, this does not mean that that process stops its execution. Only processes p_1, p_2, p_3, and p_i appear on the figures. As we will see, according to our needs p_1, p_2 or p_3 will crash in some executions (this is why the assumption $t \geq 3$ is needed). Process p_i is generic in the sense that it stands for any other process $4 \leq i \leq n$.

- Building an execution $E3$ in which the value 0 has to be decided (Figure 6.2).

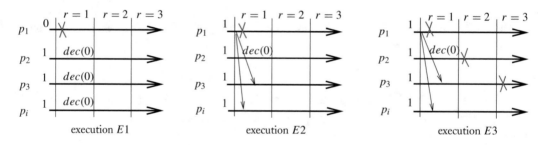

Figure 6.2: Impossibility of having both fast commit and fast abort when $t \geq 3$ (1)

- Execution $E1$. In this execution, process p_1 votes *no*, while all other processes vote *yes*. Moreover, p_1 crashes before sending any message during round $r = 1$ (hence no process will ever know its vote).

  As, by assumption, the algorithm A satisfies the fast abort property the processes p_2, p_3, and p_i have to decide 0 by the end of the first round (execution $E1$ appears at the left of Figure 6.2).

- Execution $E2$. In that execution (that appears at the center of Figure 6.2), all processes vote 1, and p_1 crashes during the broadcast of its round 1 message, and p_2 is the only process that does not receive that message. (This in indicated in the figure where the top-down arrows represent the message sent by p_1 and received by p_3 and every p_i but not received by p_2).

Let us observe that, at the end of the first round, process p_2 cannot distinguish execution $E1$ from execution $E2$: in both executions, it has received the same messages during round $r = 1$ (namely, the message broadcast by itself, the message broadcast by p_3, and the messages broadcast by every process p_i, $4 \leq i \leq n$).

It follows that p_2 has exactly the same local state at the end of the first round in $E1$ and $E2$. As the algorithm A is deterministic and p_2 decides 0 at the end of the first round of $E1$, it has to decide the very same value at end of the first round of $E2$, i.e., it decides 0.

- Execution $E3$. This execution is similar to $E2$ except that (a) p_2 crashes at the beginning of round $r = 2$ (i.e., after having decided and before sending its round 3 message), and (b) p_2 crashes at the beginning of round $r = 3$.

Let us observe that p_2 has exactly the same local state at the end of the first round in both $E2$ and $E3$. Hence, as A is deterministic, p_2 decides the same value at the end of the first round in both executions.

It follows from the NBAC agreement property of A that 0 is decided in execution $E3$ by all processes that do not crash before deciding.

- Building an execution $E5$ in which the value 1 has to be decided (Figure 6.3).

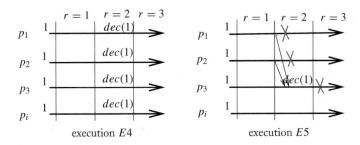

Figure 6.3: Impossibility of having both fast commit and fast abort when $t \geq 3$ (2)

- Execution $E4$. This execution is a failure-free execution in which all processes vote 1. As the algorithm A satisfies the fast commit property, it follows that the every process decides 1 by the end of the second round. Hence, p_3 decides 1.

- Execution $E5$. This execution is similar to $E4$ except that (a) p_1 and p_2 crash during the second round, and their round 2 messages are received only by p_3, and (b) p_3 crashes by at the beginning of the third round (before sending any message).

The local states of p_3 at the end of the second round of $E4$ and at the end of the second round of $E5$ are identical (p_3 has received the round 1 message and the round 2 message from every process, and its code is deterministic). It follows that, in execution $E5$, p_3 decides 1 by the end of round $r = 2$ (i.e., before crashing).

- Let us notice that, in execution $E3$ (in which 0 is decided) and execution $E5$ (in which 1 is decided), every process p_i, $4 \leq i \leq n$, receives exactly the same messages during round 1 and round 2. (More precisely, in both $E3$ and $E5$, each p_i receives the round 1 message sent by every process, and the round 2 message sent by any process but p_1 and p_2.) As p_1, p_2 and p_3 do not broadcast messages from round 3, these processes p_i will also receive the same messages in all rounds $r \geq 3$. It follows that no p_i, $4 \leq i \leq n$, can distinguish $E3$ from $E5$. Consequently, they have to decide the same way in both executions, which contradicts the fact that they decide 0 in $E3$ and 1 in $E5$, and concludes the proof.

$$\square_{Theorem\ 6.3}$$

6.2.3   WEAK FAST COMMIT AND WEAK FAST ABORT

The previous impossibility result motivates the definition of weak fast commit and weak fast abort properties that allow the design of NBAC algorithms that satisfy fast commit and weak fast abort (or fast abort and weak fast commit). This section introduces such weakened properties. The idea is to allow for one more round.

Definition 6.4   An NBAC algorithm satisfies the *weak fast abort* property if no process decides after the second round in all executions in which at least one process votes *no*.

Definition 6.5   An NBAC algorithm satisfies the *weak fast commit* property if no process decides after the third round in all crash-free executions in which all processes vote *yes*.

As we are about to see, it is possible to design NBAC algorithms that satisfy either fast commit and weak fast abort or fast abort and weak fast commit.

6.3   FAST COMMIT AND WEAK FAST ABORT ARE COMPATIBLE

This section shows that it is possible to design algorithms that are fast (as defined previously) with respect to commit (resp., abort) and weakly fast with respect to abort (resp., commit). Their very existence show that fast abort and fast commit are not entirely antagonistic. Moreover, due to the impossibility stated in Theorem 6.3, these algorithms are optimal.

6.3.1   A FAST COMMIT AND WEAK FAST ABORT ALGORITHM

This section presents an NBAC algorithm thats satisfies the fast commit property and the weak fast abort property. This means that the processes decides in two rounds if (a) all processes vote *yes* and no process crashes, or (b) a process votes *no*.

Preliminary remark As stated in Section 6.2.2, each process broadcasts a message at every round until it stops or crashes. Moreover, decide(v) and return() are two different statements; the first allows the invoking process to decide value v, while the second stops the participation of the invoking process to the algorithm.

Local variables Each process manages the following local variables.

- est_i contains the current estimate of the decision value.
- $decided_i$ is a Boolean, initialized to *fasle* that is set to true when p_i decides.
- $rec\_votes_i[r]$ is a multiset that contains the estimates of the decision values received during round r.
- $crashed_i[r]$ is the set of processes that p_i perceives as crashed at the end of round r (i.e., the process from which p_i has received a round r message).

The array-like notations $rec\_votes_i[r]$ and $crashed_i[r]$ are used for ease of exposition only.

Process behavior The algorithm is described in Figure 6.4. During the first round the processes exchange their votes (line 1). If process p_i receives less than n votes, or receives a vote *no* (coded 0) it updates its current estimate of the decision value est_i to ABORT (coded 0). Then, during a round $r, 2 \le r \le t + 1$, p_i does the following.

- If it has decided during the previous round (we have then $decided_i = true$), p_i broadcasts a message DEC(est_i) to inform the other processes, and then stops it participation to the algorithm (line 7). Otherwise, it broadcasts its current estimate of the decision value (line 8).
- If it has received a message DEC(v) during the receive phase of the current round (line 9), p_i adopts v as its decision value and decides it (line 10). If it does not crash before, p_i will then stop at line 7 of the next round.
- If p_i has neither stopped at line 7 nor received a message DEC(v), it enters lines 11-17 where it first computes the values of $rec\_votes_i[r]$ and $crashed_i[r]$. If it has received an estimate *no* (coded 0), p_i adopts ABORT (coded 0) as current decision value. Let us observe that est_i can be downgraded from 1 to 0 but never upgraded from 0 to 1.

  Then, p_i strives for deciding. If $r = 2$ and it has received only 0 estimates (line 14), it decides ABORT (line 17). It also decides if $r \le t - 1$ and it does not see more than $r - 2$ process crashes (line 15). It also decides in round t if has received estimates from at least $n - t + 1$ processes during that round (line 16). Line 15 is to ensure early decision in at most $f + 2$ rounds when f processes crash and $f \le t - 2$. Line 16 is to ensure early decision in at most $f + 1$ rounds when $f \ge t + 1$. If one is interested fast commit and weak fast abort but not in early decision in the other cases, line 16 can be suppressed.

  Finally, if r is the last round, p_i decides (if not yet done) and terminates.

```
operation nbac˙propose (vote_i):
(1)   est_i ← vote_i; decided_i ← false;
(2)   when r = 1 do
      begin synchronous round
(3)       broadcast EST(vote_i);
(4)       let rec_votes_i[1] = multiset of the votes vote_j received during the first round;
(5)       if (|rec_votes_i[1]| < n) ∨ (0 ∈ rec_votes_i[1]) then est_i ← 0 end if
      end synchronous round;
(6)   when r = 2, ..., t + 1 do
      begin synchronous round
(7)       if (decided_i) then broadcast DEC(est_i); return() end if;
(8)       broadcast EST(est_i);
(9)       if ( DEC(v) received during round r)
(10)      then est_i ← v; decide(est_i); decided_i ← true
(11)      else let rec_votes_i[r] = multiset of the estimates est_j received during r;
(12)          let crashed_i[r] ← { processes from which no message received during r};
(13)          if (0 ∈ rec_votes_i[r]) then est_i ← 0 end if;
(14)          if   ((r = 2) ∧ (1 ∉ rec_votes_i[r]))
(15)              ∨ ((r ≤ t − 1) ∧ (|crashed_i[r]| ≤ r − 2))
(16)              ∨ ((r = t) ∧ (|rec_votes_i[t]| ≥ n − t + 1))
(17)          then decide(est_i); decided_i ← true
(18)          end if;
(19)      end if;
(20)      if (r = t + 1) then if (¬decided_i) then decide(est_i) end if; return() end if
      end synchronous round.
```

Figure 6.4: Fast commit and weak fast abort NBAC despite up to $t \geq 3$ crash failures (code for p_i)

6.3.2   CORRECTNESS PROOF

Notations   A message that carries an estimate equal to 1 (resp., 0) is called "commit" (resp., "abort") message. The value of a local variable var_i of a process p_i at the end of round r is denoted $var_i[r]$.

   $CRASHED[r]$ denotes the set of processes that have crashed by the end of round r (let us observe that the value of this set is not necessarily known by a process that terminates round r).

Lemma 6.6   *If no process has decided by round $r − 1 \geq 1$, and two processes p_i and p_j that terminate round r are such that $est_i[r] \neq est_j[r]$, then $|CRASHED[r]| \geq r$.*

Proof   Let us first observe that if no process decides by round $r − 1$, then no process receives a DEC() message during round r, and consequently, any process p_i that terminates round r, update est_i during round r. This observation is implicitly used in the following proof that is is by induction on the round number r.

- Base case $r = 2$. Let us assume without loss of generality that $est_i[2] = 1$ and $est_j[2] = 0$. We have to show that $|CRASHED[2]| \geq 2$.

   Let us observe that we necessarily have $est_j[1] = 1$ (otherwise, when it receives the abort message from p_j during round $r = 2$, p_i would have changed est_i to 0 at line 13).

Hence, p_j has changed est_j from 1 to 0 during round $r = 2$, which means that it has received one abort message that p_i has not received. Consequently, there is a process p_k that that sent an abort message during round $r = 2$ and crashed before sending it to p_i. Thus, $est_k[1] = 0$.

Furthermore, as $est_i[2] = 1$, we also have $est_i[1] = 1$, from which it follows that all processes sent a commit message during the first round. As p_k has sent a commit message during the first round and an abort message during the second round, it has received less than n messages during the first round, from which we conclude that some process p_ℓ crashed during the first round. Hence, at least two processes have crashed by end of round 2, i.e., $|CRASHED[2]| \geq 2$.

- Induction. Let us assume that the lemma is satisfied from round 2 until round $r - 1$. We show it is satisfied for round r.

  Assuming that no process has decided by round r, let p_i and p_j be two processes such that $est_i[r] = 1$ and $est_j[r] = 0$. It follows from the discussion for the base case that $est_i[r - 1] = 1$. Moreover, as $est_i[r] = 1$ and both p_i and p_j terminate round r, it follows that p_i receives a commit message from p_j during round r, from which we conclude that $est_j[r - 1] = 1$. As $est_j[r] = 0$, it follows that there is a process p_k that sent an abort message during round r to p_j and crashed before sending it to p_i. Hence, $est_k[r - 1] = 0$.

  As $est_i[r - 1] = 1$ and $est_k[r - 1] = 0$, and no process has decided by round $r - 2$ (induction assumption), it follows that $|CRASHED[r - 1]| \geq r - 1$. Finally, as p_k crashes during round r, we have $|CRASHED[r]| \geq r$, which concludes the proof of the lemma.

$\square_{Lemma\ 6.6}$

Lemma 6.7   *For any round $r \geq 2$ and any process p_i that terminates round r without having ever received a DEC(() message, we have $CRASHED[r - 1] \subseteq crashed_i[r]$.*

Proof As p_i terminates round r without having ever received a DEC(() message, it executes line 12 during round r and updates $crashed_i$. The lemma then follows from the fact that, if a process p_j crashes by the end of the round $r - 1$, it does not send message during round r and p_i includes it in $crashed_i[r]$.

$\square_{Lemma\ 6.7}$

Theorem 6.8   *The round-based synchronous algorithm described in Figure 6.4 solves the NBAC problem in at most $t + 1$ rounds.*

Proof The NBAC termination property is trivial: no process blocks in a round and there are at most $t + 1$ rounds.

The NBAC obligation validity property states that if a process decides ABORT, then at least one process has voted *no* or at least one process has crashed.

If a process p_j votes *no*, then any process p_i that terminates the first round either receives the vote *no* or receives less than n messages (because p_j crashed before sending its vote *no* to p_i). Whatever the case, p_i executes line 5, and $est_i[1] = 0$. It follows that, during the second round, only abort messages are exchanged. Hence, for any process p_i that executes the second round, the predicate of line 14 is satisfied, and consequently p_i decides ABORT at line 17 of the second round.

The NBAC justification validity property states that, when all processes vote *yes* and there is no crash, the processes decide COMMIT.

If no process crashes and all processes vote *yes*, then $rec\_votes_i[1]$ contains n votes *yes* (line 4). Hence, during the second round, only commit messages are exchanged. As no process crashes, each process p_i is such that $crashed_i[2] = \emptyset$. It then follows from $3 \leq t$ and $crashed_i[2] = \emptyset$, that during round $r = 2$, the predicate of line 15 ($(r \leq t - 1) \wedge (|crashed_i[2]| \leq r - 2)$) is true at any process p_i, that consequently decides $est_i = 1$ (i.e., COMMIT) at line 17.

The NBAC agreement property states that no two different values can be decided. Let r be the smallest round during which a process decides and p_i be a process that decides during that round. Moreover, let v the value decided by p_i. The proof consists in showing that (a) any other process p_j that decides during r decides v, and (b) any process p_j that terminates round r without deciding is such that $est_j[r] = v$. To that end, four cases are considered according to the value of r. Case 1: $r = 2$, Case 2: $3 \leq r \leq t - 1$, Case 3: $3 \leq r = t$, and Case 4: $3 \leq r = t + 1$.

- Case 1: $r = 2$.
  - Subcase $v = 1$. As p_i decides 1, it did not receive abort messages. Moreover, as p_i decides during the second round, it necessarily decides at line 17, from which we conclude that the predicate at line 15 is satisfied, i.e., $crashed_i[2] = \emptyset$ (the predicate of line 14 cannot be satisfied because $1 \in rec\_votes_i[2]$, and the predicate of line 16 cannot be satisfied because $r = 2$ and $3 \leq t$).

    From $crashed_i[2] = \emptyset$, we conclude that all processes received n votes *yes* during the first round and no process crashed before the end of this round. It follows that no process decides 0 in round 2 and any process p_j that completes round 2 is such that $est_j[2] = 1$.

  - Subcase $v = 0$.
    * p_i decides because the predicate at line 14 is satisfied. In that case, we have $1 \notin rec\_vote_i[2]$. This means that p_i has received only abort messages during the second round (including itself). Since p_i completes the second round if broadcast an abort message during the second round, and any process p_j that completes this round sets $est_j[2] = 0$ at line 13. It follows that no process p_j can decide 1 during the second round of a future round.
    * p_i decides because the predicate at line 15 is satisfied. In that case, we have $crashed_i[2] = \emptyset$. We show that $(crashed_i[2] = \emptyset) \Rightarrow (1 \notin rec\_votes_i[2])$ (and we are then in the previous case).

From $crashed_i[2] = \emptyset$, we conclude that all processes have terminated the first round, and, consequently, they all have the same value in $est_x[1]$. As $est_i[2] = 0$, p_i has received at least one abort message during the second round, from which we conclude that all processes are such that $est_x[1] = 0$, i.e., we cannot have $1 \in rec\_votes_i[2]$.

- Case 2: $3 \leq r \leq t - 1$.

In that case, p_i decides at line 17 because the predicate at line 15 is satisfied. (It cannot decides at line 10 by receiving a DEC() message because, by definition, r is the first round at which a process decides.)

Let us suppose by contradiction that p_i decides v while p_j decides $1 - v$ during r or completes round r with $est_j[r] = 1 - v$.

As both complete round r, each of them receives the round r message sent by the other. If one of them (say i) has $est_i[r - 1] = 0$, then we would have $est_i[r] = est_j[r] = 0$. Hence, let us suppose that $est_i[r - 1] = est_j[r - 1] = 1$. If follows that during round r, some process p_k has sent an abort message (carrying $est_k[r - 1] = 0$) that is received by one of p_i or p_j and not by the other one. As $est_k[r - 1] = 0$ and $est_i[r - 1] = est_j[r - 1] = 1$, it follows from Lemma 6.6 that $|CRASHED[r - 1]| \geq r - 1$.

As r is the first round in which a process decides, p_i has not received a DEC() message during a round lower or equal to r. It follows from this observation and Lemma 6.7 that $CRASHED[r - 1] \subseteq crashed_i[r]$. Combined with $|CRASHED[r - 1]| \geq r - 1$, we obtain $|crashed_i|[r] \geq r - 1$, which contradicts the fact that p_i decides at line line 17 because the predicate at line 15 is satisfied (to be satisfied, this predicate requires $|crashed_i|[r] \leq r - 2$). It follows that p_j decides v during round r or completes round r with $est_j[r] = v$.

- Case 3: $3 \leq r = t$.

In that case, no process decides by round $t - 1$. If all the processes that complete round $t - 1$ have the same estimate value, then agreement follows. Hence, let us suppose that two processes p_x and p_y are such that $est_x[t - 1] \neq est_y[t - 1]$. It then follows from Lemma 6.6 that $|CRASHED[t - 1]| \geq t - 1$, from which we conclude that there are at most $n - (t - 1)$ processes that terminate round $r - 1$.

As p_i decides v during round $r = t$, it decides at line 17 due to predicate of line 16 because it has received $n - t + 1$ messages during round t. This means that exactly $n - t + 1$ processes terminate round $t - 1$.

It follows that, if another process p_j decides during the same round t, it has received the very same $n - t + 1$ messages as p_i during that round, and consequently decides also v. If p_j terminates round $r = t$ without deciding, it has received less than $n - t + 1$ messages, which means that it has received exactly $n - t$ messages (because at most t processes may crash). Hence, t processes have crashed by the end of round $r = t$. It follows that p_i is correct (because it has sent its round $r = t$ message and terminates round t). Consequently, p_j receives the DEC(v) message sent by p_i during $t + 1$ and decides v during round $t + 1$.

- Case 4: $3 \leq r = t + 1$.

  In that case, no process has decided by round $r = t$. Let us assume that two processes are such that $est_i[t + 1] \neq est_j[t + 1]$. It then follows from Lemma 6.6 that $|CRASHED[t + 1]| \geq t + 1$, which is impossible as at most t process may crash in the considered synchronous model.

  $\square_{Theorem\ 6.8}$

Theorem 6.9   *The round-based synchronous algorithm described in Figure 6.4 satisfies fast commit, weak fast abort and early decision (i.e., at most $f + 2$ rounds when $f \leq t - 2$, and $f + 1$ rounds when $f \geq t - 1$ where f is the actual number of crashes, $0 \leq f \leq t$).*

Proof Weak fast abort property. Let us consider an execution in which at least one process p_i votes *no*. Every process p_j that terminates round 1 sets est_j to 0 (because it receives the vote *no* from p_i or p_i crashes). It follows that all processes that execute the second round exchange only abort messages. It follows that the predicate of line 14 is satisfied for each process that execute the second round. Hence, any process that completes the second round decides 0 during that round.

  Early decision. We consider three cases.
- $f \leq t - 2$. Let us consider a process p_i that has completed round $f + 1$ without deciding and is executing round $f + 2$. Let us also suppose that it does not receive DEC() message during round $f + 2$ (otherwise, it would decide during that round).

  Let us first show that, when p_i executes round $f + 2$, the set $crashed_i[f + 2]$ contains only crashed processes. Suppose by contradiction that $crashed_i[f + 2]$ contains a correct process p_j. This means that p_j has stopped after it has decided and sent a DEC() message during a round $\leq f + 2$. As p_i has not received this DEC() message by round $f + 2$, it follows that $crashed_i[f + 2]$ cannot contain correct processes that would have decided. Consequently, $|crashed_i[f + 2]| \leq f$.

  When p_i executes round $r = f + 2$, there are two cases.

    - if $r = f + 2 \leq t - 1$, then the predicate of line 15 is satisfied, and, consequently, p_i decides at line 19 of that round.

    - if $r = f + 2 = t$, then p_i receives at least $n - f = n - (t - 2)$ EST() messages during round $r = t$. In that case, the predicate of line 16 is satisfied, and p_i decides at line 19 of round $r = t$.

- $f = t - 1$. In that case, a process p_i that has not decided by the end of round f and does not crash receives either a DEC() message or at least $n - f = n - (t - 1)$ EST() messages during round t. Whatever the case, it decides by the end of that round (at line 10 if it receives a DEC() message, or at line 17 -due to the predicate of line 16- otherwise).

- $f = t$. In that case, it follows from the text of the algorithm (line 20) that no process executes more than $f + 1 = t + 1$ rounds.

Fast commit property. This property follows from early decision when $f = 0$. $\square_{Theorem\ 6.9}$

6.4   OTHER ALGORITHMS

6.4.1   FAST ABORT AND WEAK FAST COMMIT

Required properties   It is possible to design an NBAC algorithm that satisfies the fast abort property and the weak fast commit property. This means that the algorithm directs the processes to decide in one round when one process votes *no*, and in three rounds when all processes vote *yes* and no process crashes.

```
operation nbac propose (vote_i):
(1)    est_i ← vote_i; decided_i ← false;
(2)    when r = 1 do
       begin synchronous round
(3)        broadcast EST(vote_i);
(4)        let rec_votes_i[1] = multiset of the votes vote_j received during the first round;
(5)*       if (|rec_votes_i[1]| < n) ∨ (0 ∈ rec_votes_i[1]) then decide(0); decided_i ← true end if
       end synchronous round;
(6)    when r = 2, ..., t + 1 do
       begin synchronous round
(7)        if (decided_i) then broadcast DEC(est_i); return() end if;
(8)        broadcast EST(est_i);
(9)        if ( DEC(v) received during round r)
(10)           then est_i ← v; decide(est_i); decided_i ← true
(11)           else let rec_votes_i[r] = multiset of the estimates est_j received during r;
(12)                let crashed_i[r] ← { processes from which no message received during r};
(13)*               if (0 ∈ rec_votes_i[r]) ∨ ((r = 2) ∧ (|rec_votes_i[r]| < n − 1))
(14)*                    then est_i ← 0 end if;
(15)*               if ((3 ≤ r ≤ t − 1) ∧ (|crashed_i[r]| ≤ r − 2))
(16)                    ∨ ((r = t) ∧ (|rec_votes_i[t]| ≥ n − t + 1))
(17)                        then decide(est_i); decided_i ← true;
(18)                    end if;
(19)        end if;
(20)        if (r = t + 1) then if (¬decided_i) then decide(est_i) end if; return() end if
       end synchronous round.
```

Figure 6.5: Fast abort and weak fast commit NBAC despite up to $t \geq 3$ crash failures (code for p_i)

An algorithm   Such an algorithm is described in Figure 6.5. It is similar to the algorithm described in Figure 6.4. The line number of the lines thta are modified are postfixed with a star.

- First line 5* forces a process to decide ABORT (i.e., 0) during the very first round if a process votes *no*.

- Then lines 13*, 14* and 15* are modified in order the processes decide in three rounds when there is no crash and all processes votes *yes* (weak fast commit), and, assuming $1 \leq f \leq t$, in $f + 2$ rounds when $f \leq t - 2$ and $f + 1$ rounds when $f \geq t - 1$.

The reader can check that Lemma 6.6 and Lemma 6.7 are still valid for the algorithm of Figure 6.5. The proofs that this algorithm solves the NBAC problem and satisfies early decision when $f \geq 1$ are case analysis similar to the one of Theorem m 6.8 and Theorem 6.9, respectively.

6.4.2   THE CASE $t \leq 2$

The impossibility result stated in Theorem 6.3 is for $t \geq 3$. When $t \leq 2$, it is possible to design an NBAC algorithm that satisfies both the fast abort property and the fast commit property.

```
operation nbac propose (vote_i):
(1)    est_i ← vote_i;
(2)    when r = 1 do
       begin synchronous round
(3)        broadcast EST(est_i);
(4)        let rec_votes_i[1] = multiset of the estimates received during the first round;
(5)        if (|rec_votes_i[1]| < n) ∨ (0 ∈ rec_votes_i[1]) then est_i ← 0; decide(0) end if
       end synchronous round;
(6)    when r = 2 do
       begin synchronous round
(7)        broadcast EST(est_i);
(8)        if (est_i = 0) then  return() end if;
(9)        let rec_votes_i[2] = multiset of the estimates received during the second round;
(10)       if (0 ∈ rec_votes_i[2]) then  decide(0); return() end if;
(11)       if (|rec_votes_i[2]| ≥ n − 1) then  decide(1) else est_i ← 0 end if;
       end synchronous round;
(12)   when r = 3 do
       begin synchronous round
(13)       broadcast EST(est_i);
(14)       if (est_i = 1) then  return() end if;
(15)       let rec_votes_i[3] = multiset of the estimates received during the third round;
(16)       if (1 ∈ rec_votes_i[3]) then  decide(1) then  decide(0) end if;
(17)       return()
       end synchronous round.
```

Figure 6.6: Fast commit and fast abort NBAC despite up to $t \leq 2$ crash failures (code for p_i)

Such an algorithm is described in Figure 6.6. It consists of three rounds. A process executes at least two rounds but can decide at any round (let us recall that it stops when it crashes or when it executes the statement return()). At the beginning of every round, p_i broadcasts its current estimate of the decision value (that initially is its vote).

- During the first round a process p_i decides 0 if it receives a vote *no* or sees a process crash. It then stop at line 8 of the second round.

- During the second round, p_i stops if it has decided ABORT. Otherwise, it decides ABORT and stops if it has received such an estimate (line 10). If it has received only estimates equal to 1, p_i decides COMMIT if it has received at least $n - 1$ such estimates; otherwise, it updates est_i to ABORT (line 11).

- Finally, if p_i has not stopped before the third round, it stops if it has already decided COMMIT in the previous round (line 14). Otherwise, p_i decides COMMIT if it has received an estimate whose value is COMMIT, and ABORT if it has not (line 16), and finally stops (line 17).

The proof of this algorithm is a simple case analysis left to the reader.

6.5 BIBLIOGRAPHIC NOTES

- As already indicated in the first chapter, the non-blocking atomic commit problem originated in databases (7; 30; 31; 48; 77).

- Timer-based NBAC algorithms suited to synchronous systems are described in (4).

- The notions of fast commit/abort and weak fast commit/abort are due to Dutta, Guerraoui and Pochon (19). The algorithms that have been presented are from the same authors.

PART III

Agreement Despite Omission or Byzantine Failures

CHAPTER 7

k-Set Agreement Despite Omission Failures

This chapter considers that, in addition to crashes, a process may forget to send messages (send omission failure model), or forget to send or receive messages (general omission failure model). Hence, an omission failure model is the crash failure model plus the possibility for processes to forget to send (or receive) messages. (These failures capture output buffer overflow and input buffer overflow, respectively). The presentation is mainly focused on the *k*-set agreement problem. Results concerning consensus can trivially be obtained by taking $k = 1$.

7.1 THE CASE OF SEND OMISSION FAILURES

A simple algorithm A simple *k*-set agreement round-based synchronous algorithm that solves the *k*-set agreement problem despite up to *t* processes that crash or commit send omission failure is described in Figure 7.1.

This algorithm is obtained by a simple modification of the non-early deciding *k*-set agreement algorithm described in Chapter 5. The processes execute $\lfloor \frac{t}{k} \rfloor + 1$ rounds, and in a round, at most *k* processes broadcast their current estimate value. More precisely, during round *r*, a process p_i broadcasts its current estimate of the decision value only if its identity *i* belongs to the interval $[(r-1)k + 1 .. r \times k]$. At the end of a round, a process updates its estimate est_i to any estimate value it has received during that round, if any. If p_i has received no value, est_i is left unchanged.

```
operation propose ($v_i$):
(1)  $est_i \leftarrow v_i$;
(2)  when $r = 1, 2, \ldots, \lfloor \frac{t}{k} \rfloor + 1$ do
     begin synchronous round
(3)      if (i is such that $(r-1)k < i \leq r \times k$) then broadcast EST($est_i$) end if;
(4)      $est_i \leftarrow$ any estimate $est_j$ received during round $r$ if any, unchanged otherwise;
(5)      if ($r = \lfloor \frac{t}{k} \rfloor + 1$) then return($est_i$) end if
     end synchronous round.
```

Figure 7.1: A simple *k*-set agreement algorithm for send omission failures (code for p_i, $t < n$)

Theorem 7.1 *Let $1 \leq t < n$. The algorithm described in Figure 7.1 solves the k-set agreement problem in synchronous systems where up to t processes may commit send omission failures.*

Proof The validity property (a decided value is a proposed value), and the termination property (any correct process decides) are trivially satisfied. Hence, let us focus on the agreement property (at most, k different value are decided).

Let $\alpha = \lfloor \frac{t}{k} \rfloor$. We have $t = \alpha \times k + \beta$, with $0 \leq \beta < k$. Let $R = \lfloor \frac{t}{k} \rfloor + 1$ (the total number of rounds). As $R \times k = \alpha \times k + k > \alpha \times k + \beta = t$, it follows that there is at least one round r with a correct sender process (say p_c).

During r, all (non-crashed) processes receive at least the estimate value of p_c, and they consequently modify their current estimate during that round. Finally, as, at most, k different estimates values can be adopted during a round, it follows that, from round r, there are at most k different values in the system, which concludes the proof of the agreement property. $\square_{Theorem\ 7.1}$

Remark on termination   According to the terminology defined in the first chapter, all the processes that neither crash nor commit receive omission failures are *good* processes (a *bad* process is a process that crashes or commits receive omission failures). It is easy to see that, in the algorithm described in Figure 7.1, not only the correct processes decide, but more generally all good processes decide a proposed value.

This property is due to the fact that a faulty process that does not crash receives at least all the messages broadcast by the correct processes.

7.2   A LOWER BOUND FOR GENERAL OMISSION FAILURES

In the general omission failure model, a faulty process can crash, omit to send messages and omit to receive messages (the send or receive omission pattern can change from round to round).

This section shows a bound on the number of processes that can be faulty in order to be able to solve k-set agreement in the general omission failure model. It first considers the case of consensus ($k = 1$) and then k-set agreement for $k \geq 1$. The first impossibility is a particular case of the second one. We nevertheless present it for a pedagogical purpose. Its proof is simpler and exhibits the main ideas (partitioning argument and indistinguishability) the impossibility relies on. Of course, the reader can skip the first proof and proceed directly to the general case.

7.2.1   THE CASE OF CONSENSUS

Theorem 7.2   *Let $t \geq n/2$. There is no algorithm that solves the consensus problem in a synchronous system where up to t processes may commit general omission failures.*

Proof The proof is by contradiction. Let us assume that there is an algorithm A that solves the binary consensus problem in a synchronous system where up to $t \geq n/2$ processes can suffer general omission failures. Let us partition the n processes into two subsets P and Q such that $|P| = t$ and $|Q| = n - t$. The important point here is that each of P and Q contains no more than t processes, which means that there are executions in which all processes of P crash, and executions in which all processes of Q crash, We first consider two executions.

- In the execution $E0$, all processes propose the value 0, and all processes in P are correct while all the processes in Q crash before taking any step (initial crashes).

  As by assumption the algorithm A solves consensus despite $t \geq n/2$, the processes of P decide (termination) the same value (agreement) and that value is 0 (validity).

- In the execution $E1$, all processes propose the value 1, and all processes in Q are correct while all the processes in P crash before taking any step (initial crashes).

  As by assumption the algorithm A solves consensus despite $t \geq n/2$, the processes of Q decide (termination) the same value (agreement) and that value is 1 (validity).

Let us now consider the following execution $E01$.

- In that execution all the processes in P are correct and propose 0, while all the processes in Q propose 1 and are faulty. Each process of Q commits the following omission failures: it "forgets" (a) to send any message it has to send to any process of P and (b) to receive any message sent by a process of P.

  This means that the subsets P and Q are partitioned. Inside each partition, all messages sent are received, while no message sent by a process in a partition is received by a process in the other partition.

  Let us consider any process $p_i \in P$. Such a process cannot distinguish if the actual execution is $E0$ or $E01$ (in both it proposes the same value and receives the same messages from the same processes). As algorithm A is correct, it follows that the processes of P have to decide 0 in the execution $E01$.

  Let us now consider any process $p_j \in Q$. Such a process cannot distinguish if the actual execution is $E1$ or $E01$ (in both it proposes the same value and receives the same messages from the same processes). As algorithm A is correct, it follows that the processes of Q have to decide 1 in the execution $E01$.

  It follows that in $E01$ some processes decide 0 while other processes decide 1, which contradicts the agreement property of A, and concludes the impossibility proof. $\square_{Theorem\ 7.2}$

7.2.2 THE CASE OF k-SET AGREEMENT

Theorem 7.3   *Let $t \geq \frac{k}{k+1}n$. There is no algorithm that solves the k-set agreement problem in a synchronous system where up to t processes may commit general omission failures.*

Proof This proof is a generalization of the previous one. In order to establish a contradiction, let us assume that $t \geq \frac{k}{k+1}n$ and there is an algorithm A that solves the k-set agreement problem in synchronous systems where at most t processes can commit general omission failures. Let us partition the set of processes into $k + 1$ subsets $S_1, \ldots, S_{k+1}$ such that $\forall 1 \leq i \leq k : |S_i| = n - t$ and $|S_{k+1}| = n - k(n - t)$. As $t \geq \frac{k}{k+1}n$, it follows that $t \geq k(n - t)$, from which we have $|S_{k+1}| = n - k(n - t) \geq n - t$. The proof consists in exhibiting an execution E of the algorithm A in which $k + 1$ distinct values are decided: a contradiction.

The execution E is as follows. Every process that belongs to the same set S_i initially proposes the same value v_i. Moreover, the values v_i are chosen such that $i \neq j \Rightarrow v_i \neq v_j$. The processes that belong to sets $S_1, \ldots, S_k$ are faulty whereas processes in set S_{k+1} are correct. The number of faulty processes is $k(n - t) \leq t$. We now describe the behavior of the faulty processes during execution E. Let p_x be a faulty process that belongs to a set S_i ($i \leq k$). From the very beginning of the execution, p_x commits.

- a send omission failure for each message it has to send to a process that does not belong to S_i,

- a receive omission failure each time it has to receive a message from a process that belongs to the set S_{k+1}.

For each $1 \leq i \leq k + 1$, we construct an execution E_i as follows. In execution E_i, every process that does not belong to set S_i crashes before sending any message. Processes in set S_i are correct. As in the execution E defined previously, all processes in S_i initially propose the same value v_i. In execution E_i, messages are only exchanged between processes in set S_i. Moreover, for any $p_x, p_y \in S_i$, each time algorithm $\mathcal{A}$ requires p_x to send a message to p_y, this message is delivered by p_y. As the processes in S_i are correct, it follows from the correction of algorithm A that they decide. Since the only value that they hear of is v_i (the only value proposed by processes in S_i), they decide that value.

Let us now consider the processes in S_i during execution E. Let us first observe (O1) that a process $p_x \in S_i$ does not receive messages sent by any process that does not belong to S_i. If $i = k + 1$ (i.e., p_x belongs to S_{k+1} and is a correct process), this is because any process p_z that does not belong to S_{k+1} commits a send omission failure each time it has to send a message to p_x. In the other case ($i \neq k + 1$), p_x does not receive messages from any $p_z \in S_j$, $j \neq i \wedge j \neq k + 1$ since these processes commit send omission failures each time they have to send a message to p_x; p_x never receives messages from any $p_z \in S_{k+1}$ since it commits a receive omission failure with respect to any process that belongs to S_{k+1}.

As in execution E_i, for any $p_x, p_y \in S_i$ each time algorithm A requires p_x to send a message to p_y, this message is delivered by p_y (O2). This is because, for any set S_i, a process that belongs to S_i does not commit omission failures with respect to the other processes of S_i. Consequently, it follows from the observations (O1) and (O2) that executions E and E_i are indistinguishable for any process that belongs to S_i. This implies that in the execution E, for each $1 \leq i \leq k + 1$, any $p_x \in S_i$ decides v_i, from which we conclude that $k + 1$ values are decided. $\square_{Theorem\ 7.3}$

7.3   GENERAL OMISSION FAILURES WHEN $t < n/2$

There is no way to force a process that commits receive omission failures to decide one of the k values decided by the correct processes. This is because, due to its faults, such a process can never know these values. In that case, the algorithm forces such processes to stop without deciding a value (let us remind that the problem requires "only" that the correct processes decide). A faulty process that does not decide, returns a default value denoted $\perp$ whose meaning is "no decision" from the k-set agreement point of view. By a language abuse we then say that such a process "decides $\perp$".

Differently, a process that does not crash and commits only send omission failures, receives the messages sent by (at least) the correct processes. Hence, the additional constraint requiring that it decides as a correct process. This has motivated (in Chapter 1) the definition of *good* process, i.e., a process that is correct or commits only send omission failures. This allows us to formally state a property requiring as many processes as possible to decide, namely any good process decides. The algorithms presented below satisfy this property.

7.3.1   A SIMPLE CONSENSUS ALGORITHM

From crash failures to general omission failures   A simple consensus algorithm that tolerates up to $t < n/2$ processes that fail by committing general omission failure is presented in Figure 7.2.

This algorithm is a simple extension of the consensus algorithm described in the first section of Chapter 2 (devoted to the crash failure model). From the first round until round $t + 1$ (lines 2-5) the processes exchange their estimates of the decision values (which are the smallest values that they have ever seen). As we can see, during a round, a process p_i broadcasts its current estimate est_i, only if est_i is a new estimate value (line 3).

The difference with the algorithm of Chapter 2 lies in the addition of one more round $r = t + 2$ (lines 8-9). During that round, a process p_i broadcasts its last value of est_i, and it waits for the estimates of the other processes. Finally if there is an estimate that is a majority value, it decides it. Otherwise, it decides the default value $\perp$.

Theorem 7.4   *The algorithm described in Figure 7.2 solves the consensus problem in a round-based synchronous system in which up to $t < n/2$ processes may commit general omission failures. Moreover, any good process decides (a proposed value).*

Proof Trivially, no process executes more than $t + 2$ rounds. Moreover, it is easy to see that, at any time, any est_i can only contain a proposed value. It follows that if a process executes return(v) at line 9, v is a proposed value.

As far as the agreement property is concerned, the same proof as for the base algorithm (Chapter 2) shows that all the correct processes have the same value at the end of round $t + 1$. Let w be that value. (The main argument of this agreement proof lies in the fact that the processes executes $t + 1$ rounds, and as a process forwards a value during a round only if that value is smaller than the

```
operation propose (v_i):
(1)  est_i ← v_i; prev_est_i ← ⊥;
(2)  when r = 1, 2, . . . , (t + 1) do
     begin synchronous round
(3)      if (est_i ≠ prev_est_i) then broadcast EST(est_i) end if;
(4)      let recval_i = {values received during round r};
(5)      prev_est_i ← est_i;
(6)      est_i ← min(recval_i ∪ {est_i});
     end synchronous round;
(7)  when r = t + 2 do % additional round %
     begin synchronous round
(8)      broadcast EST(est_i);
(9)      if (an estimate value v has been received > n/2 times) then return(v) else return(⊥) end if
     end synchronous round.
```

Figure 7.2: A simple consensus algorithm for the general omission failure model (code for p_i, $t < n/2$)

previous value it has forwarded, a value has necessarily been forwarded by a correct process in any chain of $t + 1$ forwardings.)

The fact that a good process executes return(w) at line 9 follows from the observation that because it neither crashes nor commits receive omission failures, such a process does receive the messages sent by the correct processes at any round, hence at round $t + 2$. This implies that any good process receives the value w from a majority of processes (namely the correct processes). As a single value can be a majority value, the property follows. $\square_{Theorem\ 7.4}$

Remark   Let us observe that, not only the good processes decide a proposed value, but some bad processes can also decide the value decided by the good processes. This occurs when a bad process does not crash and (whatever the receive omission failures it has committed from round 1 until round $t + 1$) does not commit receive omission failures during round $t + 2$.

7.3.2   A k-SET ALGORITHM WHERE ALL GOOD PROCESSES DECIDE IN $\lfloor \frac{t}{k} \rfloor + 1$ ROUNDS

A lower bound   The previous consensus algorithm requires $t + 2$ rounds for the good processes to decide, i.e., one more round that what is required in the crash failure model. This section shows that this additional round is not necessary.

More generally, this section presents a synchronous k-set algorithm where all good processes decide in $\lfloor \frac{t}{k} \rfloor + 1$ rounds. It follows that the good processes decide in $t + 1$ rounds when $k = 1$. Consequently, this algorithm shows that, not only the additional round used in the previous algorithm can be saved, but more importantly that $\lfloor \frac{t}{k} \rfloor + 1$ rounds is a lower bound on the number of rounds for k-set agreement when up to $t < n/2$ processes can commit general omission failures. (This follows

```
operation propose(v_i)
(1)  est_i ← v_i; trusted_i ← {1, ..., n};
(2)  when r = 1, ..., ⌊t/k⌋ + 1 do
     begin synchronous round
(3)      if (i ∈ trusted_i) then broadcast((est_i, trusted_i)) end if;
(4)      let recfrom_i = {j : (est_j, trust_j) is received from p_j during r ∧ j ∈ trusted_i};
(5)      for each j ∈ recfrom_i let W_i(j) = {ℓ : ℓ ∈ recfrom_i ∧ j ∈ trust_ℓ};
(6)      trusted_i ← recfrom_i − {j : |W_i(j)| < n − t};
(7)      if (|trusted_i| < n − t) then return(⊥) end if;
(8)      est_i ← min(est_j received during r and such that j ∈ trusted_i):
(9)      if (r = ⌊t/k⌋ + 1) then return(est_i) end if
     end synchronous round.
```

Figure 7.3: A k-set agreement algorithm for the general omission failure model (code for p_i, $t < \frac{n}{2}$)

from the fact that $\lfloor \frac{t}{k} \rfloor + 1$ is a lower bound for the crash failure model that is less severe than the general omission failure model.)

Local variables The algorithm is described in Figure 7.3. In addition to est_i, a process p_i manages three local variables whose meaning is the following:

- *trusted_i* represents the set of processes that p_i currently considers as being correct. It initial value is Π (the whole set of processes). So, $i \in trusted_i$ (line 3) means that p_i considers it is correct. (If $j \in trusted_i$ we say "p_i trusts p_j"; if $j \notin trusted_i$ we say "p_i suspects p_j".)

- $recfrom_i$ is a round local variable used to contain the identities of the processes that p_i does not currently suspect and from which it has received messages during that round (line 4).

- $W_i(j)$ is a set containing the identities of the processes that are currently trusted by p_i and that (to p_i's knowledge) trust p_j (line 5).

Process behavior The aim is for a process to decide the smallest value it has seen. But, due to the send and receive omission failures possibly committed by some processes, a process cannot safely decide the smallest value it has ever seen, it can only safely decide the smallest in "some subset" of values it has received. The crucial part of the algorithm consists in providing each process with correct rules that allow it to determine a "safe subset".

During each round r, these rules are implemented by the following process behavior decomposed in three parts according to the synchronous round-based computation model.

- If p_i considers it is correct ($i \in trusted_i$), it first sends to all processes its current local state, namely, the current pair $(est_i, trusted_i)$ (line 3). Otherwise, p_i skips the sending phase.

- Then, p_i executes the receive phase (line 4). As already indicated, when it considers the messages it has received during the current round, p_i considers only the messages sent by the processes it trusts (here, the set $trusted_i$ can be seen as a filter).

- Finally, p_i executes the local computation phase that is the core of the algorithm (lines 5-8). This phase is made up of the following statements where the value $n - t$ constitutes a threshold that plays a fundamental role.

  - First, p_i determines the new value of $trusted_i$ (lines 5-6). It is equal to the current set $recfrom_i$ from which are suppressed the processes p_j such that $|W_i(j)| < n - t$. These processes p_j are no longer trusted by p_i because there are "not enough" processes trusted by p_i that trust them (p_j is missing "Witnesses" to remain trusted by p_i, hence the name $W_i(j)$); "not enough" means here less than $n - t$.

  - Then, p_i checks if it trusts enough processes, i.e., at least $n - t$ (line 7). If the answer is negative, p_i discovers that it has committed receive omission failures and cannot safely decide. It consequently halts, returning the default value $\bot$.

  - Finally, if it has not stopped at line 7, p_i computes its new estimate of the decision value (line 8) according to the estimate values it has received from the processes it currently trusts.

The role of $W_i(j)$ and its associated predicate $|W_i(j)| < n - t$ are central to ensure the that any good process decides a proposed value. Let p_i be such a process (i.e., it neither crashes, nor commits receive omission failures). Let us observe that, at each round, such a p_i receives a message from each correct process p_j. This means that, with respect to each correct process p_j, we always have $|W_i(j)| \geq n - t$ (lines 5-6). Consequently, p_i always trusts all correct processes, and so we always have $|trusted_i| \geq n - t$. It follows that such a process p_i cannot stop at line 7, and decides consequently at line 9.

7.3.3   PROOF OF THE *k*-SET ALGORITHM: PRELIMINARIES LEMMAS

Notations   The proof assumes $t < n/2$. It uses the following notations.

- Given a set of process identities $X = \{i, j, \ldots\}$, we sometimes use $p_i \in X$ for $i \in X$.

- C is the set of correct processes in a given execution.

- $x_i[r]$ denotes the value of p_i's local variable x at the end of round r. By definition $trusted_i[0] = \Pi$.

- $Completing[r] = \{i : p_i$ proceeds to $r + 1\}$. By definition $Completing[0] = \Pi$. (If $r = \lfloor \frac{t}{k} \rfloor + 1$, "$p_i$ proceeds to $r + 1$" means that p_i executes the statement return(est_i) at line 9.)

- $EST[r] = \{est_i[r] : i \in Completing[r]\}$. By definition $EST[0]$ is the set of proposed values. $EST[r]$ contains the values that are present in the system at the end of round r.

- $Silent[r] = \{i : \forall j \in Completing[r] : i \notin trusted_j[r]\}$. It is important to remark that if $i \in Silent[r]$, then no process p_j (including p_i itself) takes into account est_i sent by p_i (if any) to update its local variables est_j at line 8 of the round r. ($Silent[0] = \emptyset$.)

The proof of the following relations are left to the reader:

$$\begin{aligned} Completing[r+1] &\subseteq Completing[r], \\ Silent[r] &\subseteq Silent[r+1], \\ \forall i \in Completing[r] : Silent[r] &\subseteq \Pi - trusted_i[r]. \end{aligned}$$

Basic Lemmas   In order not to overload the presentation, the proofs of all the lemmas are given at the end of the chapter (see Section 7.6.1). The first lemma that follows will be used to prove that a process that does not commit receive omission failure decides.

Lemma 7.5   *Let p_i be a good process. $\forall r$: (1) $C \subseteq trusted_i[r]$ and (2) $i \in Completing[r]$.*

The next two lemmas show that $n - t$ is a critical threshold related to the number of processes (1) for a process to become silent or (2) for the process estimates to become smaller or equal to some value. More explicitly, the first of these lemmas states that if a process p_x is not trusted by "enough" processes (i.e., trusted by less than $n - t$ processes.) at the end of a round $r - 1$, then that process p_x is not trusted by the processes that complete round r.

Lemma 7.6 $\forall r \geq 1 : \forall x : \left|\{y : y \in Completing[r - 1] \wedge x \in trusted_y[r - 1]\}\right| < n - t \Rightarrow x \in Silent[r]$.

The next lemma shows that if "enough" (i.e., at least $n - t$) processes have an estimate smaller than or equal to a value v at the end of a round $r - 1$, then no process $p_i \in Completing[r]$ has a value greater than v at the end of r.

Lemma 7.7   *Let v be an arbitrary value. $\forall r \geq 1 : \left|\{x : est_x[r - 1] \leq v \wedge x \in Completing[r - 1]\}\right| \geq n - t \Rightarrow \forall i \in Completing[r] : est_i[r] \leq v$.*

Finally, the next lemma states that the sequence of set values $EST[0], EST[1], \ldots$ is monotonic and never increases.

Lemma 7.8 $\forall r \geq 0 : EST[r + 1] \subseteq EST[r]$.

The lemma that follows is central to prove the agreement property, namely, at most k distinct values are decided.

Lemma 7.9   *Let r ($1 \leq r \leq \lfloor\frac{t}{k}\rfloor + 1$) be a round such that (1) $C \subseteq Completing[r - 1]$, and (2) $|EST[r]| > k$ (let v_m denote the kth smallest value in $EST[r]$, i.e., the greatest value among the k smallest values of $EST[r]$). Let $i \in Completing[r]$. We have $n - k\,r < |trusted_i[r]| \Rightarrow est_i[r] \leq v_m$.*

7.3.4   PROOF OF THE k-SET ALGORITHM: THEOREM

Theorem 7.10   *The algorithm described in Figure 7.3 solves the k-set agreement problem in the round-based synchronous model where up to $t < n/2$ processes can commit general omission failures. Moreover, no good process decides the default value $\perp$.*

Proof To prove the validity property (a decided value is a proposed value), let us first observe that a process p_i decides at line 9 of the last round. It then decides $est_i[\lfloor \frac{t}{k} \rfloor + 1]$.

The proof is an easy induction on the round number. Initially ($r = 0$), each est_i local variable contains a proposed value (line 1). Let us assume this is true until round $r - 1$. We show it is true at the end of round r. Let us notice that, due to the test of line 7, p_i updates est_i at line 8 only if $|trusted_i| \geq n - t$ (otherwise, p_i stops at line 7 without deciding). Due to line 6, $trusted_i$ is a set including only processes p_j whose value est_j has been received during the current round r. As that value is the value computed by p_j during the previous round, it follows from the induction assumption that est_i contains a proposed value.

Let us now show that any good process decides a value. Let p_i be a good process (so, either p_i is correct, or commits only send omission failures). Lemma 7.5 shows that $\forall r : C \subseteq trusted_i[r]$. We conclude from that lemma that $\forall r : |trusted_i[r]| \geq |C| \geq n - t$. It follows that p_i never exits at line 7. Consequently, p_i decides at line 9 of the last round $r = \lfloor \frac{t}{k} \rfloor + 1$. As a correct process is a good process, it follows that any correct process decides a proposed value.

To prove the agreement property (no more than k different values are decided), let us consider the set $EST[\lfloor \frac{t}{k} \rfloor + 1]$ that contains the estimate values present in the system at the end of the round $\lfloor \frac{t}{k} \rfloor + 1$. We claim $|EST[\lfloor \frac{t}{k} \rfloor + 1]| \leq k$ (Claim   C). Due to very definition of the $EST[r]$ sets, a process that decides decides a value that belongs to $EST[\lfloor \frac{t}{k} \rfloor + 1]$. This implies that at most k different values are decided.

Proof of C. Let $t = kx + y$ with $y < k$ (hence $\lfloor \frac{t}{k} \rfloor = x$). The proof is by contradiction. Let us assume that $|EST[x + 1]| > k$. Let v_m be the kth smallest values in $EST[x + 1]$ and let $i \in Completing[x + 1]$ such that $est_i[x + 1] > v_m$.

As each correct process decides, there are at least $n - t$ (correct) processes in $Completing[x + 1]$. Moreover, as $|EST[x + 1]| > k$, the assumptions of Lemma 7.9 are satisfied. Considering our assumption $est_i[x + 1] > v_m$, and applying the contrapositive of Lemma 7.9 to process p_i, we obtain $|trusted_i[x + 1]| \leq n - k(x + 1) = n - (kx + k) < n - (kx + y) = n - t$. This implies that p_i returns $\perp$ at line 7 during the round $x + 1$: a contradiction with the fact that $i \in Completing[x + 1]$.
End of proof of Claim C.

$\square_{Theorem\ 7.10}$

7.4   GENERAL OMISSION FAILURES WHEN $t < \frac{k}{k+1}n$

In that section, the notion of good process is not considered. This means that only the correct processes have to decide a non-$\perp$ value.

7.4.1   A k-SET ALGORITHM FOR $t < \frac{k}{k+1}n$

This section presents a simple algorithm that solves the k-set agreement problem despite up to t processes that commit general omission failures in a synchronous system where $t < \frac{k}{k+1}n$. This algorithm requires $t - k + 2$ rounds. To make more visible the meaning of this number, it can be rewritten as $(t + 1) - (k - 1)$. It is easy to see that for $k = 1$, this is the $t + 1$ consensus lower bound, and $t < \frac{k}{k+1}n$ becomes $t < n/2$, which is a necessary condition for the consensus problem in the general omission failure model.

This means that, in the general omission failure model, allowing up to k values to be decided instead of a single one allows the saving of $k - 1$ synchronous rounds.

```
operation propose(v_i)
(1)   est_i ← v_i; trusted_i ← {1, ..., n};
(2)   when r = 1, ..., t + 2 - k do
      begin synchronous round
(3)      broadcast(est_i) to trusted_i;
(4)      for each j ∈ trusted_i do
(5)         if (est_j received from p_j) then est_i ← min(est_i, est_j)
(6)                                      else trusted_i ← trusted_i \ {j}
(7)         end if
(8)      end do;
(9)      if (|trusted_i| < n - t) then return(⊥) end if;
(10)     if (r = t + 2 - k) then return(est_i) end if
      end synchronous round.
```

Figure 7.4: A k-set agreement algorithm for the general omission failure model (code for $p_i, t < \frac{k}{k+1}n$)

This algorithm is presented in Figure 7.4. Its design is relatively simple. Each process p_i manages a variable denoted $trusted_i$, a set containing the processes that p_i considers correct, and a variable est_i containing its current estimate of the decision value. More specifically, we have the following.

- A process p_i sends its current estimate only to the processes in $trusted_i$, and it accepts processing estimates only from them. (As we have seen in the first chapter, the broadcast of a message to a selected subset of processes during a round, can be simulated in a round-based model where where each process broadcast a message to all.) Basically, a process p_i communicates only with the processes it trusts (lines 3-8). In that way, if during a round r, p_j commits a send omission failure with respect to p_i, or if p_i commits a receive omission failure with respect to p_j, p_i and p_j will not trust each other from round $r + 1$. Interestingly, this ensures that, if p_i is correct, it will always trust at least $n - t$ processes. So, if during a round r, a process finds that it trusts less than $n - t$ processes, it can conclude that it is faulty, and consequently decides the default value $\perp$ (line 9).

- Each local variable est_i is used as in the previous algorithms. It contains the smallest value that p_i has ever received from the processes it currently trusts.

This simple management of the variables $trusted_i$ and est_i solves the k-set agreement problem despite up to $t < \frac{k}{k+1}n$ processes prone to crash and both send or receive omission failures.

Remark on which processes decide   It is easy to see that a process that neither crashes nor commits receive omission failures but commits send omission failure with respect to $t + 1$ processes, and it cannot decide a proposed value (it "decides" the default value $\perp$ at line 9). Hence, albeit such a process is a good process, it does not decide.

Differently, a faulty process that does not crash and commits (send or receive) omission failures with respect to few processes can decide. More precisely, let $suspect_i$ be the set of processes such that p_i committed an omission with respect to p_j or p_j committed an omission with respect to p_i. All the processes p_i such that $|suspect_i| \leq t$ decide.

7.4.2   PROOF FOR THE CASE $k = 1$ (CONSENSUS)

The proof of the general case is based on lemmas with long proofs. This is due to the fact that k-set agreement executions with $k > 1$ exhibit much more "combinatorics" than the case $k = 1$. Hence, this section considers the simplest case, i.e., the algorithm described in Figure 7.4 instantiated with $k = 1$.

Theorem 7.11   *When instantiated with $k = 1$, the algorithm described in Figure 7.4 solves the consensus problem in a round-based synchronous system in which up to $t < n/2$ processes may commit general omission failures, and where any process can send messages to any subset of processes.*

Proof   Let us first consider the validity and termination properties of consensus. We have to show that any correct process decides a proposed value. As a correct process neither crashes nor commits omission failures, it follows that, at every round, any correct process p_i sends a message to every correct process p_j and receives a message from it. Consequently, $trusted_i$ always contains the correct processes, hence the predicate $|trusted_i| > n/2 > t$ is always satisfied. It follows that every correct processes executes return(est_i) at line 10 when it executes round $t + 1$. Hence all correct processes decide a value $v \neq \perp$.

The fact that a value $v \neq \perp$ decided by a process p_i is a proposed value follows directly from the initialization of the estimate variables, and the min() function used at line 5. Finally, a faulty process that neither crashes, nor decides a proposed value, "decides $\perp$" at line 9 (which means that it does not decide).

As far as the agreement property is concerned, let us first prove two claims.

Claim C1. If a process p_i does not receive a message from a process p_j during a round r, it discards (if any) all the messages it receives from p_j at any round $r' > r$.
Proof of the claim. The proof is an immediate consequence of the management of the set $trusted_i$. If p_i does not receive a message from p_j, it suppresses it from $trusted_i$ (line 6) and consequently will discard all its future messages, if any (line 4). End of the proof of the claim.

Claim C2. Let p_i be a process that decides at line 10. There is a correct process $p_{c(i)}$ (called *correspondent* of p_i) such that, at every round, p_i sends a message to $p_{c(i)}$ and receives and processes the message sent by $p_{c(i)}$. (A process can have several correspondents, and a correct process is its own correspondent.)
Proof of the claim. If p_i decides at line 10, we have $|trusted_i| \geq n - t$ at the end of round $t + 1$. It follows from $t < n/2$ that $|trusted_i| > t$, and consequently $trusted_i$ contains at least one correct process $p_{c(i)}$. It follows from the management of $trusted_i$ that, at every round r, p_i sends a message to $p_{c(i)}$ and receives and processes its round r message. End of the proof of the claim.

Let us say that "process p_i learns v at round r", if (a) p_i receives the message EST(v) for the first time during that round and (b) $v < est_i$. If v is the value proposed by p_i, we say that it learns v at round 0.

The proof of the agreement property is as follows. Let v be the value decided by a process p_i at line 10. We show that the value v' decided by any process p_j at line 10 is such that $v' \leq v$. Due to symmetry we have $v \leq v'$, from which follows $v = v'$. The proof that the value v' decided by a process p_j at line 10 of round $t + 1$ is such that $v' \leq v$, is done by a case analysis.

1. Process p_i is correct and learns v during round $r = t + 1$. It follows from Claim C1 that v has been forwarded along a chain of $t + 1$ distinct processes before being learnt by p_i. This chain includes only one correct process p_x, and this process is the one that has forwarded v to p_i (otherwise, p_i would have learnt v before round $t + 1$). Hence, the t other processes are faulty. It follows that every faulty process has learnt v, and (thanks to p_x) all the correct processes learn v during the last round. Consequently, the value decided by any process p_j is $\leq v$.

2. Process p_i is a faulty process that learns v during round $r = t + 1$. In that case, there is a chain of $t + 1$ processes that have forwarded v until p_i. As p_i is faulty, this chain includes (at least) two correct processes p_x and p_y. Let us assume that p_x forwards v before p_y, i.e., p_x forwards v during round $r' \leq t$ and p_y forwards it during round $r' + 1 \leq t + 1$. During round r' any correct process p_z receives v and consequently forwards $est_z = v' \leq v$ during $r' + 1$. As $p_{c(j)}$ (the correspondent of p_j) is correct, it follows from Claim C2 that, during $r' + 1 \leq t + 1$, p_j receives and processes a value $est_{c(j)} \leq v$, which proves the case.

3. Process p_i (that is correct or faulty) learns v at round $r \leq t - 1$. We consider two cases.

- There is a correct process that learns v during round $t + 1$. The proof then follows from Item 1.
- No correct process p_j is such that $est_j \leq v$ at the end of round $t + 1$. This is impossible due to the following. As p_i decides (assumption), it sends EST(v) to its correspondent $p_{c(i)}$ during round $r + 1 \leq t$ (Claim C2) that in turn forwards EST(v') with $v' \leq v$ to all correct processes during round $r + 2 \leq t + 1$.

4. Process p_i (that is correct or faulty) learns v at round $r = t$. In that case, there is a chain of t processes that conveyed v to p_i.
    - This chain includes a process p_x that decides. Then, at the latest during round $r - 1$, process p_x learnt v, and we are then in Item 3.
    - The chain includes only processes that do not decide. This means that there are t faulty processes, and the chain includes all of them. Hence, p_i is correct and forwards v to all correct processes during round $t + 1$, which completes the proof.

$\square_{Theorem\ 7.11}$

7.4.3   PROOF OF THE ALGORITHM: GENERAL CASE

The notations are the same as the ones introduced in Section 7.3.3.

Relations   The proof of the following relations is left to the reader:

$$
\begin{aligned}
Completing[r + 1] &\subseteq Completing[r], \\
\forall i \in Completing[r + 1] : trusted_i[r + 1] &\subseteq Completing[r], \\
\forall i \in Completing[r + 1] : trusted_i[r + 1] &\subseteq trusted_i[r], \\
\forall i \in Completing[r + 1] : est_i[r + 1] &\leq est_i[r].
\end{aligned}
$$

Preliminary lemmas   In order not to overlaod the presentation, the proof of the following lemmas are given at the end of the chapter (see Section 7.6.2).

Lemma 7.12 $\forall r \geq 0 : EST[r + 1] \subseteq EST[r]$.

Lemma 7.13 $|EST[1]| \leq t + 1$.

Lemma 7.14 $\forall r, 1 \leq r \leq t - k + 2$, we have $|EST[r]| \leq t - r + 2$.

Theorem 7.15   *The algorithm described in Figure 7.4 solves the k-set agreement problem in a round-based synchronous in which up to $t < \frac{k}{k+1} n$ processes may commit general omission failures, and where any process can send messages to any subset of processes.*

Proof To prove the termination property, let us observe that it follows from the text of the algorithm that a process executes at most $t - k + 2$ rounds (line 10). A process that does not crash nor returns $\perp$ at line 7 decides when it executes the statement return() at line 10. As a correct process does not crash, we have to show that a correct process never returns $\perp$ at line 7. More precisely, we prove by induction on the round number the following property: $\forall i \in C$ (the set of correct processes in the considered execution), $\forall r : 1 \leq r \leq t - k + 2 : $ (1) $C \subseteq trusted_i[r]$ and, (2) $C \subseteq Completing[r]$. Let p_i be a correct process.

- Base case. Let us consider any correct process p_j. Let us first observe that we have initially $trusted_j[0] = \Pi$ (line 1). It follows then from line 3 that p_j sends a message to p_i during the first round. As both p_i and p_j are correct and $j \in trusted_i[0]$, this message is received and processed (at line 5) by p_i during the first round. Consequently, p_i does not remove j from $trusted_i$. Since this is true for any correct process p_j, $C \subseteq trusted_i[1]$, which proves item (1). As $|C| \geq n - t$, p_i does not return $\perp$ at line 7 during the first round, i.e., $i \in Completing[1]$, which proves item (2).

- Induction case. Let us assume that properties (1) and (2) hold from the first round until round $r - 1 (r \geq 2)$ for any correct process. First of all, let us notice that any correct process p_j sends a message to p_i during round r. This follows from the induction assumption: as $j \in Completing[r - 1]$ and $C \subseteq trusted_j[r - 1]$, p_j send a message to p_i at line 3. Moreover, as both p_i and p_j are correct and $j \in C \subseteq trusted_i[r - 1]$, this message is received and processed by p_i during round r. The proof is now the same as the base step, replacing $trusted_i[1]$ by $trusted_i[r]$, and $Completing[1]$ by $Completing[r]$.

As a correct process p_i is such that $i \in C \subseteq Completing[t - k + 2]$, it follows that it executes the statement return(est_i) at line 10.

To prove the validity property (a decided value is a proposed value) let us observe that a correct process p_i decides at line 10 the value of $est_i[t - k + 2]$. This means that the set of decided value is a subset of $EST[t - k + 2]$. Due to Lemma 7.12, $EST[t - k + 2] \subseteq EST[0]$, which is the set of proposed values.

To prove the k-set agreement property (no more than k different values are decided), let us first notice that a value decided by a correct process belongs to the set $EST[t - k + 2]$. Due to Lemma 7.14, $|EST[t - k + 2]| \leq t - (t - k + 2) + 2 = k$. Consequently, at most k distinct values are decided.
$\square_{Theorem\ 7.15}$

7.5   BIBLIOGRAPHIC NOTES

- As already indicated, the k-set agreement problem has been introduced by S. Chaudhuri (13) in the context of process crash failures. Its $\lfloor \frac{t}{k} \rfloor + 1$ lower bound for the crash failure model is proved in (14). Its early-deciding lower bound for the crash failure model is proved in (26).

- The omission failure model has been introduced by Perry and Toueg (65).

- The k-set agreement problem can be solved in the synchronous send omission failure model for any value of t, i.e., $t < n$. Moreover, it can be solved optimally in $\min(\lfloor \frac{f}{k} \rfloor + 2, \lfloor \frac{k}{k} \rfloor + 1)$ (where f is the actual number of faulty processes). An optimal algorithm can be found in (68).

- The impossibility proof (lower bound) for consensus when $t \geq n/2$ processes may commit general omission failures is from (70). A similar proof appears in (62). Its generalization to the k-set agreement problem when $t \geq \frac{k}{k+1} n$ is from (74).

- The algorithm that tolerates up to $t < n/2$ processes that commit general omission failures (Figure 7.3) is due to Raïpin Parvédy, Raynal and Travers (69).

- The algorithm that tolerates up to $t \geq \frac{k}{k+1} n$ processes that commit general omission failures (Figure 7.4) is due to Raynal and Travers (74).

- A consensus algorithm that tolerates up to $t < n/2$ processes that commit general omission failures is presented in (66).

- It is shown in (68) that $\min(\lfloor \frac{f}{k} \rfloor + 2, \lfloor \frac{t}{k} \rfloor + 1)$ is a lower bound on the number of rounds in the synchronous general omission failure model. A corresponding optimal algorithm can be found in (68).

7.6   APPENDIX: PROOF OF THE LEMMAS

7.6.1   PROOF OF THE LEMMAS FOR THE CASE $t < n/2$

Lemma 7.5 Let p_i be a good process. We have $\forall r : (1)\, \mathcal{C} \subseteq trusted_i[r]$ and $(2)\, i \in Completing[r]$.

Proof The proof is by induction on the round number r. Let p_i be a good process (i.e., it is correct or commits only send omission failures).

- Base case. Let us first observe that we have initially $\forall j : trusted_j[0] = \Pi$. The set $recfrom_i[1]$ computed by p_i at line 4 of the first round includes all the processes that did not commit send omission failure: it consequently includes (at least) all the correct processes, i.e., at least $n - t$ processes.

  Let us consider any correct process p_j. That process is such that $j \in trust_\ell$, for any p_ℓ from which p_i receives a message because $trust_\ell$ carries the value $trusted_\ell[0]$ which is equal to Π. As there are at least $n - t$ correct processes, it follows that the set $W_i(j)$ (computed at line 5) contains at least $n - t$ processes. We can then conclude that all the correct processes p_j belong to $recfrom_i[1]$ and none of them is suppressed from it when the value $trusted_i[1]$ is computed at line 6. It follows that $|trusted_i[1]| \geq n - t$, from which we conclude that p_i does not stop at line 7. This establishes the base case $r = 1$: for all the processes p_i that do not commit receive omission failures during the first round, we have $p_i \in Completing[1]$ and $\mathcal{C} \subseteq trusted_i[1]$.

- Induction case. Let us assume that the lemma is true from the first round until round $r - 1$. We show it remains true at round r. First of all, let us notice that each correct process p_j sends a message during r. This follows from the induction assumption: as $j \in Completing[r - 1]$ and $j \in trusted_j[r - 1]$, p_j executes the broadcast at line 3 of the round r.

  The proof is then the same as the second paragraph of the base step, replacing $trusted_\ell[0]$ (equal to Π) by $trusted_\ell[r - 1]$ that contains (at least) the correct processes (induction assumption) and the pair of round numbers $(0, 1)$ by the pair $(r - 1, r)$, respectively.

  $\square_{Lemma\ 7.5}$

Lemma 7.6 $\forall r \geq 1 : \forall x : \big|\{y : y \in Completing[r - 1] \wedge x \in trusted_y[r - 1]\}\big| < n - t \Rightarrow x \in Silent[r]$.

Proof Given a round $r - 1$, let p_x be a process such that $\big|\{y : y \in Completing[r - 1] \wedge x \in trusted_y[r - 1])\}\big| < n - t$. Let $p_i \in Completing[r]$. We have to show that, after p_i has executed line 6, $x \notin trusted_i[r]$.

- $x \notin trusted_i[r - 1]$ or p_i does not receive a message from p_x during round r. In that case, we have $x \notin recfrom_i[r]$. It follows from the way p_i updates its set $trusted_i$ (line 6) that $x \notin trusted_i[r]$.

- $x \in trusted_i[r-1]$ and p_i receives a message from p_x during round r (i.e. $x \in recfrom_i[r]$). Let us consider the set $W_i(x)$ computed by p_i at line 5 during round r. Let us observe that a process p_j that does not trust p_x at the end of round $r-1$ sends a pair $(est_j, trusted_j)$ such that $x \notin trusted_j$. Consequently, due to the lemma assumptions, p_i receives at most t $(est, trust)$ messages such that $x \in trust$. As $t < n/2$, we have $t < n-t$, from which it follows that $|\{j : j \in recfrom_i \wedge x \in trust_j\}| < n-t$. As $W_i(x) \subseteq \{j : j \in recfrom_i \wedge x \in trust_j\}$ (line 5), x is removed from $trusted_i$ (line 6) and consequently $x \notin trusted_i[r]$.

$\square_{Lemma\ 7.6}$

Lemma 7.7 Let v be an arbitrary value. $\forall r \geq 1 : |\{x : est_x[r-1] \leq v \wedge x \in Completing[r-1]\}| \geq n-t \Rightarrow \forall i \in Completing[r] : est_i[r] \leq v$.

Proof Let v be a value such that at least $n-t$ processes p_j are such that $est_j[r-1] \leq v$. Let p_j be one of these (at least $n-t$) processes that belongs to $Completing[r]$ and sends a message during r. Let us observe that the pair $(est_j, trusted_j)$ sent during r by p_j is such that $est_j \leq v$.

Let $p_i \in Completing[r]$. Due to the very definition of $Completing[r]$, p_i does not stop by returning $\perp$ at line 8, and consequently, $|trusted_i[r]| \geq n-t$. This implies that the set of the est_j values received by p_i during round r and used to compute its new estimate (at line 8) contains at least $n-t$ values. Due to the "majority of correct processes" assumption ($n-t > t$) and, to the fact that two majorities always intersect, at least one of these est_j is such that $est_j \leq v$. The min() function used by p_i to update est_i at line 8 allows concluding that $est_i[r] \leq v$. $\square_{Lemma\ 7.7}$

Lemma 7.8 $\forall r \geq 0 : EST[r+1] \subseteq EST[r]$.

Proof The lemma follows directly from the fact that, during a round, values can only disappear because (1) the new value of est_i computed by a process is the smallest of values it has received, and (2) some processes may stop sending or receiving messages. $\square_{Lemma\ 7.8}$

Lemma 7.9 Let r ($1 \leq r \leq \lfloor \frac{t}{k} \rfloor + 1$) be a round such that (1) $C \subseteq Completing[r-1]$, and (2) $|EST[r]| > k$ (let v_m denote the kth smallest value in $EST[r]$, i.e., the greatest value among the k smallest values of $EST[r]$). Let $i \in Completing[r]$. We have $n - k\,r < |trusted_i[r]| \Rightarrow est_i[r] \leq v_m$.

Proof Let us first consider the case $r = 1$. As $p_i \in Completing[r]$ and $n - k < |trusted_i[r]|$, p_i misses at most $k-1$ values during the first round. It follows that $est_i[1] \leq v_m$.

The rest of the proof addresses the case $r \geq 2$. To prove the lemma, we prove the contrapositive, namely $est_i[r] > v_m \Rightarrow |trusted_i[r]| \leq n - k\,r$. In the following, r and p_i denote the round number and the processes introduced in the lemma statement. Let us consider the following set of processes:

$$P(v, x) = \{p_\ell : \exists x' \leq x \text{ such that } \ell \in Completing[x'] \wedge est_\ell[x'] \leq v\}$$

where v is a proposed value and x, $0 \leq x \leq \lfloor \frac{t}{k} \rfloor + 1$, a round number. ($P(v, x)$, $x > 0$ is the set of processes that have processed a value $v' \leq v$ during some round $x' \leq x$; $P(v, 0)$ is the set of processes whose initial value is smaller than or equal to v.)

Let $r \geq 1$. We claim $k\, r \leq |P(v_m, r - 1)|$ (Claim *C1*) and $P(v_m, r - 1) \subseteq \Pi - trusted_i[r]$ (Claim *C2*). The lemma follows directly from these claims, as combining *C1* and *C2* we obtain $k\, r \leq |P(v_m, r - 1)| \leq |\Pi - trusted_i[r]|$, from which we conclude that $|trusted_i[r]| \leq n - k\, r$.

The proofs of *C1* and *C2* are based on the following properties (implicitly defined in the context of the assumptions of the lemma, for $r \geq 2$):
Property P1: $\forall\, r' \leq r - 2 : P(v_m, r') \subseteq Silent[r' + 2]$,
Property P2: $\forall\, r' \leq r - 2 : k \leq |P(v_m, r' + 1) - P(v_m, r')|$.
We first prove P1 and P2, and then prove the two claims.

Property P1: $\forall\, r' \leq r - 2 : P(v_m, r') \subseteq Silent[r' + 2]$.
Proof of P1. Let $r' \leq r - 2$. We consider two cases, namely $r' < r - 2$ and $r' = r - 2$.

- $r' < r - 2$. Let $p_x \in P(v_m, r')$. From the definition of the $P(v_m, r')$ set, there is a round $r'' \leq r'$ such that $est_x[r''] \leq v_m$. We claim that, at the end of round $r'' + 1$, at least $n - t$ processes do not trust p_x, which allows us to conclude from Lemma 7.6 that $x \in Silent[r'' + 2]$. The fact that $Silent[r'' + 2] \subseteq Silent[r' + 2]$ completes the proof.

  Proof of the Claim. Let p_c be a correct process that has not decided by the end of round $r - 1$. Due to the lemma assumptions, such a correct process does exist. In order to obtain a contradiction, let us suppose that p_c trusts p_x at the end of round $r'' + 1$ (i.e., $x \in trusted_c[r'' + 1]$). This implies that p_c receives and processes a message $(est_x, -)$ from p_x during round $r'' + 1$, and due to the min() function used to compute a new estimate, we have $est_c[r'' + 1] \leq v_m$.

  Let us observe that (O1) all the correct processes have started the round r (by assumption), (O2) a correct process is trusted by every correct process (Lemma 7.5 and O1), and (O3) a correct process p_y is such that $\forall d, d' : d' < d \Rightarrow est_y[d] \leq est_y[d']$ (this is because a correct process always receives and processes a message from itself).

  Let p_y a correct process. As p_y trusts p_c at round $r'' + 2$ (Observation O2), p_c sends an estimate $v \leq v_m$ during round $r'' + 2$, and due to the min() function used to compute a new estimate, we have $est_y[r'' + 2] \leq v_m$. Moreover, until it decides, p_y is then such that $est_y \leq v_m$ (Observation O3). In particular, at the end of the round $r - 1$, every correct process p_y is such that $est_y[r - 1] \leq v_m$.

  Moreover, as there are at least $n - t$ correct processes that belong to $Completing[r - 1]$ (lemma assumption), it follows from Lemma 7.7 that all the processes p_y that belong to $Completing[r]$ are such that $est_y[r] \leq v_m$. As p_i belongs to $Completing[r]$ (lemma assumption), we have $est_i[r] \leq v_m$: a contradiction (remind that the proof assumes initially that

$est_i[r] > v_m$). Thus, at the end of round $r'' + 1$, for each correct process p_c, $x \notin trusted_c[r'' + 1]$. As at least $n - t$ correct processes belong to $Completing[r'' + 1]$, we conclude that $n - t$ processes do not trust p_x at the end of round $r'' + 1$. End of proof of the Claim.

- $r' = r - 2$. Let $p_x \in P(v_m, r') - P(v_m, r' - 1)$ (if $p_x \in P(v_m, r' - 1)$, the previous case applies). As $i \in Completing[r]$ and $est_i[r] > v_m$, taking the contrapositive of Lemma 7.7, we obtain $|\{y : y \in Completing[r - 1] \wedge est_y[r - 1] \le v_m\}| < n - t$. It follows that, even if p_x sends $est_x[r - 2] \le v_m$ during $r - 1$, strictly less than $n - t$ processes receive and process that message from p_x during $r - 1$. This implies that $|\{y : x \in trusted_y[r - 1]\}| < n - t$, from which we conclude by applying Lemma 7.6, that $x \in Silent[r]$. End of proof of property P1.

Property P2: $\forall 0 \le r' \le r - 2 : k \le |P(v_m, r' + 1) - P(v_m, r')|$.

Proof of P2. Let r' be a round number, $0 \le r' \le r - 2$ and $p_x \in P(v_m, r')$. From property $P1$, we know that $p_x \in Silent[r' + 2]$. Thus, during $r' + 2$, any process $p_j \in Completing[r' + 2]$ (possibly including p_x itself) ignore the round $r' + 1$ estimate of p_x (i.e., $est_x[r' + 1]$) to compute $est_j[r' + 2]$. It follows that, if all the processes p_j such that $est_j[r' + 1] \le v_m$ were such that $p_j \in P(v_m, r')$, then no value $v \le v_m$ would belong to $EST[r' + 2]$. This means that the only possibility for such values to belong to $EST[r' + 2]$, is to be adopted during $r' + 1$ by some $p_y \notin P(v_m, r')$.

As $EST[r] \subseteq EST[r' + 2]$ (Lemma 7.8), and $EST[r]$ contains k values smaller than or equal to v_m (lemma assumption), we can conclude that $EST[r' + 2]$ contains at least k values smaller than or equal to v_m. It follows that, during round $r' + 1$, at least k processes p_j such that $p_j \in Completing[r' + 1] \wedge p_j \notin P(v_m, r')$ adopt an estimate smaller than or equal to v_m. This implies that $|P(v_m, r' + 1) - P(v_m, r')| \ge k$. End of proof of Property P2.

Claim C1: $k\, r \le |P(v_m, r - 1)|$.

Proof of C1. The proof is by induction on the round number r'.

- Base case $r' = 1$: By assumption, there are k distinct values smaller than or equal to v_m in $EST[r]$. As no new value appears in a round, at least k distinct values smaller than or equal to v_m were initially proposed, it follows that $k \le |P(v_m, 0)|$.

- Induction case: $k\, r' \le |P(v_m, r' - 1)|$ is satisfied for $1 \le r' < r$.
  As $k \le |P(v_m, r') - P(v_m, r' - 1)|$ (Property $P2$) and as $P(v_m, r' - 1) \subseteq P(v_m, r')$ (from the definition of the $P(v, x)$ sets), we have $k + |P(v_m, r' - 1)| \le |P(v_m, r')|$ (A).

  Combining $k(r - 1) \le |P(v_m, r - 2)|$ (induction assumption) with A, we obtain $k\, r \le |P(v_m, r - 1)|$. End of proof of Claim C1.

Claim C2: $P(v_m, r - 1) \subseteq \Pi - trusted_i[r]$.

Proof of C2. The claim is trivially satisfied if $trusted_i[r] = \emptyset$. In the other case, let us observe that, as $p_i \in Completing[r]$, we have $Silent[r] \subseteq \Pi - trusted_i[r]$ (see the notations defined at the beginning of Section 7.3.3). Combining this inclusion with $P(v_m, r-2) \subseteq Silent[r]$ (Property $P1$), we obtain $P(v_m, r-2) \subseteq \Pi - sender_i[r]$ (B).

Due to the property $P2$, the set $P(v_m, r-1) - P(v_m, r-2)$ has at least k elements. Hence, it is not empty. Let $p_x \in P(v_m, r-1) - P(v_m, r-2)$. We consider two cases. If p_x does not send a message to p_i or p_i fails to receive the message of p_x during r, we have $x \notin recfrom_i[r]$ which implies $x \in \Pi - trusted_i[r]$ (line 6). If p_x sends a message to p_i in round r, it sends $v = est_x[r-1] \leq v_m$. Due to the min() function used to compute its new estimate (line 8) and the fact that p_i is such that $est_i[r] > v_m$, p_i does not process v during r. It follows that $x \in \Pi - trusted_i[r]$. So, for each process p_x such that $p_x \in P(v_m, r-1) - P(v_m, r-2)$, we always have $x \in \Pi - trusted_i[r]$ (C). Combining B and C, we obtain $P(v_m, r-1) \subseteq \Pi - trusted_i[r]$ which proves the claim.
End of proof of Claim C2.
$\hfill \square_{Lemma\ 7.9}$

7.6.2   PROOFS OF THE LEMMAS FOR THE CASE $t < \frac{k}{k+1}n$

Lemma 7.12 $\forall r \geq 0 : EST[r+1] \subseteq EST[r]$.

Proof The lemma follows directly from the fact that, during a round, values can only disappear because (1) the new value of est_i computed by a process is the smallest of values it has received, and (2) some processes may stop sending or receiving messages.
$\hfill \square_{Lemma\ 7.12}$

Lemma 7.13 $|EST[1]| \leq t + 1$.

Proof Let $v_{min} = \min\{est_i[0], i \in C\}$. The proof uses the following sets of processes/values:
$\mathcal{F}_- = \{i \in \Pi - C : est_i[0] < v_{min}\}$,
$\mathcal{F}_+ = \{i \in \Pi - C : est_i[0] > v_{min}\}$,
$V_- = \{v : \exists i \in \mathcal{F}_- \text{ such that } v = est_i[0]\}$,
$V_+ = \{v : \exists i \in \mathcal{F}_+ \text{ such that } v = est_i[0]\}$.
$\mathcal{F}_-$ (resp., $\mathcal{F}_+$) is the set of faulty processes that propose a value strictly smaller (resp., strictly greater) than v_{min}. V_- (resp., V_+) is the set of values strictly smaller (resp., strictly greater) than v_{min} that are proposed by faulty processes.

Let p_i be a correct process. During the first round, it receives and processes all the values proposed by the correct processes. As a process updates its estimate by taking the smallest value it has received (line 5), we have $est_i[1] \leq v_{min}$. It follows that p_i can update its estimate only to v_{min} or a value sent by a process $p_j : j \in \mathcal{F}_-$, i.e., $\{est_i[1] : i \in C\} \subseteq \{v_{min}\} \cup V_-$ (O1).

Let $i \in \mathcal{F}_-$. As $est_i[0] < v_{min}$, p_i can update its estimate only to a value received from a process that belong to $\mathcal{F}_-$. This implies that $\{est_i[1] : i \in \mathcal{F}_-\} \subseteq V_-$ (O2).

Let $i \in \mathcal{F}_+$. In that case, p_i can adopt a value from any process in Π. It follows that, at the end of the first round, there are at most $|\mathcal{F}_+|$ distinct values among the processes that belong to $\mathcal{F}_+$ (O3). From (O1) and (O2), we obtain: $\{est_i[1] : i \in C \cup \mathcal{F}_-\} \subseteq \{v_{min}\} \cup V_-$. Moreover, we have

$|V_-| \leq |F_-|$ (O4). From (O3), (O4) and the fact that $|F_-| + |\mathcal{F}_+| \leq t$, we conclude that at the end of the first round we have $|\{est_i[1] : i \in Completing[1]\}| \leq t + 1$. $\square_{Lemma\ 7.13}$

Lemma 7.14 $\forall r, 1 \leq r \leq t - k + 2$, we have $|EST[r]| \leq t - r + 2$.

Proof The proof is by induction on the round number r. For all r, $1 \leq r \leq t - k + 2$, let $HR(r)$ be the predicate $|EST[r]| \leq t - r + 2$. The base case of the induction (i.e., $HR(1)$) follows directly from Lemma 7.13 So, considering the induction assumption (namely, $HR(x)$ is satisfied for all x such that $1 \leq x < r$), we prove that $HR(r)$ is satisfied. Let us first observe that if $|EST[r - 1]| < t - (r - 1) + 2$, $HR(r)$ follows directly from Lemma 7.12 as $|EST[r]| \leq |EST[r - 1]| \leq t - r + 2$. So, the rest of the proof assumes $|EST[r - 1]| = t - (r - 1) + 2 = t - r + 3$.

In the following, we consider a particular value $v_m \in EST[r - 1]$ and the set of processes that have an estimate equal to v_m at the end of the round $r - 1$. The value v_m is defined as follows:

$$v_m = \max\{v : |P_=(v, r - 1)| < n - t\}$$

(among the values of $EST[r - 1]$, v_m is the greatest one that is the estimate of less than $n - t$ processes that complete the round $r - 1$).

We claim that v_m exists (Claim C1) and $v_m \notin EST[r]$ (Claim C2). Assuming these claims, it follows from $v_m \in EST[r - 1]$, and $|EST[r - 1]| = t - r + 3$ (Case assumption), that $|EST[r]| = t - r + 2$, which proves $HR(r)$, from which the Lemma follows. The rest of the proof concerns the claims C1 and C2.

Claim C1: $\exists v$ such that $|P_=(v, r - 1)| < n - t$.
Proof of the Claim C1. As $r \leq t - k + 2$ (Lemma assumption), we have $t - r + 2 \geq k$. Combining this with $|EST[r - 1]| = t - r + 3$ (Case assumption), we obtain $|EST[r - 1]| > k$.

We now show the existence of v by contradiction. Let us suppose that each value $v' \in EST[r - 1]$ is such that $|P_=(v', r - 1)| \geq n - t$ (i.e., there are at least $n - t$ copies of each value present in the system at the end of round $r - 1$). As $|EST[r - 1]| > k$ and at most n processes complete round $r - 1$, the inequality $n \geq (k + 1)(n - t)$ must hold. Thus, $(k + 1)t \geq (k + 1)n - n$ from which we obtain that $t \geq \frac{kn}{k+1}$. This contradicts the upper bound on t, namely, $\frac{kn}{k+1} > t$. End of Proof of Claim C1.

Claim C2: $v_m \notin EST[r]$.
Proof of Claim C2. If $est_i[0] = v$, we say "p_i learns v during the (fictitious) round 0". More generally, for $d \geq 1$, we say "p_i learns v during round d" if p_i (1) completes the round d, (2) has never received v by the end of round $d - 1$, and (3) has an estimate equal to v at the end of round d. This means that (1) $i \in Completing[d]$, (2) $\forall d' < d : est_i[d'] > v$ and, (3) $est_i[d] = v$. We consider two cases: no process learns v_m during round $r - 1$ (case 1); a process learns v_m during

round $r - 1$ (case 2).

Case 1: No process learns v_m during $r - 1$.
We claim (Sub-claim C2.1) $est_i[r] = v_m \Rightarrow |trusted_i[r]| < n - t$. The proof that $v_m \notin EST[r]$ follows directly from this claim as then a process p_i that sets its estimate to v_m after having executed the lines 4-8 during round r necessarily returns $\perp$ at line 9. This implies that any process p_i that completes round r is such that $est_i[r] \neq v_m$, i.e., $v_m \notin EST[r]$.

The proof of C2.1 is based on the following properties (implicitly defined in the context of the case assumption):
Property P1: $\forall i \in P_>(v_m, r - 1) : P_=(v_m, r - 1) \subseteq \Pi - trusted_i[r - 1]$.
This property states that any process p_x completing the round $r - 1$ with an estimate value equal to v_m, is not trusted by any process p_i that completes the round $r - 1$ with an estimate value greater than v_m.
Property P2: $(x \in Completing[r]) \wedge (est_x[r] = v_m) \Rightarrow x \in P_=(v_m, r - 1)$.
This property states that any process p_x completing the round r with an estimate value equal to v_m, was such that $est_x[r - 1] = v_m$.
We prove first P1 and P2, and then C2.1.

Property P1: $\forall i \in P_>(v_m, r - 1) : P_=(v_m, r - 1) \subseteq \Pi - trusted_i[r - 1]$.
Proof of P1. Let $i \in P_>(v_m, r - 1)$ and $x \in P_=(v_m, r - 1)$. Let us first observe that it follows from the fact that no process learns v_m during round $r - 1$ that $P_=(v_m, r - 1) \subseteq P_=(v_m, r - 2)$. Consequently, $x \in P_=(v_m, r - 2)$ and thus a message sent by p_x during round $r - 1$ carries $v_m (= est_x[r - 2])$ (line 3).

As $est_i[r - 1] > v_m$ and p_x sends v_m during round $r - 1$, it follows from the min() function used to compute new estimates (line 5) that either p_i does not receive the message from p_x during round $r - 1$ or p_i does not trust p_x at the beginning of round $r - 1$. In both cases, p_i does not trust p_x at the end of round $r - 1$, i.e., $x \in \Pi - trusted_i[r - 1]$. End of Proof of P1.

Property P2: $(x \in Completing[r]) \wedge (est_x[r] = v_m) \Rightarrow x \in P_=(v_m, r - 1)$.
Proof of P2. Let $x \in Completing[r]$ such that $est_x[r] = v_m$. Due to the min() function used by a process to update its estimate (line 5), $x \notin P_<(v_m, r - 1)$ (1).

Consider now a process p_i that belongs to $P_>(v_m, r - 1)$. Let us observe that only the processes in $P_=(v_m, r - 1)$ can send v_m during the round r. Due to property P1, when p_i completes the round $r - 1$, it does not trust the processes belonging to $P_=(v_m, r - 1)$. Consequently, p_i does not consider the messages sent during the round r by the processes in $P_=(v_m, r - 1)$. It follows that $est_i[r] \neq v_m$, from which we conclude that $x \notin P_>(v_m, r - 1)$ (2).

As the sets $P_<(v_m, r - 1)$, $P_=(v_m, r - 1)$ and $P_>(v_m, r - 1)$ define a partition of $Completing[r - 1]$, and $x \in Completing[r] \subseteq Completing[r - 1]$, it follows from (1) and (2) that $x \in P_=(v_m, r - 1)$. End of Proof of P2.

Claim C2.1: $est_x[r] = v_m \Rightarrow |trusted_x[r]| < n - t$.

Proof of Claim C2.1. Let $x \in Completing[r]$ such that $est_x[r] = v_m$. Let us first consider a process p_i that belongs to $P_<(v_m, r - 1)$. If p_i sends messages during round r, these messages necessarily carry a value $< v_m$ (line 3). Since $est_x[r] = v_m$, either p_x does not receive this message from p_i (lines 5-7) or p_x does not trust p_i at the beginning of round r. In both cases, we have $i \notin trusted_x[r]$, from which we conclude that $P_<(v_m, r - 1) \subseteq \Pi - trusted_x[r]$ (1).

Let now p_i be a process that belongs to $P_>(v_m, r - 1)$. Due to property P2, $x \in P_=(v_m, r - 1)$. Consequently, $x \notin trusted_i[r - 1]$ (property P1). This implies that p_i does not send a message to p_x during round r (line 3). Thus, $i \notin trusted_x[r]$. Since this holds for any process that belongs to $P_>(v_m, r - 1)$, we have $P_>(v_m, r - 1) \subseteq \Pi - trusted_x[r]$ (2).

By combining (1) et (2), we obtain $trusted_x[r] \subseteq \Pi - (P_<(v_m, r - 1) \cup P_>(v_m, r - 1))$. Moreover, as only processes that belong to $Completing[r - 1]$ may send messages during round r, it follows from the fact that the sets $P_<(v_m, r - 1)$, $P_=(v_m, r - 1)$ and $P_>(v_m, r - 1)$ define a partition of $Completing[r - 1]$ that $trusted_x[r] \subseteq P_=(v_m, r - 1)$. Finally, due to the definition of v_m, we have $|P_=(v_m, r - 1)| < n - t$ from which we conclude that $trusted_x[r]| < n - t$. End of Proof of Claim C2.1.
End of Proof of Case 1 of Claim C2.

Case 2: There is a process that learns v_m during round $r - 1$.
We claim (Claim C2.2), in the case assumptions, $v_m = \max(EST[r - 1])$. We prove by contradiction that $v_m \notin EST[r]$. Let us assume that there is a process p_x such that $x \in Completing[r] \wedge est_x[r] = v_m$. Due to the min() function used by p_x to update its estimate (line 5), p_x receives during round r from the processes it trusts only values $\geq v_m$. As (1) only processes that belong to $P_\geq(v_m, r - 1)$ can send values $\geq v_m$ during round r and (2) $P_\geq(v_m, r - 1) = P_=(v_m, r - 1)$ (Claim C2.2), p_x can only trust processes that belong to $P_=(v_m, r - 1)$. Moreover, due to the very definition of v_m, $|P_=(v_m, r - 1)| < n - t$. This implies that $|trusted_x[r]| < n - t$ from which we conclude that p_x returns $\perp$ at line 10: a contradiction with $x \in Completing[r]$.

Claim C2.2: $v_m = \max(EST[r - 1])$. (Let us remind that, in the context of this claim, $|EST[r - 1]| = t - r + 3$ and at least one process learns v_m during $r - 1$.)
Proof of Claim C2.2. Let $\alpha = |\{v : v \in EST[r - 1] \wedge v < v_m\}|$ and, $\beta = |\{v : v \in EST[r - 1] \wedge v > v_m\}|$. To prove that v_m is the greatest value in $EST[r - 1]$, the rest of the proof establishes $\beta = 0$. Let us notice that $|EST[r - 1]| = \alpha + \beta + 1 = t - r + 3$.

Let us define three sets of processes, denoted A, B and C, as follows:

- Let $A = \{i : est_i[0] < v_m\}$. A is the set of processes that propose a value strictly smaller than v_m. Since values can only disappear while rounds progress (Lemma 7.12), clearly $|A| \geq \alpha$.

- Let $B = \{i : est_i[r-1] > v_m \quad \wedge \quad i \in Completing[r-1]\}$ (or $B = \bigcup_{v \in EST[r-1] \wedge v > v_m} P_=(v, r-1)$). B is the set of processes that have an estimate strictly greater than v_m at the end of round $r-1$. Due to the very definition of v_m, for each $v \in EST[r-1]$ such that $v > v_m$, we have $|P_=(v, r-1)| \geq n - t$. It follows that $|B| \geq \beta(n-t)$.

- Let p_x be a process that learns v_m during round $r-1$. We claim (Claim C2.3) that there is a chain of r distinct processes $p_{v_m(0)}, \ldots, p_{v_m(r-1)}(= p_x)$ such that $\forall \ell : 1 \leq \ell \leq r-1 : p_{v_m(\ell)}$ learns v_m at round ℓ from $p_{v_m(\ell-1)}$ (hence, $est_{v_m(\ell)}[\ell] = v_m$). The set C is the set of processes that participate in the chain that carries v_m to p_x. More precisely, $C = \{v(0), \ldots, v(r-1) = x\}$. We clearly have $|C| = r$.

We now show that any pair of sets A, B and C has an empty intersection.

- $A \cap B = \emptyset$ and $A \cap C = \emptyset$.
  Let $a \in A$ ($est_a[0] < v_m$) and $x \in B \cup C$. There is a round $d \leq r-1$ such that $est_x[d] \geq v_m$ (O1). (This follows from the following observations. If $x \in B$, taking $d = r-1$ establishes (O1). If $x \in C$, (O1) follows from the definition of the set C, namely, p_x learns v_m during some round $d \leq r-1$, at the end of which $est_x[d] = v_m$.)

  It follows from (O1) and the relation $\forall \ell, \ell' : 0 \leq \ell < \ell' \leq r-1 \Rightarrow est_x[\ell] \geq est_x[\ell']$ that $est_x[0] \geq v_m$. Consequently, as $est_a[0] < v_m$ (definition A), we have $A \cap B = \emptyset$ and $A \cap C = \emptyset$.

- $B \cap C = \emptyset$.
  Let p_x be a process that belongs to C. If $x \notin Completing[r-1], x \notin B$ (a process that belongs to B completes round $r-1$). If $x \in Completing[r-1]$, as there is a round $\ell, 1 \leq \ell \leq r-1$, such that $est_x[\ell] = v_m$, and due to the min() function an estimate value can only decrease, we have $est_x[r-1] \leq v_m$. Consequently, as every process p_y that belongs to B is such that $est_y[r-1] > v_m$, we have $x \notin B$, from which we conclude that $B \cap C = \emptyset$.

We have established the following relations:

- (1) $A \cap B = \emptyset$, $A \cap C = \emptyset$ and $B \cap C = \emptyset$,

- (2) $|A| \geq \alpha$, $|B| \geq \beta(n-t)$ and $|C| = r$,

- (3) $\alpha + \beta + 1 = t - r + 3$.

By combining (1) and (2) we obtain: $n \geq \alpha + \beta(n-t) + r$, i.e., $n - \beta(n-t) - r \geq \alpha$. The last inequality combined with (3) gives $n - \beta(n-t) - r \geq t - r + 3 - \beta - 1$ from which we have: $n - t - 1 > \beta(n - t - 1)$, which implies $\beta = 0$. Since β is the number of values greater than v_m in $EST[r-1]$, it follows that v_m is the greatest value that belongs to $EST[r-1]$. End of Proof of Claim C2.2.

Claim C2.3: Let p_i be a process that learns a value v at round $d \geq 1$. There is a chain of $d+1$ distinct processes $p_{v(0)}, \ldots, p_{v(d)}(= p_i)$ such that $\forall \ell, 1 \leq \ell \leq d : p_{v(\ell)}$ learns v at round ℓ from $p_{v(\ell-1)}$.

Proof of Claim C2.3. We prove the claim by induction on d. Base case: $d = 1$. Suppose that a process p_i learns a value v during the first round. Then, a process $p_{v(0)}$ has sent v to p_i during that round. It follows that there are two distinct processes p_i and $p_{v(0)}$ such that $p_{v(0)}$ learned v during the round 0 and p_i learns it during the first round.

Induction case: $d > 1$. Suppose the claim holds for $1 \leq d' < d$. Let p_i be a process that learns a value v at round d from some process p_x. During the round d, p_i can process messages only from processes it has never suspected from the first round until the round $d-1$ (included). It follows that p_i has received a message from p_x at each round $1, \ldots, d-1$. Since a process that learns a value during a round forwards that value during the next round, we conclude that p_x learnt v at round $d-1$. By applying the induction hypothesis to p_x, we conclude that there is a chain of $d+1$ distinct processes that participated in forwarding the value v to p_i (that learns it at round d).

End of Proof of Claim C2.3.

End of Proof of Case 2 of Claim C2.

$\square$ *Lemma 7.14*

CHAPTER 8

Consensus Despite Byzantine Failures

This chapter addresses the interactive consistency problem and the consensus problem in a system where processes can be Byzantine, i.e., can behave in an arbitrary way.

A simple interactive consistency algorithm is first presented that works for $n = 4$ processes, one of them being potentially Byzantine. The chapter then shows that $n > 3t$ is an upper bound on the maximal number of processes that may be faulty when one wants to solve the consensus (or interactive consistency) problem in a synchronous round-based model. This upper bound has to be compared with the corresponding bounds for the crash failure model and the omission failure models (see Table 8.1).

Table 8.1: Upper bounds on the number of faulty processes (Consensus problem)	
Failure model	Upper bound
Crash failure	$t < n$
Send omission failure	$t < n$
General omission failure	$t < n/2$
Byzantine failure	$t < n/3$

The chapter presents then two algorithms that solve the Byzantine consensus problem. The first algorithm is optimal with respect to the value of t (i.e., $t < n/3$) and the number of rounds (namely, $t + 1$), but it requires messages, the number of which increases exponentially with respect to t. Differently, the second algorithm uses constant size message but assumes $t < n/4$ and requires $2(t + 1)$ rounds.

8.1 INTERACTIVE CONSISTENCY FOR 4 PROCESSES DESPITE ONE BYZANTINE PROCESS

This section presents a simple algorithm that solves the interactive consistency (IC) problem in a set of $n = 4$ processes in which one of them ($t = 1$) can be Byzantine.

Let us remember that in the Byzantine IC problem each process proposes a value and the correct processes have to agree on the same vector $D[1..n]$, this vector being such that $D[i] = v_i$ if p_i is a correct process.

In the crash failure model or the omission failure model, the text of an algorithm is for any process p_i. A process fails by stopping prematurely or omitting to send or receive messages only. Differently, in the Byzantine failure model, as a faulty process can behave arbitrarily, the algorithm that is described is only for correct processes.

8.1.1   AN ALGORITHM FOR $n = 4$ AND $t = 1$

Let p_1, p_2, p_3 and p_4 be the four processes. The aim of every correct process p_i is to compute a local vector $view_i[1..4]$ such that $view_i[1..4] = D[1..4]$. As in previous algorithms, $\perp$ is a default value that cannot be proposed by a process.

Local variables   To that end, each process p_i manages two local arrays.

- $rec1_i[1..4]$ is a one-dimensional array; $rec1_i[j]$ is destined to contain the value proposed by p_j, as known by p_i. If p_i does not know it, we have $rec1_i[j] = \perp$. Otherwise, $rec1_i[j] = v$ means "p_j has said to p_i that its proposed value is v".

- $rec2_i[1..4, 1..4]$ is a two-dimensional array whose meaning is the following: $rec2_i[x, j] = v$ means "p_x has told p_i that p_j sent it value v".

```
operation  propose (v_i):
(1)  when r = 1 do
     begin synchronous round
(2)      broadcast EST1(v_i):
(3)      for each j ∈ {1, 2, 3, 4} do
(4)          if (a value v has been received from p_j) then rec1_i[j] ← v else rec1_j[j] ← ⊥ end if
(5)      end for
     end synchronous round;
(6)  when r = 2 do
     begin synchronous round
(7)      broadcast EST2(rec1_i):
(8)      for each j ∈ {1, 2, 3, 4} do
(9)          if (an array rec1_j has been received from p_j) then rec2_i[j] ← rec1_j else rec2_i[j] ← [⊥, ⊥, ⊥, ⊥] end if;
(10)     end for;
(11)     for each j ∈ {1, 2, 3, 4} do
(12)         let a, b and c the three values in rec2_i[x, j] with x ≠ j;
(13)         if (there is a majority value v in a, b and c) then view_i[j] ← v else view_j[1] ← ⊥ end if
(14)     end for;
(15)     return(view_i)
     end synchronous round.
```

Figure 8.1: Interactive consistency for 4 processes despite one Byzantine process (code for p_i)

Behavior of a (correct) process   The algorithm is described in Figure 8.1. Each process p_i executes two rounds. During the first round p_i first broadcasts the value it proposes (message EST1(v_i), line 2). Then, if it receives a value v from process p_j, it updates $rec1_i[j]$ to v; otherwise, it assigns $\perp$ to $rec1_i[j]$.

During the second round, each process p_i broadcasts what it has learnt during the first round (message EST2($rec1_i$), line 7). Then, if it receives a vector $rec1_j$ from p_j, is updates $rec2_i[j]$ (i.e., line j of the two-dimensional array $rec2_i[1..4, 1..4]$). Otherwise, it assigns the default vector $[\perp, \perp, \perp, \perp]$ to $rec2_i[j]$ (line 9). Finally, according to the values in the array $rec2_i$, p_i computes the value of the vector $view_i$ returned as local output.

The value of $view_i[j]$ is computed as follows. Let $\{x1, x2, x3\} = \{1, 2, 3, 4\} \setminus \{j\}$, and $rec2_i[x1, j] = a, rec2_i[x2, j] = b$, and $rec2_i[x3, j] = c$. As an example, $rec2_i[x1, j] = a$ means that a is the value that p_{x1} has received from p_j during the first round and then forwarded to p_i during the second round. If p_{x1} has not received a value from p_j during the first round or has not send a message to p_i during the second round, $a = \perp$. If there is a majority value v among a, b and c (i.e., at least two of a, b and c are equal to v), p_i assigns v to $view_i[j]$. Otherwise, it assigns it the default value $\perp$.

As we are about to see, if p_j is correct, v is the value it has proposed. On the contrary, if $view_i[j] = \perp$, then p_i is faulty. Let us observe that p_j can be faulty while we have $view_i[j] = v$ (in that case, it is possible that the faulty process p_j sent v to some process and v' to another one).

8.1.2   PROOF OF THE ALGORITHM

Theorem 8.1   *The algorithm described in Figure 8.1 solves the interactive consistency problem in a round-based synchronous model made up of 4 processes in which one of them can have a Byzantine behavior.*

Proof The termination property follows directly from the synchrony assumption.

Proving the validity property consists in showing that, for any two correct processes p_i and p_j, we have $view_i[j] = v_j$ (where v_j is the value proposed by p_j). In addition to p_i, let p_k and p_ℓ be two distinct correct processes (these processes exist by assumption). As p_i, p_k, p_ℓ and p_j are correct (p_j is one of p_i, p_k or p_ℓ, or the fourth process if it is correct), it follows from the algorithm that:

- $rec1_i[j] = rec1_k[j] = rec1_\ell[j] = v_j$ at the end of the first round, and
- $rec2_i[i, j] = rec2_i[k, j] = rec2_i[\ell, j] = v_j$, at the end of the second round.

Let us consider the three values a, b and c obtained by suppressing $rec2_i[j, j]$ from $rec2_i[1, j]$, $rec2_i[2, j]$, $rec2_i[3, j]$ and $rec2_i[4, j]$ (line 12). It follows from the previous observation that at least two of these values are equal to v_j. Hence, $view_i[j] = v_j$ (line 13), which completes the proof of the validity property.

For the agreement property we have to show that if p_i and p_k are two correct processes, then $\forall j : view_i[j] = view_k[j]$. If p_j is correct, the proof follows from the validity property where it has been shown that $view_i[j] = v_j$ and $view_k[j] = v_j$ as soon as p_i, p_k and p_j are correct.

Hence, let us assume that p_j is a faulty process. Let p_x denote the third process that, in addition to p_i and p_k, is correct. If $view_i[j] = view_k[j] = view_x[j] = \bot$, the agreement property follows. Hence, let consider that some process (e.g., p_k) computes $view_k[j] = v \neq \bot$. This means that at least two of the values in $rec2_k[i, j]$, $rec2_k[k, j]$ and $rec2_k[x, j]$ are equal to v. Let us consider two cases.

- Case 1 (left part of Figure 8.2). During the second round, process p_k has received $v \neq \bot$ from both p_i and p_x. This means that, as p_i is correct, we have $rec1_i[j] = v$ and p_i sent v to both p_k and p_x during the second round. We can also conclude that, as p_x is correct, we have $rec1_x[j] = v$ and p_x sent it to both p_k and p_i during the second round.

  It follows that p_i is such that $rec2_i[i, j] = rec2_i[x, j] = v$, i.e., v appears at least twice in $rec2_i[i, j]$, $rec2_i[k, j]$ and $rec2_i[x, j]$. Then, due to lines 12-13, p_i assigns v to $view_i[j]$, which concludes the case.

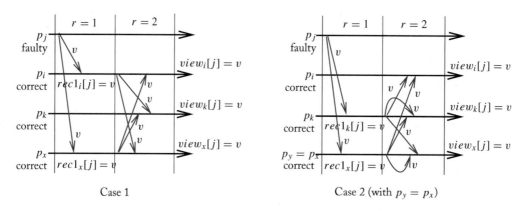

Case 1   Case 2 (with $p_y = p_x$)

Figure 8.2: Proof of the interactive consistency algorithm with $n = 4$ and $t = 1$

- Case 2 (right part of Figure 8.2). During the second round, process p_k has received $v \neq \bot$ from only one of p_i and p_x (say p_y where $y = i$ or $y = x$). Hence, we have $rec2_k[y, j] = rec1_y[j] = v$. As $view_k[j] = v \neq \bot$, it follows from lines 12-13 that p_k has received $v \neq \bot$ from at least two processes (different from p_j), from which we conclude that it has received $rec1_k[j] = v$ from itself and consequently $rec2_k[k, j] = rec1_k[j] = v$. As p_i is correct, it has received $rec1_y[j] = v$ and $rec1_k[j] = v$ and we have $rec2_i[y, j] = rec2_i[y, j] = v$. Hence, p_i is such that $rec2_i[y, j] = rec2_i[k, j] = v$, and it assigns v to $view_i[j]$, which concludes the proof of the agreement property.

$\square$ _Theorem_ 8.1

8.2   AN UPPER BOUND ON THE NUMBER OF BYZANTINE PROCESSES

This section presents a fundamental result related to Byzantine failures, namely, it is impossible to solve the interactive consistency problem (and the consensus problem) in a synchronous system made up of n processes where up to t can be Byzantine when $t \geq n/3$.

This impossibility is proved in two steps. First, a lemma shows that there is no synchronous consensus algorithm for $n = 3$ processes when one of them is Byzantine. Then, a theorem extends the result to n processes where $n \leq 3t$. This theorem is based on a classical simulation-based problem reduction.

Preliminary remark   Clearly, the processes have to exchange messages. The content of a message is under the control of its sender. As the underlying network is fully connected (every pair of processes is a bi-directional channel), a process can (only) check which is the sender of a message.

Lemma 8.2   *There is no algorithm that solves the interactive consistency (or consensus) problem in a synchronous system composed of 3 processes, where one of them can have a Byzantine behavior.*

Proof The proof is by contradiction. Let us assume that there is an algorithm A that solves the problem for 3 processes p_1, p_2 and p_3, one of them being Byzantine. Without loss of generality, let us also suppose that the values that can be proposed are 1 and 0. Moreover, to be as general as possible, each process is assumed to have an "infinite" computational power in the sense that it is a Turing machine that can execute any local computation in 0 time unit (only communication takes times).

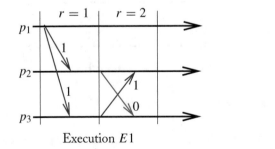
Execution $E1$

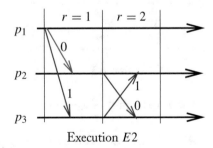
Execution $E2$

Figure 8.3: Impossibility of agreement for 3 processes one of which is Byzantine (1)

Let us consider the two executions depicted in Figure 8.3 where, considering the interactive consistency problem, we focus on the value proposed by process p_1.

- Execution $E1$. In that execution, process p_1 and p_3 are correct, while process p_2 is Byzantine. Moreover, p_1 proposes value 1 and consequently sends that value to p_2 and p_3. During the second round, each of p_2 and p_3 reports to the other what it has received from p_1. Hence, p_3

sends to p_2 a message saying "during the first round p_1 told me that it has proposed value 1". As far as the Byzantine process p_2 is concerned, it sends to p_3 a message saying "during the first round p_1 told me that it has proposed value 0". (Let us observe that no more round does help because each process has already conveyed what it knows.) As p_1 and p_3 are correct, it follows from the validity property of the algorithm A that we need to have $view_3[1] = 1$.

- Execution $E2$. This execution is similar to execution $E1$, but it is now process p_1 that is Byzantine, while p_2 and p_3 are correct. Process p_1 sends different values to p_2 and p_3. During the second round, p_2 and p_3 exchange what they received form p_1.

In both $E1$ and $E2$, process p_3 has the same local state at the end of the second round (and, as already indicated, no more round can help because each process has already conveyed what it knows.) Hence, p_3 has to decide $view_3[1] = 1$ at the end of the second round of $E2$. Moreover, as p_2 is correct, due to the agreement property of A, we need to have $view_2[1] = 1$ in execution $E2$.

Let us now consider the executions $E3$ and $E4$ depicted in Figure 8.4. Similarly to executions $E1$ and $E2$, the Byzantine process is p_1 in execution $E3$, while it is p_1 in execution $E4$.

When looking execution $E3$, as p_1 and p_2 are correct it follows from the validity property of A that p_2 has to decide $view_2[1] = 0$ (same reasoning as before). Let us now look at execution $E4$ in which the faulty process is p_1. At the end of the second round, process p_2 cannot distinguish if the execution is $E3$ or $E4$. Hence as it decides $view_2[1] = 0$ in $E3$, it has to decide the same in $E4$.

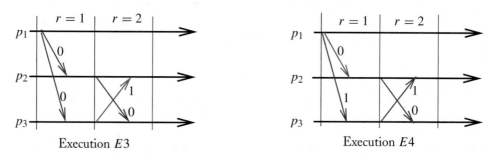

Execution $E3$ Execution $E4$

Figure 8.4: Impossibility of agreement for 3 processes one of which is Byzantine (2)

Let us finally consider the executions $E2$ and $E4$. It is easy to see that they are the very same execution. But, we have shown that p_2 decides $view_2[1] = 1$ in $E2$ and decides $view_2[1] = 0$ in $E4$. As $E2$ and $E4$ are the same execution, this is clearly impossible, from which we conclude that there is no algorithm A that solves interactive consistency for three processes, one of them being Byzantine. (The same kind of reasoning holds for consensus). $\square_{Lemma\ 8.2}$

Theorem 8.3   *There is no algorithm that solves the interactive consistency (or consensus) problem in a synchronous system composed of n processes, where t of them are Byzantine, when $n \leq 3t$.*

Proof Let $ICB(n \leq 3t, t)$ denote the interactive consistency (or consensus) problem in a set of $n \leq 3t$ processes that contains up to t Byzantine processes, and $ICB(3, 1)$ the problem for a set of 3 processes, one of them being a Byzantine process.

The proof is by contradiction. It is based on problem reduction. More specifically, the problem $ICB(3, 1)$ is reduced to $ICB(n \leq 3t, t)$. This means that, if there is an algorithm A that solves $ICB(n \leq 3t, t)$, that algorithm can be used to solve $ICB(3, 1)$. (Let us observe that nothing prevents us from having an algorithm A that would work only for specific values of n et t, e.g., for $n = 9$ and $t = 4$. This means that we cannot assume that it is possible to instantiate A with $n = 3$ and $t = 1$.) Then, as $ICB(3, 1)$ has no solution (Lemma 8.2), it follows that $ICB(n \leq 3t, t)$ cannot have a solution either, which proves the theorem.

The reduction is as follows. Let us partition the n processes into three sets S_1, S_2 and S_3, each of size at most t. Let q_1, q_2 and q_3 be the three processes involved in $ICB(3, 1)$. Each of q_i, $1 \leq i \leq 3$, simulates the execution of A by the (at most) t processes $p_x \in S_i$ (e.g., q_i executes one step of each process $p_x \in S_i$ in a round-robin order). If one process q_i is faulty, then at most t processes p_x are faulty in $ICB(n \leq 3t, t)$. Moreover, a correct process q_i simulates correctly a group of at most t processes p_x, i.e., it simulates correctly the steps (send events, receive events, intra-set and inter-set communication events) of each process $p_x \in S_i$.

It follows from this reduction from $ICB(3, 1)$ to $ICB(n \leq 3t, t)$ that the algorithm A used to solve $ICB(n \leq 3t, t)$ can be used to solve $ICB(3, 1)$. (This can be easily obtained as follows: for every i, the value proposed in A by each process of S_i is the the value proposed by q_i.) Hence, taking the contrapositive of the last statement, we conclude from the fact that $ICB(3, 1)$ cannot be solved, that $ICB(n \leq 3t, t)$ cannot be solved either whatever the values of n and t (as long as these values are such that $n \leq 3t$). $\square_{Theorem\ 8.3}$

8.3 A BYZANTINE INTERACTIVE CONSISTENCY ALGORITHM FOR $n > 3t$

This section presents a general interactive consistency algorithm that meets two bounds, namely (a) the upper bound on the number of processes that can exhibit a Byzantine behavior ($t < n/3$) and (b) the lower bound on the number of rounds ($t + 1$). Differently, as it uses an exponential number of messages, $O(n^t)$, this algorithm is not efficient from a message point of view.

This algorithm is a non-trivial generalization of the particular algorithm presented in section 8.1 that has considered the specific pair $(n, t) = (4, 1)$.

8.3.1 FROM THE BYZANTINE GENERALS PROBLEM TO INTERACTIVE CONSISTENCY

To simplify the presentation, and without loss of generality, we consider that only one process p_j proposes a value and the processes have to agree on that value. This means that we focus only on the variable $view_i[j]$ of each correct process p_i. At the end of the algorithm the local variables $view_i[j]$

and $view_k[j]$ of any pair of correct processes p_i and p_k have to be (a) equal, and (b) equal to v_j (the value proposed by p_j) is p_j is correct.

Byzantine Generals (BG) problem   The previous problem actually consists for the processes to agree on the value proposed by a given predetermined process. As seen in ther first Chapter, this is the *Byzantine Generals* (BG) problem (the process that proposes a value is the *Commander* while the other processes are called its *Lieutenants*).

Let $BG(n, t, j)$ denotes the BG problem where n and t have their usual meaning and j is the identity of the commander process.

Multiplexing n BG instances, one per process, provides us with a solution to the interactive consistency problem, which in turn can be used to solve the consensus problem.

Majority function   The algorithm uses a function majority$(a, b, \ldots, h)$ defined as follows. If there is a value v that appears a majority of times in $a, b, \ldots, h$, then majority$(a, b, \ldots, h)$ returns it. If there is no majority value, majority$(a, b, \ldots, h)$ returns $\perp$. (Let us recall that, if a value v is a majority value in a collection of x values, it appears strictly more than $x/2$ times.)

8.3.2   PRESENTING THE ALGORITHM WITH AN EXAMPLE

Let us consider the pair $(n, t) = (7, 2)$, which means that there are 7 processes $p_1, p_2, p_3, p_4, p_5, p_6$ and p_7, and up to two of them can exhibit Byzantine behavior. Let p_3 be the process that proposes its value (p_3 is the commander while the six other processes are lieutenants). Hence, this problem is $BG(7, 2, 3)$.

In order to agree on the value proposed by p_3, the processes execute $t + 1 = 3$ rounds during which they do the following (see Figure 8.5).

- Round $r = 1$. During that round, p_3 broadcasts to all the value it proposes. The aim is then for the six other processes p_1, p_2, p_4, p_5, p_6 and p_7 to agree on the same value that will be considered as the value sent by p_3. This is done as follows in the next rounds.

- Round $r = 2$. Each of the $n - 1 = 6$ processes p_1, p_2, p_4, p_5, p_6 and p_7 acts as a commander in a separate Byzantine Generals subproblem in which at most $t - 1 = 1$ process(es) are assumed to fail. Hence, there are now $n - 1 = 6$ subproblem instances to be solved, namely, $BG(6, 1, 1), BG(6, 1, 2), BG(6, 1, 4), BG(6, 1, 5), BG(6, 1, 6)$ and $BG(6, 1, 7)$.

  Let $X = \{1, 2, 4, 5, 6, 7\}$ and $x \in X$. Solving problem $BG(6, 1, x)$ will provide each process $p_y, y \in X$, with a value v_x that represents the value that the associated commander process p_x is assumed to have proposed in that instance (if p_x is correct, that value is the value that p_x has received from p_3 in the first round, or the default value $\perp$ if it has received no value from p_3 in the first round).

  When the 6 subproblems $BG(6, 1, x)$, $x \in X$, will have been solved (see the next round), every process $p_y, y \in X$, will be able to compute the value assigned to $view_y[3]$. Let v_y^x be the value obtained by p_y from $BG(6, 1, x)$, $x \in X$. Process p_y will assign to $view_y[3]$ the

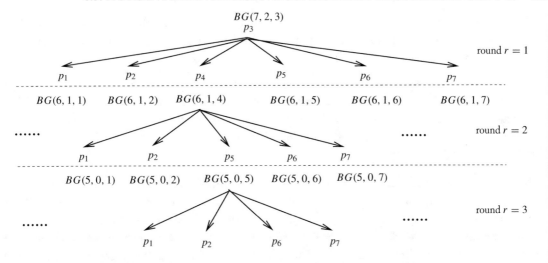

Figure 8.5: Representing an execution with a tree (partially described)

value majority(v_y^1, v_y^2, v_y^4, v_y^5, v_y^6, v_y^7). This is the value that p_y considers as being the value proposed by p_3. As we will in the proof, for any pair of correct processes p_y and p_z we have majority(v_y^1, v_y^2, v_y^4, v_y^5, v_y^6, v_y^7)= majority(v_z^1, v_z^2, v_z^4, v_z^5, v_z^6, v_z^7). Moreover, this is the value proposed by p_3 if it is correct.

- Round $r = t + 1 = 3$. For each $x \in X$, let $X_x = X \setminus \{3, x\}$. During that round, each of $n - 1 = 6$ subproblem instances $BG(6, 1, x), x \in X$, generates $n - 2 = 5$ sub-subproblem instances $BG(5, 0, x'), x' \in X_x$, which means that we have then $6 \times 5 = 30$ problem instances (see round 3 in Figure 8.5).

In each subproblem $BG(5, 0, x'), x' \in X_x$, process $p_{x'}$ acts as a commander, and each of the 4 remaining processes of X_x acts as a lieutenant. As this round is the last one, every lieutenant considers that the value that has been broadcast by $p_{x'}$ in that $BG(5, 0, x')$ instance is the value it has received from $p_{x'}$ in that instance (or $\perp$ if it has received no value). Looking at Figure 8.5, and assuming that p_5 is correct, this means that the correct processes in p_1, p_2, p_6 and p_7 consider the value w_5 they receive from p_5 as the value broadcast by that process in the corresponding $BG(5, 0, 5)$ instance.

More generally, let us consider the five $BG(5, 0, x')$ instances generated by each of the processes p_1, p_2, p_5, p_6 and p_7 of the $BG(6, 1, 4)$ instance (level 2 of the tree). These processes use the majority function to agree on the value broadcast by p_4 at the beginning of the second round as follows: v_y^4 =majority(w_1, w_2, w_5, w_6, w_7) (where each $w_{x'}$ has been computed from the corresponding $BG(5, 0, x')$ instance as described just previously).

As we have seen previously, the value v_y^4 is then used to compute the value that the processes consider as being the value initially proposed by p_3 (that is by definition the commander process in the instance $BG(7, 2, 3)$).

On the number of messages   When considering the previous example, it is easy to see that 6 messages are sent in the first round, $6 \times 5 = 30$ messages are sent in the second round (6 instances with 5 messages each), and $6 \times 5 \times 4 = 120$ messages are sent in the third round (30 instances with 4 messages each). As we will see later, the number of messages increases exponentially with respect to t.

Identifying the messages   Let us observe that every instance $BG(m, u, w)$ can be uniquely identified by the path of the tree it belongs to, as depicted in Figure 8.5. The messages associated with the instance $BG(6, 1, 4)$ appearing on the figure can consequently be prefixed unambiguously with the sequence of process identities $< 3, 4 >$. Similarly, the messages associated with the instance $BG(5, 0, 5)$ can be prefixed with $< 3, 4, 5 >$. It is easy to see that no two instances can have the same prefix. Consequently, when during a round a process receives a message, it easily recognizes which BG instance this message belongs to.

Let us also observe that the length of the prefix of a message received during round r is r. Hence, if during a round a process receives a message whose prefix length is not r, it knows that the sender is faulty and consequently considers $\perp$ as the received value. A process can also discard a message that contains several times the same process identity (this is due to the fact that in the tree, no prefix as defined by the tree can contain twice the same process identity).

8.3.3   A RECURSIVE FORMULATION OF THE ALGORITHM

Preliminary remarks   Let us recall that the underlying network is reliable (a Byzantine process has no access to it), and a process knows which is the sender of a message (point-to-point channels).

Let us also recall that a Byzantine process can send erroneous messages or send no message at all. Thanks to the synchrony assumption of the round-based model, the absence of a message can be detected. In that case, the receiver considers $\perp$ as the received value.

The majority function that is used is the one that has been previously defined.

A recursive formulation   The algorithm is described in Figure 8.6. This description is based on a recursive formulation that adopts a global point of view and makes the description particularly concise.

Initially (first round), and each process invokes byz˙general(n, t), one of the processes being the commander associated with that BG instance. At the end of the execution of byz˙general(n, t), each participating process will obtain a value that will be considered as the value proposed by the commander.

Let us consider a message containing the value v and prefixed $< i_1, i_2, \ldots, i_r >$ that arrives at process p_i during a round r. The intuitive meaning associated with this message is the following: "p_{i_r} tells p_i that $p_{i_{r-1}}$ told it that $p_{i_{r-2}}$ told it ... that p_{i_2} told it that p_{i_1} sent it value v".

operation byz general(n, t) locally returns a value:
(1)   **let** BG_inst be the corresponding BG instance;
(2)   The commander of BG_inst broadcasts its value to the other processes of BG_inst;
(3)   **if** $(t = 0)$
          then if (a value v is received from the commander of BG_inst)
(4)   **then** returns(v) **else** returns$(\bot)$
(5)   **end if**
(6)   **else for** any process p_i participating to BG_inst **do**
(7)   **if** (a value v is received from the commander of BG_inst)
(8)   **then** $v_i \leftarrow v$ **else** $v_i \leftarrow \bot$
(9)   **end if**;
(10) p_i acts as the commander in algorithm byz general$(n - 1, t - 1)$ associated
                  with the sub-instance including the same processes as BG_inst but its
                  commander. In that sub-instance, p_i broadcasts v_i to the $n - 2$ other lieutenants
(11)   **end for**;
(12)   **for** any process p_i participating to BG_inst **do**
(13)   **for each** $p_j \neq p_i$ participating to BG_inst **do**
(14)   **if** (p_i has received a value w at line 10 of the current BG_inst
                          sub-instance in which p_j was the commander)
(15)   **then** $w_j \leftarrow v$ **else** $w_j \leftarrow \bot$
(16)   **end if**;
(17)   **end for**;
(18)   return$\big($majority$($ values w obtained at line 15$)\big)$
(19)   **end for**
(20) **end if**.

Figure 8.6: An algorithm for the Byzantine Generals problem

Each recursive call corresponds to a new round, and there are consequently $t + 1$ rounds. As we have seen previously, during every round $r > 1$, a process participates in several BG instances.

More precisely, byz general(n, t) invokes $n - 1$ independent parallel executions of byz general$(n - 1, t - 1)$, each associated with a specific instance of the BG problem involving $n - 1$ processes. In turn, each byz general$(n - 1, t - 1)$ call invokes $n - 2$ independent parallel executions of byz general$(n - 2, t - 2)$, etc.

As the recursion unfolds, each invocation byz general$(n - k, t - k)$ (which occurs at round $r = k + 1$) entails the sending of a message to $n - (k + 1)$ processes, namely, the processes that are in the same BG instance as the corresponding commander process. As there are $(n - 1)(n - 2) \cdots (n - k)$ parallel executions of byz general$(n - k, t - k)$ during round $r = k + 1$, those give rise to $(n - 1)(n - 2) \cdots (n - (k + 1))$ messages that are sent in that round.

8.3.4   PROOF OF THE ALGORITHM

Assuming that the commander process is p_j, the proof must show that (a) the same value v is returned at each correct process p_i (and p_i will assign v to $view_i[j]$), and (b) if p_j is correct $v = v_j$ (the value proposed by p_j). To that end, a lemma is first proved. It is then used to prove the algorithm.

Lemma 8.4   *For any pair (k, m), the algorithm* byz·general(n, m) *described in Figure 8.6 ensures that, in synchronous systems made up of $n > 2k + m$ processes where at most k are Byzantine, if the commander process p_j is correct, the same value v is returned at each correct process, and v is the value proposed by p_j.*

Proof Let us emphasize that, in the lemma statement, the number of faulty processes is k (not m). The proof is by induction on the lemma parameter m. The proof of the base case $m = 0$ is trivial. If the commander process p_j is correct and $m = 0$, the value v sent by p_j is received and returned by each correct process at line 4.

Induction step. Let us assume that the lemma is true for $m - 1$ with $m > 0$ and let us prove it for m. As the commander p_j of the instance $BG(n, k, j)$ is correct, it sends its proposed value v to the $n - 1$ other processes (lines 2 and 6-8), and every correct process p_i invokes byz·general$(n - 1, m - 1)$ (line 10).

As $n > 2k + m$, we have $n - 1 > 2k + (m - 1)$, from which we can apply the induction hypothesis to conclude that each correct process p_i obtains (line 14) the value v from every of the $n - 1$ BG instances byz·general$(n - 1, m - 1)$ whose commander is correct. (these invocations line 10).

As there are at most k Byzantine processes, and $n - 1 > 2k + (m - 1) \geq 2k$, it follows that there is a majority of byz·general$(n - 1, m - 1)$ instances whose commander is correct. Consequently, there is a majority of the $n - 1$ instances of byz·general$(n - 1, m - 1)$ that return v to each correct process that participates in these instances (lines 13-17). It follows that the value v is a majority value when a correct process p_i executes line 18, which concludes the proof of the lemma.

$\square_{Lemma\ 8.4}$

Theorem 8.5   *For any m, the algorithm* byz·general(n, m) *described in Figure 8.6 solves the Byzantine General problem in synchronous systems made up of $n > 3m$ processes and where, at most, m can be Byzantine.*

Proof As previously shown, the proof is by induction on m but, differently from the lemma, here m is an upper bound on the number of Byzantine processes.

Let us first consider the base case $m = 0$. If there is no faulty process, the algorithm byz·general$(n, 0)$ trivially satisfy the properties on the BG problem: it follows directly from lines 1-5 that all the correct processes return the value proposed by the commander process.

Induction step. Let us assume that the theorem is true for $m - 1$ with $m > 0$ and let us prove it for m. Let us first consider the case were the commander process associated with the invocation byz˙general(n, m) is correct. In that case, taking $k = m$, the proof follows immediately from Lemma 8.4.

Let us now consider the case were the commander process is Byzantine. This means that at most $m - 1$ lieutenant processes are Byzantine. As $n - 1 > 3m - 1 > 3(m - 1)$, we can apply the induction assumption to each of the $n - 1$ invocations of byz˙general$(n - 1, m - 1)$ (launched at line 10) that solves its associated instance of the BG problem for $n - 1$ processes and at most $m - 1$ Byzantine processes. Hence, any two correct processes obtain the same $n - 1$ values at line 18, and as the function majority() is deterministic, they return the same value, which concludes the proof of the theorem. $\square_{Theorem\ 8.5}$

8.3.5   COMPLEXITY MEASURES

Time complexity   As we seen, as far as the time complexity is concerned, the algorithm terminates in $t + 1$ rounds. It is important to notice that the synchrony assumption prevents a process from blocking forever waiting for a message from a process that has crashed or has not sent a message in a BG instance during which it should have.

Message size   A message from a correct process contains at most $t + 1$ process identities (a new one being added at each round).

Number of messages   As far the message complexity is concerned, each invocation byz˙general$(n - k, t - k)$ generates $n - (k + 1)$ messages (by the correct processes). As the are $(n - 1)(n - 2) \cdots (n - t)$ such invocations the total number of messages sent by the correct processes is

$$(n - 1) + (n - 1)(n - 2) + \cdots + [(n - 1)(n - 2) \cdots (n - (t + 1))].$$

Hence , the total number of messages belongs to $O(n^t)$. It increases exponentially with respect to the number of processes that can exhibit a Byzantine behavior.

Local memory   The value returned by byz˙general(n, t) depends on the values returned by the $n - 1$ invocations byz˙general$(n - 1, t - 1)$, each of which in turn depends on the values returned by $n - 2$ invocations of byz˙general$(n - 2, t - 2)$, etc. until the $(n - 1)(n - 2) \cdots (n - t)$ invocations of byz˙general$(n - t, 0)$. As all intermediate values are necessary for a process to compute the value it returns from byz˙general(n, t), it follows that the size of local memory required at each process is $O(n^t)$.

8.4 A SIMPLE CONSENSUS ALGORITHM WITH CONSTANT SIZE MESSAGES

8.4.1 FEATURES OF THE ALGORITHM

The previous algorithm meets two bounds associated with consensus in synchronous Byzantine systems, namely the upper bound on the number of faulty processes ($t < n/3$), and the lower bound on the number of rounds ($t + 1$). Unfortunately, in addition to a complex design, it requires processes to exchange a number of messages exponential with respect to the number of faulty processes ($O(n^t)$).

This section presents a simple consensus algorithm in which processes exchange a linear number of messages (with respect to t). Moreover, each message has a constant size (it carries a single proposed value). This algorithm requires $n > 4t$, and processes decide after $2(t + 1)$ rounds.

As far as consensus validity is concerned (see Chapter 1), the algorithm ensures that, when all correct processes propose the same value, then that value is decided (weak validity).

8.4.2 PRESENTATION OF THE ALGORITHM

Rotating coordinator paradigm and underlying principle   The algorithm is based on the *rotating coordinator* paradigm (which has proved to be a valuable paradigm in the design of a lot of distributed algorithms). This means that some rounds are (partially) under the control of some processes, each of these rounds being appropriately *coordinated* by a single process. The identity of the process that coordinates a given round r is predetermined from the value of r.

The algorithm is presented in Figure 8.7. Each process maintains a current estimate (est_i) of the decision value. In order to ensure the consensus validity property, it is based on the following principle.

1. If the occurrence number of the most current estimate value bypasses some threshold, that value will be the decided value.

2. Otherwise, the coordinator paradigm is used to force an estimate value to be adopted by enough processes in order its occurrence number bypasses the given threshold in order the previous requirement become satisfied (during the next round).

Implementing the principle   To implement the previous principle, the algorithm uses a sequence of stages, each made up of two rounds, each of them being related to item 1 or item 2 stated previously. During each stage, a process p_i computes a new estimate of the decision value (kept in the local variable est_i, initialized to the value v_i it proposes). The aim of the sequence of stages is to guarantee that a value eventually becomes "present enough" to bypass the threshold. More precisely, we have the following.

- The first round of stage k (i.e., the round whose number is $r = 2k - 1$) is an estimate determination. The processes exchange their current estimate values est_i, and each process p_i determines the one it sees the most often and keeps it in $most\_freq_i$. (If several values are equally "most common", one is deterministically selected, and saves it in $most\_freq_i$.)

- The second round of stage k (i.e., the round whose number is $r = 2k$) is an estimate adoption. For each process p_i, as indicated previously, if the occurrence number of the estimate v it has seen the most often bypasses the threshold, p_i adopts it as new estimate. The other case is solved by the rotating coordinator paradigm as follows. During round $r = 2k$, process p_k acts a coordinator role: it broadcasts its $most\_freq_k$ value to all processes p_i (that saves it in $coord\_val_i$) in order they adopt it in case they cannot adopt their $most\_freq_i$ value.

Let us notice that, as at most t processes are faulty, $t + 1$ stages necessarily include a stage whose coordinator is correct. So, this coordinator will impose the same estimate value to the correct processes if, up to this stage, no estimate value was "present enough" to bypass the threshold.

---

operation propose(v_i)
(1) $est_i \leftarrow v_i$;
(2) **when** $r = 1, 3, \ldots, 2t - 1, 2t + 1$ **do**
    begin synchronous round
(3)   broadcast ESTI(est_i);
(4)   **let** rec_i = multiset of values received during round r;
(5) $most\_freq_i \leftarrow$ most frequent value in rec_i;
(6) $occ\_nb_i \leftarrow$ occurrence number of $most\_freq_i$
    end synchronous round;
(7) **when** $r = 2, 4, \ldots, 2t, 2(t + 1)$ **do**
    begin synchronous round
(8)   **if** $(i = r/2)$ **then** broadcast EST2($most\_freq_i$) **end if**;
(9)   **if** (a value v is received from $p_{r/2}$) **then** $coord\_val_i \leftarrow v$ **else** $coord\_val_i \leftarrow v_i$ **end if**;
(10)   **if** $(occ\_nb_i > n/2 + t)$ **then** $est_i \leftarrow most\_freq_i$ **else** $est_i \leftarrow coord\_val_i$ **end if**
(11)   **if** $(r = 2(t + 1))$ **then** return(est_i) **end if**
    end synchronous round.

Figure 8.7: Byzantine Consensus (code for p_i, $t < n/4$)

The threshold value is $n/2 + t$. As shown by Lemma 8.6, this threshold value is required to guarantee the agreement property of consensus despite up to t Byzantine processes. Let us notice that

$$(n > 4t) \Leftrightarrow (2n > n + 4t) \Leftrightarrow \left(n > \frac{n}{2} + 2t\right) \Leftrightarrow \left(n - t > \frac{n}{2} + t\right).$$

The algorithm uses a multiset denoted rec_i. It is a set in which the same value can appear several times (e.g., $\{a, b, a, c\}$ is a multiset that contains three different values, a that appears twice while b and c appear once).

8.4.3 PROOF AND PROPERTIES OF THE ALGORITHM

Lemma 8.6 *Let $t < n/4$, and consider the situation where, at the beginning of stage k, the correct processes have the same estimate value v. They will never change their estimate value, thereafter.*

Proof It follows from the lemma assumption that the multiset rec_i of any correct process p_i (line 4) contains at least $n - t$ copies of v at the end of the first round of stage k (round $r = 2k - 1$). Hence, we have $occ\_nb_i \geq n - t$ (line 6).

Moreover, as $n > 4t$, we have $n - t > n/2$, from which it follows that v is the single most common value in rec_i. Consequently, the local variable $most\_freq_i$ is assigned value v (line 5).

From $n > 4t$, we obtain $n - t > n/2 + t$ (see above), from which we conclude that during the second round of stage k (round $r = 2k$) the estimate est_i of each correct process p_i is set to $most\_freq_i$, i.e., keeps the value v. $\qquad\qquad\qquad\qquad\qquad\qquad\qquad\square_{Lemma\ 8.6}$

Theorem 8.7 *Let $f < n/4$. The algorithm described in Figure 8.7 satisfies the termination, agreement and weak validity properties of consensus in presence of up to t Byzantine processes. It requires $2(t + 1)$ rounds.*

Proof The weak validity property (if all correct processes propose the same value, that value is decided) is an immediate consequence of Lemma 8.6. The termination property follows from the synchrony assumption: a correct process decides at line 11 at the end of round $2(t + 1)$.

Let us now prove that the algorithm satisfies the consensus agreement property. Since there are $t + 1$ stages and at most t Byzantine processes, there is at least one stage coordinated by a correct process. Let k be the first stage coordinated by a correct process (say p_x), and p_i be any correct process. At the end of stage k, p_i has some value v in est_i. Let us consider two cases according to the value assigned to est_i by p_i at line 10.

- Process p_i executes $est_i \leftarrow most\_freq_i$. In that case, due to the predicate used in line 10, we conclude that at least $n/2 + t + 1$ processes sent v as estimate value at the beginning of stage k. Therefore, as at most t processes are Byzantine, the coordinator p_x of stage k (which is correct) received at least $n/2 + 1$ copies of v from correct processes, which means that p_x has seen a single most frequent value (namely a majority value). Consequently, p_x has broadcast $most\_freq_x = v$ (line 8 during the second round of stage k).

  Let us consider any correct process $p_j \neq p_i$ when it executes line 10 during the second round of stage k.

    - Case 1: p_j executes $est_j \leftarrow coord\_val_j$. As $coord\_val_j = most\_freq_x$, p_j assigns v to est_j, which proves the property for that case.
    - Case 2: p_j executes $est_j \leftarrow most\_freq_j$. It follows from the fact that p_i has received $n/2 + t + 1$ copies of v during the first round of stage k, that p_j has received at least $n/2 + 1$ copies of v. Hence, p_j has executed $most\_freq_j \leftarrow v$ at line 5 of the first round of stage k. In that case also, p_i and p_j adopts the same value for their estimates.

- No correct process p_i executes $est_i \leftarrow most\_freq_i$. In that case, all correct processes have executed $est_i \leftarrow coord\_val_i$, and consequently, they all have the same estimate value at the end of stage k (remind that, as p_x is correct, it sent the same value to all the processes).

In both cases, due to Lemma 8.6, the correct processes will not modify these estimates in the future, from which the consensus agreement property follows. $\square_{Theorem\ 8.7}$

Properties of the algorithm   A noteworthy property of this algorithm is its simplicity. Another one lies in the fact that each message has a bounded size (equal to the number of bits needed to encode a proposed value).

The algorithm requires $2(t + 1)$ rounds and $(t + 1)[n(n - 1) + (n - 1)] = (t + 1)(n^2 - 1)$ messages (assuming the messages that a process sends to itself are saved).

8.5   BIBLIOGRAPHIC NOTES

- The notions of Byzantine failure and the Byzantine Generals problem have been introduced by Lamport, Shostack and Pease in the early eighties (45; 47; 64). The same authors have proved the $n > 3t$ upper bound on t (the maximal number of processes that can be faulty) (64).

  Their initial motivation was the fact that a malfunctioning component can give different values to different processes which makes majority voting ineffective (majority voting requires that each component gives the same value to every voting entity).

- The $t + 1$ lower bound on the number of rounds (communication steps) for Byzantine consensus has been proved by Fischer and Lynch for Byzantine consensus in which processes exchange unauthenticated messages (22). The corresponding proof for signed messages is due to Dolev and Strong (18).

- The synchronous algorithm for unauthenticated messages presented in Section 8.3 is due to Lamport, Shostack and Pease (47).

- The synchronous algorithm for unauthenticated messages with constant size presented in Section 8.4 is due to Berman and Garey (6).

- There is a algorithm that solves the consensus problem in synchronous systems made up of n processes where up to t processes can be Byzantine that (a) satisfies the $n > 3t$ upper bound on t, (b) requires $t + 1$ rounds, and (c) needs only polynomial number of messages. This algorithm is due to Garey and Moses (27).

- Byzantine synchronous and asynchronous consensus algorithms are described in the following books (3; 28; 44; 49). A short introduction to Byzantine agreement is presented in (63).

- Early stopping despite Byzantine failures is addressed in (5; 17).

CHAPTER 9

Byzantine Consensus in Enriched Models

This chapter considers that the underlying synchronous system is enriched with additional assumptions. The first enrichment is an underlying binary consensus algorithm. While from a computability point of view this does not add any computational power, it allows for the design of multivalued consensus with interesting properties. The second enrichment adds computational power to the synchronous system. It consists in the possibility for a process to sign the messages it sends. This prevents a faulty process from forging messages that could be attributed to correct processes. Signatures restrict the possible behavior of a Byzantine process to fail to relay messages or send bad values only.

9.1 FROM BINARY TO MULTIVALUED BYZANTINE CONSENSUS

9.1.1 MOTIVATION

This section presents an algorithm that, assuming $n > 3t$, builds a synchronous multivalued consensus algorithm on top of of a synchronous binary consensus algorithm. Such a construction has two main advantages.

- The first advantage is related to bit complexity. As we will see, the construction that is presented leads to substantial savings of bits when compared to a multivalued Byzantine consensus that would be build directly on top of a bare round-based synchronous model. It is nevertheless important to signal that this gain in bit complexity is not obtained for free, two additional rounds are required.

- The second advantage concerns the value that is decided by the correct processes. The construction allows the correct processes to never decide the value proposed by a Byzantine process (but if it is also proposed by a correct process).

    More precisely, the value decided by the correct processes is either the value proposed by a correct process (and this is always the case when the correct processes propose the same value) or the default value $\perp$. Hence, as an interesting side effect, when a correct process decides $\perp$, it learns that no all correct processes have proposed the same value.

(As a simple example, let us consider a set of sensors that are sensing the same area, e.g., its temperature. The previous property means that even when t sensors reports arbitrary values, these bad values will never corrupt the state of the sensing system.)

9.1.2   A CONSTRUCTION

The algorithm is described in Figure 9.1. In order to prevent confusion, the operation of the multi-valued consensus that is built is denoted mv˙propose(), while the operation of the underlying binary consensus is denoted bin˙propose().

The underlying binary consensus   It is assumed that the binary values are 1 and 0. The binary consensus is assumed to satisfy the following properties: (a) termination (any correct process decides), (b) agreement (no two correct processes decide differently), and (c) weak validity (if all correct processes propose the same value, that value is decided).

The weak validity property is crucial for the multivalued consensus construction. As we will see, this is due to the following lemma.

Lemma 9.1   *Let $v \in \{0, 1\}$. If the value v is decided, then at least one correct process has proposed v.*

Proof The proof is by contradiction. Let $\bar{v} = 1 - v$. Let us assume that value v is decided by the correct processes, while no correct process has proposed v. Hence, all correct processes have proposed $\bar{v}$. It then follows from the weak validity property that they decide $\bar{v}$, which contradicts the initial assumption and concludes the proof of the lemma. $\square_{Lemma\ 9.1}$

From binary to multivalued consensus   The idea of the construction is for the processes to first exchange the values they propose and compute a binary value from these exchanges. After each process has computed a binary value, the processes execute the underlying binary agreement, and finally, according to binary value that is returned, decide either a value proposed by a correct process or $\perp$. That default value is used to prevent the processes from deciding a value proposed only by faulty processes.

From an operational point of view, when looking at Figure 9.1, the underlying binary consensus appears at line 14. It is prefixed by two additional rounds. From a round-based synchrony point of view, line 15 (that is a simple local statement) is considered as being part of the last round of the underlying binary consensus (as there is no message exchange, there is no need to consider that this line requires another round). More precisely, we have the following. let $\mathcal{C}$ denote the set of processes that are correct in the considered execution.

- First, additional round (lines 2-5). A process p_i first broadcasts the value v_i it proposes. It then computes an auxiliary value aux_i from the proposed values it has received. If there is a proposed value v that it has received at least $n - t$ times, it saves s it in aux_i; otherwise, it considers the default value $\perp$. The aim of this round is to establish the following property (Lemma 9.2):

```
operation mv⸱propose(v_i)
(1)   est_i ← v_i;
(2)   when r = 1 do
      begin synchronous round
(3)       broadcast EST1(est_i);
(4)       let rec1_i = multiset of values received during the first round;
(5)       if (∃v : #_v(rec1_i) ≥ n − t) then aux_i ← v else aux_i ← ⊥ end if
      end synchronous round;
(6)   when r = 2 do
      begin synchronous round
(7)       broadcast EST2(aux_i);
(8)       let rec2_i = multiset of values received during the second round;
(9)       if (∃v ≠ ⊥ : #_v(rec2_i) ≥ n − t) then bp_i ← 1 else bp_i ← 0 end if;
(10)      if (∃v ≠ ⊥ : v ∈ rec2_i) then let v = most frequent non-⊥ value in rec2_i;
(11)                              res_i ← v
(12)                          else res_i ← ⊥
(13)      end if
      end synchronous round;
(14)  b_dec_i ← bin⸱propose(bp_i);
(15)  if (b_dec_i = 1) then return(res_i) else return(⊥) end if.
```

Figure 9.1: From binary to multivalued Byzantine consensus (code for p_i, $t < n/3$)

$$PR1 \equiv \big[\forall i, j \in \mathcal{C} : \big((aux_i \neq \bot) \wedge (aux_j \neq \bot)\big) \Rightarrow$$
$$(aux_i = aux_j = v) \wedge (v \text{ has been proposed by at least one correct process})\big].$$

Hence, from a global point of view, this additional round replaces the set of values proposed by the processes by a non-empty set including at most two values (namely a value v proposed by a correct process and $\bot$).

• Second additional round (lines 6-13). The exchange pattern of this round is similar to the previous one where est_i is replaced by aux_i. The aim of this round is twofold.

  – First p_i computes the binary value bp_i it will propose to the underlying binary consensus (bp_i stands fro *binary proposal*). If p_i has received the same proposed value ($aux = v \neq \bot$) from at least $n - t$ processes, it has received enough copies of v to be certain that v is the most frequent non-$\bot$ value received by any correct process, hence $bp_i = 1$. Otherwise, $bp_i = 0$.

  – Then p_i computes the value that it will return if the binary consensus returns the value 1. That value, kept in res_i, is either the most frequent non-$\bot$ value that p_i has received during that round, or $\bot$ if it has received only messages carrying $\bot$. (If several non-$\bot$ values appear equally as most frequent, one of them is arbitrarily selected.)

As we will see in the proof, this round establishes the following property (Lemma 9.3):

$$PR2 \equiv \big[(\exists i \in \mathcal{C} : bp_i = 1) \Rightarrow (\forall j \in \mathcal{C} : res_j = res_i = v \neq \bot)\big].$$

- Using the binary consensus (lines 14-15). Finally, p_i proposes bp_i to the underlying binary consensus. If 1 is returned, p_i decides the value it has previously saved in res_i (that is either a value $v \neq \bot$ or $\bot$). If 0 is returned, p_i decides $\bot$ whatever the content of res_i.

9.1.3 CORRECTNESS PROOF

Let us recall that C denotes the set of processes that are correct in the considered execution. Moreover, it is assumed that $n > 3t$.

Lemma 9.2 $\forall i, j \in C : \big[(aux_i \neq \bot) \wedge (aux_j \neq \bot)\big] \Rightarrow \big[(aux_i = aux_j = v) \wedge (v \text{ has been proposed by at least one correct process})\big]$.

Proof Let p_i and p_j be two correct processes such that $(aux_i \neq \bot) \wedge (aux_j \neq \bot)$. It follows from $aux_i \neq \bot$ that there is a proposed value v such that $\#_v(rec1_i) \geq n - t$ (line 5). In the worst case, at most t copies of v received by p_i are from faulty processes. Hence, any correct process (e.g., p_j) has received at least $n - 2t$ copies of v. As $n > 3t$, we have $n - 2t > t$, which means that p_j has received at least $t + 1$ copies of v (Observation O1).

Similarly, it follows from $aux_j \neq \bot$ that there is a proposed value w such that $\#_w(rec1_j) \geq n - t$. Hence, p_j has received at least $n - t$ messages with a copy of w (Observation O2).

It follows from O1 and O2 that p_j has received $\geq t + 1$ copies of v and $\geq n - t$ copies of w. This means that if $v \neq w$, p_j has received values from at least $n + 1$ processes. (Let us recall that communication is point-to-point, and, consequently, when a message arrives, the receiver knows which is the sender process. Hence if a faulty process sends several messages during the same round, it is immediately discovered.) A contradiction with the fact that there are exactly n processes from which follows that $w = v$.

The fact that v has been proposed by a correct process follows from the observation that p_i has received v from a set of (at least) $n - t$ processes, and as $n > 3t \Rightarrow n - t > 2t > t$, this set includes at least one correct process. $\square_{Lemma\ 9.2}$

Lemma 9.3 $(\exists i \in C : bp_i = 1) \Rightarrow (\forall j \in C : res_j = res_i = v \neq \bot)$.

Proof Let p_i be a correct process such that $bp_i = 1$. It follows from line 9 that there is a non-$\bot$ value v such that p_i has received at least $n - t$ messages EST2(v). It follows from the second part of Lemma 9.2 that v has been proposed by a correct process.

As the system is synchronous and there are at most t faulty processes, any correct process p_j receives at least $n - 2t$ messages EST2(v) during the second round. Moreover, (due to the first part of Lemma 9.2) a correct process sends either EST2(v) or EST2($\bot$). It follows that a correct process receives at most t messages EST2(w) with $w \neq v$.

The worst case scenario is depicted in Figure 9.2. Process p_i receives $n - t$ messages EST2(v) ($n - 2t$ from correct processes and t from Byzantine processes) and t messages EST2($\bot$) (from correct processes). Process p_j receives $n - 2t$ messages EST2(v) (from correct processes), t messages EST2(w) with $w \neq v$ (from Byzantine processes), and t messages EST2($\perp$) (from correct processes).

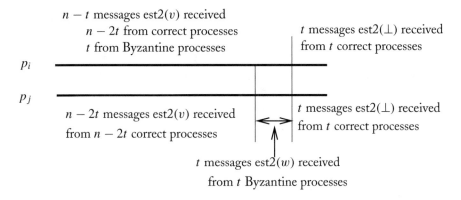

Figure 9.2: Proof of Property *PR2*

As $n - 2t > t$, it follows that v is the most frequent non-$\perp$ value received by p_j during the second round (and similarly for p_i). Hence, both p_i and p_j execute line 11, and we have $res_i = res_j = v \neq \perp$. $\square$ *Lemma 9.3*

Theorem 9.4   *The algorithm described in Figure 9.1 satisfies the termination, agreement and weak validity property of the multivalued consensus problem. Moreover, it satisfies the following additional property: no value proposed only by Byzantine processes can be decided.*

Proof As for the other synchronous algorithms, the termination property follows directly from the synchrony property of the underlying system.

Let us consider the weak validity property (if all correct processes propose the same value, that value is decided). Hence, let us assume that all correct processes propose value v. As there are at least $n - t$ correct processes, any correct process p_i is such that $\exists v : \#_v(rec1_i) \geq n - t$ (line 5) and consequently sets aux_i to v. Consequently, there are at least $n - t$ processes that broadcasts EST2(v). It follows that each correct process p_i assigns 1 to bp_i and v to res_i (lines 9-11). As all correct processes propose 1 to the underlying binary consensus, it follows from its weak validity property that they all decide 1 (line 14). hence, v is decided by each correct process (line 15).

Let us now prove that no two correct processes decide differently (agreement property). If all correct processes decide $\perp$, the agreement property is trivially satisfied. So, let us consider that a correct process p_i decides a value $v \neq \perp$, which means that p_i decides 1 from the underlying binary consensus. It follows then from Lemma 9.1 that at least one correct process p_j has proposed

$bp_j = 1$. The agreement property follows then immediately from Lemma 9.3 and the fact that a correct p_x process decides the value kept in res_x.

Let us finally show that the value proposed by a Byzantine process (and not proposed by a correct process) is never decided. (Let us notice that it is possible that all Byzantine processes propose the same value whil each correct process propose its own value.) If follows from Lemma 9.1 that, if a non-$\perp$ value v is decided by a correct process, there is a correct process p_i that has proposed $bp_i = 1$. It then follows that p_i has received $n - t$ messages EST2(v) with $v \neq \perp$ (line 9). Finally, we conclude from Lemma 9.2 that v is a value that has been proposed by a correct process.

$\square_{Theorem\ 9.4}$

9.1.4   AN INTERESTING PROPERTY OF THE CONSTRUCTION

Let v be the value that is most proposed by the correct processes (it is possible that several values are equally most proposed), and $\#_v$ the number of correct processes that propose it. The previous algorithm has the following interesting property (that follows from Lemma 9.2, Lemma 9.3 and Theorem 9.4).

- If $\#_v \geq n - t$, then v is decided by the correct processes (let us observe that, in that case, there is a single most proposed value).

- If $\#_v < n - 2t$, then $\perp$ is decided by the correct processes.

- If $n - 2t \leq \#_v < n - t$, then which value (v or $\perp$) is decided by the correct processes depends on the behavior of the Byzantine processes.

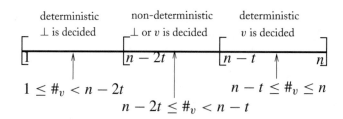

Figure 9.3: Deterministic vs non-deterministic scenarios

Let us consider an omniscient oberver that would know which are the correct processes and the values they propose. In the first and the second cases, this omniscient observer can compute the result in a deterministic way. Differently, it cannot in the last case. The value that is decided depends actually on the behavior of the Byzantine processes (that can favor values proposed by correct processes, or entail a $\perp$ decision). These different cases are depicted on Figure 9.3.

9.2   ENRICHING THE SYNCHRONOUS MODEL WITH MESSAGE AUTHENTICATION

9.2.1   SYNCHRONOUS MODEL WITH SIGNED MESSAGES

Digital signatures   This section considers that processes can safely sign the messages they send. This means that a sender can append it signature to every message it sends. This signature contains a sample portion of the message encoded in such a way that a receiver can always verify that the message is authentic (it has not been modified by an other process). Let us remember that, as every channel is point-to-point, a receiver always knows which is the process that sent the message it receives.

It is assumed that no process p_i can forge the signature of another process p_j undetectably, and consequently cannot change the content of the messages send by any other process. This results in restricting the possible behavior of a Byzantine process. Such a process can only crash or fail to relay messages.

Signatures define a more restricted model   The round-based synchronous model enriched with signatures is a computation model strictly more restricted than the round-based synchronous model.

This is due to the following observation. On the one side, breaking signatures requires theoretically an "infinite" computation power. On the other side, a round-based synchronous model enriched with signatures assumes that no process has enough power to break signatures. More specifically, a synchronous model enriched with signatures provides the processes with a strong security abstraction (signatures) that by assumption can never be defeated. Such an assumption is not considered in the base synchronous model, and consequently processes are not prevented from having an "infinite computing power" in such a base system in order to break signatures if they were used.

Using signatures: notion of a valid message   In a signature-based algorithm each process signs every message it broadcasts. During the first round a process sends a signed message containing its value. Then, at every round r, a process that receives a message signs and forwards it during round $r + 1$.

A message m received during round r by a process p_i is *valid* if (a) it carries a value v with a list of r signatures (b) that are pairwise different and (c) different from the signature of p_i. Such a message m is denoted $[v : p_a : p_b : \cdots : p_x]$, where v is a value signed by p_a, and then the pair $[v : p_a]$ has been signed by p_b giving $[v : p_a : p_b]$, etc.

Its meaning is the following. During the first round process p_a has sent the signed message $[v : p_a]$ to process p_b, that during the second round sent the signed message $[v : p_a : p_b]$ to process p_c, etc., until p_x that during round r sent the signed message $[v : p_a : p_b : \cdots : p_x]$.

In all signature-based algorithms, a process discards systematically all the messages that it received that are not valid. When writing an algorithm, the elimination of the messages that are not valid is left implicit. It is easy to see that signatures restrict the faults of Byzantine processes to crash or to relay messages.

9.2.2 WHAT IS THE GAIN OBTAINED FROM SIGNATURES

Upper bound on t for the Byzantine Generals problem When solving the Byzantine Generals problem, the gain provided by signatures is that the upper bound $t < n/3$ on the number of faulty processes collapses. We have then $t < n$ as in the crash and the send omission failure models.

Upper bound on t for the consensus problem As far as the consensus problem is concerned, the constraint on t becomes $t < n/2$. This is in agreement with what has been seen in chapter 7 devoted to the omission failure model where it has been shown that the constraint $t < n/2$ defines the upper bound on t associated with the consensus problem in the general omission failure model (which is a model less severe than Byzantine failures as seen in chapter 1). This is not counter-intuitive as signatures restrict the possible behavior of a faulty process to only crashing or failing to relay messages, which are exactly the failures allowed in the general omission failure model.

Albeit consensus has the same upper bound on t in both models, let us nevertheless recall that the consensus validity and agreement properties have different definitions in both models. More precisely, we have the following.

- Agreement property.
    - Failure omission model: no two processes decide differently.
    - Byzantine failure model: no two correct processes decide differently.

- Validity property.
    - Failure omission model: a decided value is a proposed value.
    - Byzantine failure model: if all correct processes propose the same value, no other value can be decided by a correct process.

Lower bound on the number of rounds On another side, as in the previous models, $t + 1$ is a lower bound for the number of rounds to solve the Byzantine Generals, interactive consistency or consensus problem in presence of up to t Byzantine processes. This means that signatures are not computationally strong enough to allow for a reduction of the number of rounds.

9.2.3 SIGNATURES VS ERROR DETECTING CODES

Byzantine behaviors include malicious behaviors from processes that do their best to pollute the computation of the correct processes. This is not always the case in practice. When Byzantine behavior is not intentional, signatures can be replaced by error-detecting codes. From an implementation point if view, the advantage is that error-detecting codes are much less expensive than signatures.

9.3 A CONSENSUS ALGORITHM BASED ON SIGNATURES

9.3.1 THE ALGORITHM AND ITS COST

Description of the algorithm A consensus algorithm based on signatures is described in Figure 9.4. First each process p_i builds a message made up of the value it proposes signed by it (line 2).

Then the processes execute $t + 1$ synchronous rounds. When it starts a new round a process p_i broadcasts the messages in the set to_sent_i (line 4). This set contains the valid messages m that p_i has received during the previous round and to which it has appended its signature (lines 6-8).

Finally, when it executes round $t + 1$, p_i decides a value (lines 9-17). For each process p_j, process p_i first computes the value v_j proposed by p_j. If p_j is correct, such a value belongs to all the valid messages received during the round $t + 1$ whose first signature is p_j's signature 10-14). If there is such a value p_i saves it $rec\_val_i[j]$. If there is a single most common value in rec_val_i, p_i decides it, otherwise it decides the default value $\perp$.

Remark on the underlying communication model As formulated in the algorithm described in Figure 9.4, a process broadcasts a set of messages during every round (line 4) and receives each message separately (line 6). This formulation simplifies the presentation of the algorithm.

An exponential number of messages Let us assume that all processes are correct. There are n messages during the first round, n^2 during the second round, etc., until n^{t+1} messages during the last round. Hence the number of messages exchanged is $O(n^t)$.

---

operation propose(v_i)
(1) $est_i \leftarrow v_i$; $rec\_val_i[1..n] \leftarrow [\perp, \ldots, \perp]$;
(2) $to\_send_i \leftarrow \{$ message made up of est_i signed by $p_i \}$;
(3)   **when** $r = 1, 2, \cdots, t + 1$ **do**
        begin synchronous round
(4)   broadcast EST(to_send_i);
(5) $to\_send_i \leftarrow \emptyset$;
(6)   **for** every valid message m received during round r **do**
(7)   add m' to to_send_i where m' is m signed by p_i
(8)   **end for**;
(9)   **if** $(r = t + 1)$ **then**
(10)   **foreach** $j \in \{1, \ldots, n\}$ **do**
(11)   **if** (all the valid messages m received during round $t + 1$ starting with p_j's signature carry v)
(12)   **then** $rec\_val_i[j] \leftarrow v$ **else** $rec\_val_i[j] \leftarrow \perp$
(13)   **end if**
(14)   **end for**;
(15)   **if** (there is a single most common value v in $rec\_val_i[1..n]$) **then** $dec_i \leftarrow v$ **then** $dec_i \leftarrow \perp$ **end if**;
(16)   return(dec_i)
(17)   **end if**
        end synchronous round.

Figure 9.4: A Byzantine signature-based consensus algorithm (code for p_i, $t < n/2$)

9.3.2   PROOF OF THE ALGORITHM

Theorem 9.5 *Let $t < n/2$. The algorithm described in Figure 9.4 solves the consensus problem in synchronous systems prone to up to t Byzantine failures, enriched with message authentication.*

Proof The termination property follows from the synchrony assumption.

To prove the weak validity property, we have to show that, if all the correct processes propose the same value v, then v is decided. Let us consider a correct process p_i that proposes value v. Due to $n > 2t$, we have $n - t \geq t + 1$ from which follows that there is a path of $t + 1$ correct processes from p_i to any other correct process. Thus, at round $t + 1$, each correct process p_j receives at least one valid message that carries v and originated at p_i. Moreover, due to signatures, no valid message with prefix $[v : p_i]$ can have been corrupted by a faulty process. Hence, any correct process p_j is such that $rec\_val_j[i] = v$ at the end of round $t + 1$. It then follows from the $n > 2t$ assumption that, if all correct processes propose the same value v, a majority of entries of $rec\_val_j[1..n]$ are equal to v, and consequently, all correct processes decide v.

For the agreement property, we have to show that no two correct processes decide different values. To that end, we show that $rec\_val_i = rec\_val_j$ for any two correct processes. Let $rec\_val_i[x] = v$. If p_x is correct, the proof that $rec\_val_j[x] = v$ is the same as for the weak validity property. Hence, let us assume that p_x is faulty. As $rec\_val_i[x] = v$, there is a round $r \leq t$ during which there is a correct process p_y that has received a valid message $m = [v : p_x : \ldots]$; as this message is valid, it carries r distinct signatures. As $n - t \geq t + 1$, there is a path of $t + 1 - r$ correct processes from p_y (included) to p_j (excluded) that have not yet signed and forwarded the message. Due to the algorithm, during the rounds from $r + 1$ to $t + 1$, the correct processes on this path sign and forward this message from p_y to p_j, and, consequently, we have $rec\_val_j[x] = v$ at the end of round $t + 1$, which proves the agreement property. $\square_{Theorem\ 9.5}$

9.4   A BYZANTINE GENERALS (BG) ALGORITHM BASED ON SIGNATURES

9.4.1   A BYZANTINE GENERALS ALGORITHM

Valid messages Let p_a be the commander process. This is known by all processes. Hence, process p_a is the only process that broadcast a message during the first round. This signed message is $[v : p_a]$. It follows that all valid messages will be of the form $[v : p_a : \cdots]$.

The algorithm The algorithm is described in Figure 9.5. During the first round, the commander process p_a signs the value v it proposes and broadcasts the message $[v : p_a]$. If a process p_i receives a message from p_a, it processes it only if it is valid (i.e., the message contains a value signed by p_a).

Then, during each round r, a process considers only the valid messages that it receives during that round. Moreover, from a more global point of view, a process forwards (after having signed it) only the first two messages that carries different values. To understand the way the algorithm works, let us consider two cases.

- The commander is correct. In that case, the commander has sent the same signed value v to all the processes that can only forward it (after having appended their signatures). This is because no process can forge the signature of another process. Hence, the single value v can be received by the correct processes.

- The commander is faulty. In that case, the commander can have sent different signed values to different processes and no message to other processes. This means that if a process p_i receives several valid messages carrying different values, as these values necessarily originated from the commander, p_i knows that the commander is faulty. For the other correct processes to be aware of that, p_i needs to forward (after having signed them) only the first two messages it has received that carry different values.

It follows that at most $(n - 1) + (n - 1)(n - 2)$ messages are sent if the commander is correct, while at most $(n - 1) + 2(n - 1)(n - 2)$ messages are sent if it is faulty. Hence, the algorithm requires $O(n^2)$ messages.

---

operation propose(v_i)
(1) $rec\_val_i \leftarrow \emptyset; rec\_msg_i \leftarrow \emptyset;$
(2)   **when** $r = 1$ **do**
       begin synchronous round
(3)   **if** (p_i is the commander) **then** broadcast EST($[v_i : p_i]$); return(v_i) **end if**;
(4) $rec\_msg_i \leftarrow$ { valid messages received during first round };
(5) $rec\_val_i \leftarrow recval_i \cup$ { values in the messages $\in rec\_msg_i$}
       end synchronous round;
(6)   **when** $r = 2, \cdots, t + 1$ **do**
       begin synchronous round
(7)   **if**   (no two different values have yet been forwarded)
(8) $\wedge$ (at round $r - 1$ at least one new value has been added to rec_val_i)
(9)   **then let** w be a new value received during round $r - 1$;
(10)   **let** m be the message received at round $r - 1$ that was carrying value w;
(11)   **let** m_w the message m signed by p_i;
(12)   **let** $dest$ = the set of $n - (r + 1)$ processes whose signatures are not in m_w;
(13)   broadcast EST(m_w) to $dest$;
(14)   **if** (since the second round only w has been forwarded by p_i
                    and there is another new value w' received during $r - 1$)
(15)   **then** execute again lines 10-13 with w' replacing w
(16)   **end if**;
(17)   **end if**:
(18) $rec\_msg_i \leftarrow$ { valid messages received during round r};
(19) $rec\_val_i \leftarrow recval_i \cup$ { values in the messages $\in rec\_msg_i$};
(20)   **if** $r = t + 1$ **then**
(21)   **if** $|val\_rec_i| = 1$ **then** return(v) where $val\_rec_i = \{v\}$ **else** return($\bot$) **end if**
(22)   **end if**
       end synchronous round.

Figure 9.5: A Byzantine Generals algorithm based on signed messages (code for $p_i, t < n$)

Remark Two broadcasts can be done at line 13. This occurs when at round r, p_i receives two new values (carried by valid messages), while it has not received valid messages before round r. Of course, p_i can compute first the messages m_w and $m_{w'}$ it has to broadcast and only then broadcast them to the appropriate processes. For the processes p_x to which both m_w and $m_{w'}$ have to be sent, p_i pack them into a single message that is sent to p_x. When, during round $r + 1$, p_x receives such a message, it unpacks it in order to obtain m_w and $m_{w'}$.

Theorem 9.6 *The algorithm described in Figure 9.5 solves the Byzantine general problem in a round-based synchronous system enriched with message authentication.*

Proof Let us first observe that the termination property follows directly from the synchrony assumption.

Let us first prove the validity property (if the commander is correct), all correct processes returns the value it has proposed). Hence, let us assume that the commander p_a is correct. It follows that it signs the value it proposes and sends the signed message $m = [v : p_a]$ to all processes. It follows that during the first round each correct process p_i adds v to the empty set rec_val_i. During the second round, the correct processes exchange message such as $m = [v : p_a : p_i]$, which does not modify the sets rec_val_i. On another side, as a faulty process cannot imitate the signature of p_a, no value different from v can belong to a valid message. It follows that the set rec_val_i of all correct processes remain such that $val\_rec_i = \{v\}$. It then follows from line 21 that all correct processes return v.

Let us now prove the agreement property (no two processes return different values). If the commander is correct, agreement follows from the validity property. If it sends no value during the first round, there are no valid messages and all sets val_rec_i remain empty forever, and all correct processes decide $\perp$ at line 21.

Hence, let us consider any correct processes p_i and p_j and p_i receives a value v (carried by a valid message m) for the first time during round r. We consider two cases.

- The signature of p_j appears in m. In that case, p_j has already received a valid message containing v and has then added v to rec_val_j if this set was containing less than two values.
- The signature of p_j does not appear in m, and $r < t + 1$. In that case, p_i forwards an appropriate valid message to p_j during round $r + 1$. Hence, p_j will add v to rec_val_j if this set contains less than two values.
- The signature of p_j does not appear in m, and $r = t + 1$. In that case, there is no more round for p_i to forward v to p_j within an appropriate valid message to p_j. But, as the message containing v is valid, it contains $t + 1$ signatures, hence it contains the signature of a correct process p_x that received a valid message containing v during a round $r < t + 1$. It follows that p_x has forwarded v (within a valid message) during $r + 1 \leq t + 1$.

It follows from this case analysis that (a) if a correct process p_i has inserted only one value v into rec_val_i, then any other correct process p_j has also inserted only v into rec_val_j; and (b) if a correct process p_i has inserted several values into rec_val_i, then any other correct process p_j has also inserted several into rec_val_j (let us notice that the two values inserted by p_i into rec_val_i are not necessarily the same as the one inserted by p_j into rec_val_j). The agreement property follows.

$\square_{Theorem\ 9.6}$

9.4.2   FROM BYZANTINE GENERALS (BG) TO CONSENSUS

As we have seen, it is easy to solve consensus despite Byzantine failures in a synchronous system as soon as one has an algorithm that solves the Byzantine Generals problem. Multiplexing n BG instances (one per process) solves the interactive consistency problem from which a solution to consensus is trivially obtained. But, while the constraint $t < n$ defines the upper bound on the maximal number of faulty processes for each Byzantine General instance in the synchronous model enriched with signatures, the previous multiplexing requires $t < n/2$.

9.5   BIBLIOGRAPHIC NOTES

- The algorithm solving multivalued Byzantine consensus on top of synchronous binary Byzantine consensus is due to Turpin and Coan (79).

- The consensus algorithm described in Section 9.2 is a variant of an algorithm described in (5).

- The Byzantine general algorithm for authenticated messages presented in Section 9.4 is due to Dolev and Strong (18). This algorithm is an improvement of an algorithm described in (47) that requires an exponential number of signed messages, namely $O(n^t)$.

- Readers interested in messages authentication are referred to (29; 75; 78).

Bibliography

[1] Aguilera M.K., Le Lann G. and Toueg S., On the Impact of Fast failure Detectors on Real-Time Fault-Tolerant Systems. *Proc. 16th Symposium on Distributed Computing (DISC'02)*, Springer-Verlag LNCS #2508, pp. 354-369, 2002. DOI: 10.1007/3-540-36108-1_24 52

[2] Aguilera M.K. and Toueg S., A Simple Bi-valency Proof that t-Resilient Consensus Requires $t + 1$ Rounds. *Information Processing Letters*, 71:155-158, 1999. DOI: 10.1016/S0020-0190(99)00100-3 29

[3] Attiya H. and Welch J., Distributed Computing: Fundamentals, Simulations and Advanced Topics, (2d Edition), *Wiley-Interscience*, 414 pages, 2004. 12, 29, 78, 141

[4] Babaoğlu O. and Toueg S., Understanding Non-Blocking Atomic Commitment. In *Distributed Systems*, ACM Press, pp. 147-168, 1993. 12, 95

[5] Bar-Noy A., Dolev D., Dwork C. and Strong H.R., Shifting Gears: Changing Algorithms on the Fly to Expedite Byzantine Agreement. *Information & Computation*, 97:205-233, 1992. DOI: 10.1016/0890-5401(92)90035-E 141, 155

[6] Berman P. and Garay J.A., Cloture Voting: $n/4$-Resilient Distributed Consensus in $t + 1$ Rounds. *Mathematical System Theory*, 26(1):3-19, 1993. DOI: 10.1007/BF01187072 141

[7] Bernstein Ph.A., Hadzilacos V. and Goodman N., Concurrency Control and Recovery in Database Systems. *Addison Wesley Publishing Company*, 370 pages, 1987. 12, 95

[8] Bonnet F. and Raynal M., Conditions for Set Agreement with an Application to Synchronous Systems. *Springer-Verlag Journal of Computer Science and Technology*, 24(3):418-433, 2009. DOI: 10.1007/s11390-009-9234-3 79

[9] Borowsky E. and Gafni E., Generalized FLP Impossibility Results for t-Resilient Asynchronous Computations. *Proc. 25th ACM Symposium on Theory of Computation (STOC'93)*, ACM Press, pp. 91-100, 1993. DOI: 10.1145/167088.167119 78

[10] Chandra T.D., Hadzilacos V. and Toueg S., The Weakest Failure Detector for Solving Consensus. *Journal of the ACM*, 43(4):685-722, 1996. DOI: 10.1145/234533.234549 52

[11] Chandra T.D. and Toueg S., Unreliable Failure Detectors for Reliable Distributed Systems. *Journal of the ACM*, 43(2):225-267, 1996. DOI: 10.1145/226643.226647 52

[12] Charron-Bost B. and Schiper A., Uniform Consensus is Harder than Consensus. *Journal of Algorithms*, 51(1):15-37, 2004. DOI: 10.1016/j.jalgor.2003.11.001 52

[13] Chaudhuri S., More *Choices* Allow More *Faults:* Set Consensus Problems in Totally Asynchronous Systems. *Information and Computation*, 105:132-158, 1993. DOI: 10.1006/inco.1993.1043 12, 78, 113

[14] Chaudhuri S., Herlihy M., Lynch N. and Tuttle M., Tight Bounds for k-Set Agreement. *Journal of the ACM*, 47(5):912-943, 2000. DOI: 10.1145/355483.355489 79, 113

[15] Delporte-Gallet C., Fauconnier H., Guerraoui R. and Pochon S., The Perfectly Synchronized Round-based Model of Distributed Computing. *Information and Computation*, 205:783-815, 2007. DOI: 10.1016/j.ic.2006.11.003 29

[16] Dolev D., The Byzantine Generals Strike Again. *Journal of the Algorithms*, 3:14-30, 1982. DOI: 10.1016/0196-6774(82)90004-9 12

[17] Dolev D., Reischuk, R. Strong H.R., Early Stopping in Byzantine Agreement. *Journal of the ACM*, 37(4):720-741, 1990. DOI: 10.1145/96559.96565 12, 29, 52, 63, 141

[18] Dolev D. and Strong H.R., Authenticated Algorithms for Byzantine Agreement. *SIAM Journal of Computing*, 12(4):656-666, 1983. DOI: 10.1137/0212045 29, 141, 155

[19] Dutta P., Guerraoui R. and Pochon B., Fast Non-blocking Atomic Commit: an Inherent Tradeoff. *Information Processing Letters*, 91(4):195-200, 2004. DOI: 10.1016/j.ipl.2004.04.006 95

[20] Dwork C. and Moses Y., Knowledge and Common Knowledge in a Byzantine Environment: Crash failures. *Information and Computation*, 88(2):156-186, 1990. DOI: 10.1016/0890-5401(90)90014-9 12, 29, 63

[21] Fagin R., Halpern, J.Y., Moses Y. and Vardi M., Reasoning about Knowledge, *MIT Press*, Cambridge (MA), 491 pages, 2003. 63

[22] Fischer M. and Lynch N., A Lower Bound for the Time to Ensure Interactive Consistency. *Information Processing Letters*, 14:183-186, 1982. DOI: 10.1016/0020-0190(82)90033-3 29, 141

[23] Fischer M.J., Lynch N.A. and Paterson M.S., Impossibility of Distributed Consensus with One Faulty Process. *Journal of the ACM*, 32(2):374-382, 1985. DOI: 10.1145/3149.214121 29, 52

[24] Friedman R., Mostéfaoui A., Rajsbaum S. and Raynal M., Distributed Agreement Problems and their Connection with Error-correcting Codes. *IEEE Transactions on Computers*, 56(7):865-875, 2007. DOI: 10.1109/TC.2007.1043 52

[25] Gafni E., Round-by-round Fault Detectors: Unifying Synchrony and Asynchrony. *Proc. 17th ACM Symposium on Principles of Distributed Computing (PODC'98)*, ACM Press, pp. 143-152, 1998. DOI: 10.1145/277697.277724 79

[26] Gafni E., Guerraoui R. and Pochon B., From a Static Impossibility to an Adaptive Lower Bound: The Complexity of Early Deciding Set Agreement. *Proc. 37th ACM Symposium on Theory of Computing (STOC'05)*, Baltimore (MD), pp.714-722, May 2005. DOI: 10.1145/1060590.1060696 79, 113

[27] Garay J. and Moses Y., Fully Polynomial Byzantine Agreement for $n > 3t$ Processes in $t + 1$ Rounds. *SIAM Journal of Computing*, 27(1):247-290, 1998. DOI: 10.1137/S0097539794265232 141

[28] Garg V.K., Elements of Distributed Computing. *Wiley-Interscience*, 423 pages, 2002. 12, 29, 141

[29] Goldreich O., Fundations of Cryptography, Basic Tools. *Cambridge University Press*, 372 pages, 2001. 155

[30] Gray J., Notes on Database Operating Systems: and Advanced Course. *Springer Verlag*, LNCS #60, pp. 10-17, 1978. 12, 95

[31] Gray J. and Reuter A., Transaction Processing: Concepts and Techniques. *Morgan Kaufmann Pub.*, 1045 pages, 1993. 95

[32] Guerraoui R., Revisiting the Relationship Between Non-Blocking Atomic Commitment and Consensus. *Proc. 9th Int'l Workshop on Distributed Algorithms (WDAG'95)*, Springer Verlag LNCS #972, pp. 87-100, 1995. DOI: 10.1007/BFb0022140 12

[33] Guerraoui R., Failure Detectors. *Encyclopedia of Algorithms*, Springer Verlag, pp. 304-308, 2008. 52

[34] Guerraoui R., Herlihy M. and Pochon B., A Topological Treatment of Early-Deciding Set Agreement. *Proc. 10th Int'l Conference On Principles Of Distributed Systems (OPODIS'06)*, Springer-Verlag LNCS #4305, pp. 20-35, 2006. DOI: 10.1007/11945529_3 79

[35] Guerraoui R. and Rodrigues L., Introduction to Reliable Distributed Programming. *Springer*, 299 pages, 2006. 12

[36] Hadzilacos V., On the Relationship Between the Atomic Commitment and Consensus Problems. *Asilomar Workshop on Fault-Tolerant Distributed Computing*, Springer Verlag LNCS #448, pp. 201-208, 1990. DOI: 10.1007/BFb0042336 12

[37] Hadzilacos V. and Toueg S., Fault-Tolerant Broadcasts and Related Problems. In *Distributed Systems*, ACM Press, pp. 97-145, 1993. Extended version: A Modular Approach to Fault-Tolerant Broadcasts and Related Problems. *Tech Report 94-1425*, 83 pages, Cornell University, Ithaca (USA), 1994. 12

[38] Halpern J.Y. and Moses Y., Knowledge and Common Knowledge in a Distributed Environment; *Journal of the ACM*, 37(3):549-587, 1990. DOI: 10.1145/79147.79161 63

[39] Herlihy M.P. and Rajsbaum S., Algebraic Spans. *Mathematical Structures in Computer Science*, 10(4): 549-573, 2000. DOI: 10.1017/S0960129500003170 79

[40] Herlihy M.P. and Shavit N., The Topological Structure of Asynchronous Computability. *Journal of the ACM*, 46(6):858-923, 1999. DOI: 10.1145/331524.331529 78

[41] Izumi T. and Masuzawa T., Condition Adaptation in Synchronous Consensus, *IEEE Transactions on Computers*, 55(7):843-853, 2006. DOI: 10.1109/TC.2006.99 52

[42] Izumi T. and Masuzawa T., A Weakly-adaptive Condition-based Consensus Algorithm in Asynchronous Distributed Systems. *Information Processing Letters*, 100(5):199-205, 2006. DOI: 10.1016/j.ipl.2006.07.003 52

[43] Keidar I. and Rajsbaum S., A simple Proof of the Uniform Consensus Synchronous Lower Bound. *Information Processing Letters*, 85(1):47-52, 2003. DOI: 10.1016/S0020-0190(02)00333-2 52

[44] Ksemkalyani A. and Singhal M., Distributed Computing: Principles, Algorithms, and Systems. *Cambridge University Press*, 738 pages, 2008. 12, 29, 141

[45] Lamport L., The Weak Byzantine Generals Problem. *Journal of the ACM*, 30(4):668-676, 1983. DOI: 10.1145/2402.322398 12, 141

[46] Lamport L. and Fischer M., Byzantine Generals and Transaction Commit Protocols. *Technical Report 62*, SRI International, 16 pages, 1982. 29

[47] Lamport L., Shostack R. and Pease M., The Byzantine Generals Problem. *ACM Transactions on Programming Languages and Systems*, 4(3)-382-401, 1982. DOI: 10.1145/357172.357176 12, 141, 155

[48] Lampson B., Atomic Transactions. *Springer Verlag*, LNCS #105, pp. 246-265, 1981. 95

[49] Lynch N.A., Distributed Algorithms. *Morgan Kaufmann Pub.*, San Francisco (CA), 872 pages, 1996. 12, 29, 78, 141

[50] Mizrahi T. and Moses Y., Continuous Consensus via Common Knowledge. *Distributed Computing*, 20(5):305-321, 2008. DOI: 10.1007/s00446-007-0049-6 63

[51] Moses Y., Dolev D. and Halpern J.Y., Cheating Husbands and other Stories: A Case Study of Knowledge, Action, and Communication, *Distributed Computing*, 1(3):167-176, 1986. DOI: 10.1007/BF01661170 63

[52] Moses Y. and Rajsbaum S., A Layered Analysis of Consensus. *SIAM Journal of Compuitng*, 31(4):989-1021, 1998. DOI: 10.1137/S0097539799364006 29

[53] Moses, Y. and Raynal M., No Double Discount: Condition-based Simultaneity Yields Limited Gain. *Proc. 22th Int'l Symposium on Distributed Computing (DISC'08)*, Springer-Verlag LNCS #5218, pp. 423-437, 2008. DOI: 10.1007/978-3-540-87779-0_29 63

[54] Moses, Y. and Raynal M., Revisiting Simultaneous Consensus with Crash Failures. *Journal of Parallel and Distributed Computing*, 69:400-409, 2009. DOI: 10.1016/j.jpdc.2009.01.001 12, 63

[55] Moses Y. and Tuttle M.R., Programming Simultaneous Actions Using Common Knowledge. *Algorithmica*, 3:121-169, 1988. DOI: 10.1007/BF01762112 63

[56] Mostéfaoui A., Rajsbaum S. and Raynal M., Conditions on Input Vectors for Consensus Solvability in Asynchronous Distributed Systems. *Journal of the ACM*, 50(6):922-954, 2003. DOI: 10.1145/950620.950624 52, 79

[57] Mostéfaoui A., Rajsbaum S. and Raynal M., Synchronous Condition-Based Consensus. *Distributed Computing*, 18(5):325-343, 2006. DOI: 10.1007/s00446-005-0148-1 52

[58] Mostéfaoui A., Rajsbaum S., Raynal M. and Roy M., A Hierarchy of Conditions for Asynchronous Interactive Consistency. *7th Int'l Conference on Parallel Computing Technologies (PaCT'03)*, Springer Verlag LNCS #2763, pp. 130-140, 2003. DOI: 10.1007/978-3-540-45145-7_11 52

[59] Mostéfaoui A., Rajsbaum S., Raynal M. and Roy M., Condition-Based Consensus Solvability: a Hierarchy of Conditions and Efficient Protocols. *Distributed Computing*, 17(1):1-20, 2004. DOI: 10.1007/s00446-003-0093-9 52

[60] Mostéfaoui A., Rajsbaum S., Raynal M. and Travers C., The Combined Power of Conditions and Information on Failures to Solve Asynchronous Set Agreement. *SIAM Journal of Computing*, 38(4):1574-1601, 2008. DOI: 10.1137/050645580 52

[61] Mostéfaoui A., Raynal M. and Travers C., Narrowing Power vs Efficiency in Synchronous Set Agreement: Relationship, Algorithms and Lower Bound. *Theoretical Computer Science*, 411(1):58-69, 2010. DOI: 10.1016/j.tcs.2009.09.002 79

[62] Neiger G. and Toueg S., Automatically Increasing the Fault-Tolerance of Distributed Algorithms. *Journal of Algorithms*, 11:374-419, 1990. DOI: 10.1016/0196-6774(90)90019-B 114

[63] Okun M., Byzantine Agreement. *Springer Verlag Encyclopedia of Algorithms*, pp. 116-119, 2008. 141

[64] Pease M., R. Shostak R. and Lamport L., Reaching Agreement in the Presence of Faults. *Journal of the ACM*, 27:228-234, 1980. DOI: 10.1145/322186.322188 12, 141

[65] Perry K.J. and Toueg S., Distributed Agreement in the Presence of Processor and Communication Faults. *IEEE Transactions on Software Engineering*, SE-12(3):477-482, 1986. 114

[66] Raïpin Parvédy Ph. and Raynal M., Optimal Early Stopping Uniform Consensus in Synchronous Systems with Process Omission Failures. *Proc. 16th ACM Symposium on Parallel Algorithms and Architectures (SPAA'04)*, ACM Press, pp. 302-310, 2004. DOI: 10.1145/1007912.1007963 114

[67] Raïpin Parvédy Ph., Raynal M. and Travers C., Early-Stopping k-set Agreement in Synchronous Systems Prone to any Number of Process Crashes. *8th Int'l Conference on Parallel Computing Technologies (PaCT'05)*, Springer Verlag LNCS #3606, pp. 49-58, 2005. 79

[68] Raïpin Parvédy Ph., Raynal M. and Travers C., Decision Optimal Early-Stopping k-set Agreement in Synchronous Systems Prone to Send Omission Failures. *Proc. 11th IEEE Pacific Rim Int'l Symposium on Dependable Computing (PRDC'05)*, IEEE Computer Press, pp. 23-30, 2005. 114

[69] Raïpin Parvédy Ph., Raynal M. and Travers C., Strongly Terminating Early-Stopping k-set Agreement in Synchronous Systems with General Omission Failures. *Theory of Computing Systems*, 47(1):259-287, 2010. DOI: 10.1007/s00224-008-9157-3 114

[70] Raynal, M., Consensus in Synchronous Systems: a Concise Guided Tour. *Proc. 9th IEEE Pacific Rim Int'l Symposium on Dependable Computing (PRDC 2002)*, IEEE Computer Press, pp. 221-228, 2002. DOI: 10.1109/PRDC.2002.1185641 29, 52, 114

[71] Raynal M., Set Agreement. *Springer-Verlag Encyclopedia of Algorithms*, pp. 829-831, 2008. 12, 78

[72] Raynal M., Failure Detectors for Asynchronous Distributed Systems: an Introduction. *Wiley Encyclopedia of Computer Science and Engineering*, Vol. 2, pp. 1181-1191, 2009 (ISBN 978-0-471-38393-2). 52

[73] Raynal M., Communication and Agreement Abstractions for Fault-Tolerant Asynchronous Distributed Systems. *Morgan & Claypool Publishers*, 251 pages, 2010. DOI: 10.2200/S00236ED1V01Y201004DCT002 12

[74] Raynal M. and Travers C., Synchronous Set Agreement: a Concise Guided Tour (including a new algorithm and a list of open problems). *Proc. 12th IEEE Pacific Rim Int'l Symposium*

on Dependable Computing (PRDC'05), IEEE Computer Press, pp. 267-274, Riverside (CA), 2006. DOI: 10.1109/PRDC.2006.59 78, 114

[75] Rivest R.L., Shamir A. and Adelman L., A method for Obtaining Digital Signatures and Public Key Cryptosystems. *Communications of the ACM*, 21:1210-126, 1978. DOI: 10.1145/359340.359342 155

[76] Saks M. and Zaharoglou F., Wait-Free k-Set Agreement is Impossible: The Topology of Public Knowledge. *SIAM Journal on Computing*, 29(5):1449-1483, 2000. DOI: 10.1137/S0097539796307698 78

[77] Skeen D., Non-blocking Commit Protocols. *Proc. ACM SIGMOD Int'l Conference on Management of Data*, ACM Press, pp. 133-142, 1981. DOI: 10.1145/582318.582339 12, 95

[78] Srikanth T.K. and Toueg S., Simulating Authenticated Broadcasts to Derive Simple Fault-tolerant Algorithms. *Distributed Comuting*, 2:80-94, 1987. DOI: 10.1007/BF01667080 155

[79] Turpin R. and Coan B.A., Extending Binary Byzantine Agreement to Multivalued Byzantine Agreement. *Information Processing Letters*, 18:73-76, 1984. DOI: 10.1016/0020-0190(84)90027-9 155

[80] Wang X., Teo Y.M. and Cao J., A Bivalency Proof of the Lower Bound for Uniform Consensus. *Information Processing Letters*, 96:167-174, 2005. DOI: 10.1016/j.ipl.2005.08.002

[81] Zibin Y., Condition-Based Consensus in Synchronous Systems. *Proc. 17th Int'l Symposium on Distributed Computing*, Springer-Verlag LNCS #2848, pp. 239-248, Sorrento (Italy), 2003. 52

Author's Biography

MICHEL RAYNAL

Michel Raynal is a professor of computer science at the University of Rennes, France. His main research interests are the basic principles of distributed computing systems. Michel Raynal is a world leading researcher in the domain of distributed computing. He is the author of numerous papers on distributed computing and is well-known for his distributed algorithms and his books on distributed computing.

He has chaired the program committee of the major conferences on the topic, such as the IEEE Int'l Conference on Distributed Computing Systems (ICDCS), the Symposium on Distributed Computing (DISC), the Int'l Colloquium on Structural Information and Communication Complexity (SIROCCO), and the Int'l Conference on Principles of Distributed Systems (OPODIS). He has also served on the program committees of many international conferences, and is the recipient of several "Best Paper" awards. Michel Raynal has been invited by many universities all over the world to give lectures on distributed computing.

Index

Printed in the United States
by Baker & Taylor Publisher Services